THE BRITISH BOARD OF FILM CENSORS

The British Board of Film Censors

FILM CENSORSHIP IN BRITAIN,1896~1950

James C. Robertson

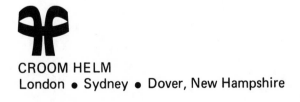

CROOM HELM
London • Sydney • Dover, New Hampshire

© 1985 James C. Robertson
Croom Helm Ltd, Provident House, Burrell Row,
Beckenham, Kent BR3 1AT

Croom Helm Australia Pty Ltd, First Floor,
139 King Street, Sydney, NSW 2001, Australia

British Library Cataloguing in Publication Data

Robertson, James C.
   The British Board of Film Censors: film
   censorship in Britain 1896-1950.
   I. Title
   791.43   PN1994.A5G7
   ISBN 0-7099-2270-1

Croom Helm, 51 Washington Street, Dover,
New Hampshire 03820, USA

Library of Congress Cataloging in Publication Data

Robertson, James C.
   The British Board of Film Censors.

   Bibliography: p.
   Includes index.
   1. British Board of Film Censors — History.
I. Title.
PN1994.A5G837 1985 354.410085'4 85-403
ISBN 0-7099-2270-1

Printed and bound in Great Britain by
Biddles Ltd, Guildford and King's Lynn

CONTENTS

BLACK AND WHITE PLATES

1. Confessions of a Nazi Spy

   On his return to the USA from Nazi Germany,
   where he received instructions from Dr Göbbels
   in person, Paul Lukas reviews a parade of the
   German-American Bund in Confessions of a Nazi
   Spy (Warner Brothers, 1939). Despite its
   committed anti-Nazi content the BBFC sanctioned
   the film prior to the outbreak of the Second
   World War.

2. Dawn

   Dame Sybil Thorndike as Edith Cavell defies the
   Huns in Dawn (British Dominions Film
   Corporation, 1927-8). To circumvent censorship,
   director Herbert Wilcox outmanoeuvred the
   Cabinet and the BBFC in 1928.

3. King of Kings

   Christ suffers on the cross in King of Kings
   (Pathé, 1927). The BBFC banned films material-
   ising Christ but did not receive the opportunity
   to ban Cecil B. De Mille's epic because the
   distributors submitted it successfully direct to
   the local authorities.

4. Mission to Moscow

   Stalin criticises the pre-war Anglo-French
   appeasement of Hitler to American Ambassador
   Joseph E. Davies in Mission to Moscow (Warner
   Brothers, 1943). The BBFC on Foreign Office
   advice probably deleted much of this dialogue.

BLACK AND WHITE PLATES

5. ## Nosferatu

    Max Schreck as the terrifying Dracula in
    Friedrich Murnau's Nosferatu (Germany, 1922),
    the only silent horror film which the BBFC
    banned outright.

6. ## Red-Headed Woman

    Shameless hussy Jean Harlow breaks up Chester
    Morris's engagement in order to marry him
    herself in Red-Headed Woman (MGM, 1932). Her
    brazen sexuality in this film brought about a
    BBFC ban from 1932 to 1965.

7. ## She Done Him Wrong

    Mae West about to announce herself as the
    'prettiest girl who ever walked the streets' in
    She Done Him Wrong (Paramount, 1933). The BBFC
    made so many cuts that no complete print exists
    in Britain.

8. ## This Above All

    Class-conscious British deserter Tyrone Power
    sees the light and gives himself up to Sgt Rhys
    Williams in This Above All (Twentieth Century-
    Fox, 1942). Despite the questioning in the film
    of Britain's motives for fighting Nazi Germany,
    the BBFC allowed it in full.

    All stills are reproduced by courtesy of the
    National Film Archive Stills Library. The
    permission of the film company copyright
    holders to reproduce is gratefully acknowledged.

ABBREVIATIONS

BBFC   British Board of Film Censors
BFI   British Film Institute
CEA   Cinematograph Exhibitors Association
FBI   Federal Bureau of Investigation
FO   Foreign Office
GFD   General Film Distributors
HO   Home Office
IRA   Irish Republican Army
LCC   London County Council
LPMC   London Public Morality Council
MGM   Metro-Goldwyn-Mayer
MoI   Ministry of Information
MPPDA   Motion Picture Producers and Distributors
        Association (of America)
NAMPI   National Association of the Motion Picture
        Industry
PCA   Production Code Administration
PRO   Public Record Office
TCF   20th Century-Fox

ACKNOWLEDGEMENTS

I am very grateful indeed to James Ferman, the
Secretary of the British Board of Film Censors, for
his permission to scrutinise the Board's registers,
to publish their information and to quote from the
Board's correspondence with government departments
held in the Public Record Office. Without his
invaluable co-operation this book could not have
been written. I am also greatly indebted to the
Board's Office Manager, Bert Mayell, who helped me
to cut through some of the secrecy in which the
Board shrouded itself and which was so great initially that before 1948 its premises did not even
display a street nameplate.[1] He permitted me to
encroach on his time, and our always interesting
talks yielded information of a kind which often
eludes the written record. I cannot omit the staffs
of the Board, the British Film Institute Library,
the National Film Archive and the Public Record
Office, whose cheerfully given help was indispens-
able. Finally Crown copyright records in the Public
Record Office are reproduced by permission of the
Controller of H.M. Stationery Office, while the film
stills are reproduced by courtesy of the Stills
Division of the National Film Archive.

Letchworth   Jim Robertson

---

1.   Verbal testimony of Bert Mayell to the author,
     6 August 1982.

Chapter 1

THE FORMATIVE YEARS, 1896-1918

Before 1896 films in Britain were shown in circuses,
fairgrounds and mobile music halls. Such itinerant
exhibitions did not die out until 1904, but their
eventual death was guaranteed by the 1896 arrival of
moving films in London and Manchester music halls and
variety theatres. The pioneer film-makers comprised
a mixture of lower middle class producers and
individual music hall or variety theatre showmen.
The latter were proletarians whose businesses did not
outlast their own generation but who had sown the
seeds for a new communication medium among the lowest
educational and income groups. The first purpose-
built cinema was completed in 1906 and by 1910 there
were about 1,600 British cinemas, almost a third of
them in London. The other high attendance areas
were the industrial cities and towns of northern
England, Scotland and South Wales where in the late
19th century the working class had gained shorter
working hours without an income reduction and cinema
admission prices were low.
    In the early days of British cinema no clear
distinctions existed within the industry between
production, distribution and exhibition. Initially
the producers sold films to the various types of
exhibitor, but as the industry organised itself into
trade associations during the years before the First
World War, film sale came to be replaced by renting
and firms came into being which specialised in distribution through renting. Between 1906 and 1914 the
producers established the Kinematograph Manufacturers
Association, the exhibitors the Cinematograph
Exhibitors Association (CEA) and the distributors the
Incorporated Association of Film Renters. The
exhibitors in particular greatly expanded from three
registered companies in 1908 to more than 1,800 by
1914. This progress arose from both the growing

popularity of the cinema and an abortive 1910 secret agreement between the producers and the distributors to control the market through price fixing and limitation of film circulation. This agreement had to be abandoned due to opposition from the smaller distributors and the exhibitors, but the struggle deepened the industry's compartmentalisation tendencies, the only pre-1914 British example of integration between production, distribution and exhibition being Provincial Cinematograph Theatres. This was a rare instance of professional investment capitalism in cinema as performed by financier Sir William Bass, but on the whole cinema capital investment centred on local exhibitors and was derived from local sources. No single branch of the industry predominated, and as yet American penetration of British distribution was in its infancy, although by 1914 American films constituted 60 per cent of the films shown in British cinemas compared to 30 per cent in 1909.[1]

The British film industry's organisation into the various trade associations from 1906 to 1914 was also influenced by a simultaneous fear of official censorship and a consequent profit reduction all round. As the cinemas mushroomed after 1906, objections to film content soon arose. In March 1908 there were press criticisms and private protests to the Home Office about a film on show in London dealing with the criminal activities of murderer Charles Peace. In February 1909 the Metropolitan Police Commissioner urged the Home Office to initiate control over cinemas because fire precautions were inadequate and many films glorified crime.[2] However, although some fires had occurred in the new cinemas, there had been nothing remotely comparable to the 1897 annual Paris Charity Bazaar catastrophe in which 140 eminent people had lost their lives. In March 1909 Home Secretary Herbert Gladstone drew a place in the ballot for a private member's measure to be introduced into the House of Commons and tabled a bill for cinema control ostensibly on safety grounds. Gladstone did not have top priority among the fortunate 1909 private members, and under normal circumstances his bill would have stood little chance to become law, but Prime Minister Herbert Asquith's Liberal Cabinet decided to take up the bill as an official government act. At first sight this decision seems curious, for the Liberal government had just embarked upon a bitter clash with the Conservatives over Chancellor David Lloyd George's controversial budget. This was contested

clause by clause and consumed much Commons time which
would otherwise have been used for other government
legislation. However, when viewed from a background
of steadily rising unemployment, the Labour Party's
recent emergence as a force in the Commons and the
first signs of the serious labour unrest which was to
plague Britain until 1914, the government's decision
to proceed with cinema control seems less strange.
The cinemas were patronised mainly by working class
audiences, but why the Home Office evidently believed
that control over film content was important remains
obscure in the absence of reliable attendance statistics. In 1916 weekly attendance was estimated at
over 20 millions, but by then the number of cinemas
had more than doubled to 3,500 since 1910.

Herbert Samuel, the Home Office Parliamentary
Under-Secretary, introduced the second reading of the
bill in the Commons on 21 April. He explained that
the bill intended to confer powers on all local
authorities to take steps to avoid cinema fires. He
argued that the matter was urgent because if no such
action was taken, sooner or later there would be
serious loss of life. However, he did not expressly
mention the 1897 Paris disaster, and when one MP
questioned the need for the projected legislation and
asked why the cinemas were being singled out for
prompt attention when other entertainment places
using gas were equally at risk, Samuel offered no
convincing answer.[3] The Home Office documents suggest he greatly exaggerated the danger of cinema fires
to evade too probing a Commons discussion, and at
committee stage on 25 August 1909 T.M. Healy MP
clearly suspected that the bill's real purpose was
film censorship.[4] Supporting evidence for Healy's
suspicion that Gladstone was not averse to seeing
local authorities use safety powers for control over
the arts when these were transmitted to the discont-
ented masses, some of whom possessed votes, can be
found in a near contemporary protest to the Home
Office from the Association of Travelling Portable
Theatre Managers. This pointed out to Gladstone
that local authorities were harassing itinerant
theatrical groups on social grounds under safety
pretexts,[5] but it brought no response from the Home
Office. Safety measures for theatres had been a
legal requirement since 1878, and many theatres had
been situated in working class districts. The Cinematograph bill eventually passed its third Commons
reading on 31 August, while after two cursory discussions in the House of Lords during September and
October it received the royal assent to become law in

3

November 1909.
     In outward form the Cinematograph Act dealt
purely with safety regulations and was so headed,
but a December 1910 legal judgment ruled that the
safety heading did not limit the act's scope. This
ruling came about because, as the Home Office had
almost certainly foreseen on the basis of experience
with theatres, certain local authorities were exercising their new powers to grant licences to cinemas
in such a way as to control film content. When the
film industry challenged the legality of such policies, the courts invariably supported the local
authorities. By 1912 local authority pressure on
film content was sufficiently strong for the film
industry to fear the imposition of central government
censorship, as some local authorities wished. To
forestall such a measure, the film industry approached the Home Office, and as a result Home Secretary
Reginald McKenna and several permanent officials -
including a future President of the British Board of
Film Censors (BBFC), Sir Sidney Harris, then plain
Mr S.W. Harris - received a film deputation on 22
February 1912. This represented producers, exhibitors and distributors. Included among its thirteen
members were one MP and the noted film-maker Cecil
Hepworth who, together with fellow film pioneer
William C. Barker, had initiated the overtures to the
Home Office.
     The deputation proposed the formation of a Board
of Film Censors by the film industry itself, with a
Home Office-appointed official chief censor who would
act as an arbiter between the new Board and producers
unwilling to accept the Board's decision. The chief
censor's decision would be final. The deputation
also conceded that all the Board's censors should be
appointed subject to Home Office approval. McKenna
agreed in principle to a Board, but as he would state
in the Commons on 22 April 1912, he was opposed to an
official Home Office censorship. He also raised
questions concerning the Board's relations with the
local authorities.[6] However, despite differences of
detail the deputation was sufficiently encouraged by
McKenna's general response to go ahead, and in
November 1912 the film industry appointed G.A.
Redford as the first BBFC President. Whether he was
a Home Office nominee or a film industry appointment
which McKenna simply approved is unclear, but the
mechanics of his selection were academic, for the
film industry was so keen to secure Home Office backing for its new Board that it inevitably chose some-
one as President who would unquestionably meet with

McKenna's approval. Redford's prime qualification
for the post seems to have been that he possessed a
lengthy experience of stage censorship through his
duties on the Lord Chamberlain's staff, there being
no evidence that his knowledge of films or the film
industry was extensive. Shortly after Redford's
appointment a further film deputation went to the
Home Office on 13 November 1912 to discuss the additional BBFC personnel. Permanent Under-Secretary Sir
William Byrne declined to become involved beyond a
recommendation that there should be at least one
woman among the four censors.[7] The Home Office
remained unwilling to become involved with the new
Board or the appointment of its staff. This explains
the appointment as BBFC Secretary of Joseph Brooke
Wilkinson, who had been a journalist with the North-
cliffe press when he and Hepworth had first met and
who was currently the CEA secretary, a post he had
held for several years. He thus had the knowledge of
the film world that Redford seemingly lacked.
        The BBFC was financed by the film industry on
the basis of a set fee per foot of film viewed. Its
work began on 1 January 1913, although its decisions
were applicable only to films released after 1 March.
It had been established without a written constitution, in the light of which its initial development
in offices at 75-77 Shaftesbury Avenue in London
would rest on the personalities and energies of its
two chief officers as well as on the readiness or
otherwise of the producers and the local authorities
to accept its rulings. Liaison with the film industry was maintained through a small committee of
producers, exhibitors and distributors which met
often until at least the early 1920s to keep the
BBFC's work under constant review. Evidence on the
working relationship between Redford, who was 66 at
the time of his appointment, and Brooke Wilkinson,
who was 42, is exceedingly sparse. However, by
September 1916 Redford was seriously ill, was
possibly lax in consequence and was called upon for
a final decision only when two censors wished to ban
a film.[8] It is thus likely that Brooke Wilkinson
was the de facto BBFC ruler, and that Redford's
authority was largely drawn upon only as a last
resort. The BBFC was empowered to issue a film with
either an 'A' (adult) or 'U' (universal) certificate
or to withhold a certificate altogether. A certificate denoted merely that a film was suitable for both
adults and children ('U') or for adults only ('A')
and was intended to serve merely as a guide to local
authorities. This system covered only feature films

and no producer was legally obliged to submit films
to the BBFC, although it appears that most producers
had promised to do so during the 1912 negotiations
which had led to the BBFC's foundation. Moreover,
local authorities possessed the statutory power
either to allow a film when the BBFC had rejected it
or to ban a film which the BBFC had allowed.

Since most of the BBFC records were destroyed by
German bombs in May 1941, the names of two original
censors may never be traced. In 1913 there were four
censors. Two, who served with the BBFC until the
early 1920s, bore the initials CCR and OC, while the
other two were Benham Blaxland, who remained with the
BBFC until his death in 1926, and C. Hubert Husey,
who was chief censor until his death in February 1930
and BBFC Vice-President after November 1916. At
least two censors viewed each film, and before the
emergence of sound it was normal practice for two
films to be projected simultaneously in the same
room, so that each film was seen by all four censors.
The chief projectionist was William Hines until 1954.
Brooke Wilkinson designated two responsible censors
for each film. When they disagreed, they referred to
Brooke Wilkinson for a decision. Redford was evidently referred to only in the exceptional cases where
two censors favoured a ban. The censors were given
the bare minimum of guidance, for only two specific
rules were laid down - no nudity and no portrayal of
Jesus Christ.[9] Before 1913 much of the local
authority pressure against film content had concentrated on morality issues, while in 1912 Robert
Henderson Bland had played Jesus in From the Manger
to the Cross (Kalem, 1912, director Sidney Olcott).
This reverential biography of Christ had opened in
London at both the Queen's Hall and the Albert Hall
during December 1912 and despite some public criticism was still running when the BBFC came into existence. The film was shown every day except Sunday
for three months in both halls, but the BBFC retained
the general rule banning the portrayal of Jesus
presumably for fear of parliamentary or public
controversy. From the Manger to the Cross was not
submitted to the BBFC until November 1918 when it was
passed uncut with a 'U' certificate. However, under
wartime emergency powers which were to lapse shortly
afterwards the BBFC passed it for export only. After
the war Henderson Bland bought the rights to the film
and revived it with additional footage at the Albert
Hall at Easter during April 1922. This move was to
prove so successful that a tour of British cities
and towns ensued. On 16 April 1922 the Bishop of

London's sermon at St Paul's Cathedral described it as a beautiful film, but despite this recommendation from on high within the church and the 1922 benevolence of local authorities towards From the Manger to the Cross, the BBFC did not drop its ban on the materialisation of Christ until well after the Second World War.

Additional rules during 1913 were thus a response to films submitted. Furthermore, the practical politics of inducing local authorities to accept the BBFC as Britain's major film censorship organisation without simultaneously alienating the film industry could never be wholly ignored. The first local authority to announce publicly that it would not pass a film which had not received a BBFC certificate took this action as early as April 1913 and by the end of 1914 23 other local authorities had followed suit, but only a further twelve were to do so in 1915 despite a much higher figure of promises. Since there were several hundred authorities empowered to grant licences to cinemas, the BBFC was far from established after three years of operations, and local authority pressure on film content was soon revived under First World War exigencies.

During 1913 the BBFC refused a certificate to 22 films (See Appendix 3). To quote from its first annual report, published in 1914, the BBFC's general principle was the elimination of 'anything repulsive and objectionable to the good taste and better feelings of English audiences'. The report specified 22 grounds on which films had been either cut or banned. These are worth listing in full as the social values of upper class late Victorian and Edwardian Britain which came to form the core of the BBFC's standard rules until 1938:   (1) cruelty to animals; (2) indecorous dancing; (3) vulgarity and impropriety in conduct and dress; (4) indelicate sexual situations; (5) scenes suggestive of immorality; (6) situations accentuating delicate marital relations; (7) gruesome murders; (8) excessively gruesome details in crime or warfare; (9) indecently morbid death scenes; (10) scenes tending to disparage public characters and institutions; (11) medical operations; (12) executions; (13) painful scenes in connection with insanity; (14) cruelty to women; (15) confinements; (16) drunken scenes carried to excess; (17) scenes calculated to act as incentive to crime; (18) indecorous sub-titles; (19) indelicate accessories; (20) native customs in foreign lands abhorrent to British ideas; (21) irreverent treatment of sacred or solemn subjects; (22) the materialisation of Christ or the

7

Almighty. The report pointed out that the 22 rejected films had infringed rules one, two, three, four,
five, ten, twelve, sixteen, nineteen, twenty and
twenty-two. The BBFC particularly deprecated that
ministers of religion had been ridiculed which
apparently violated rule ten. It seems that none of
the 22 banned 1913 films now exists,[10] so that it is
impossible to judge their content in plot and style.
    The 22 rejected films turned out to be the high-
est number in any full peacetime year before 1931.
Whether the relatively high figure represented early
enthusiasm or ultra caution on the part of the
censors, an unwarranted producers' optimism as to
what the BBFC would tolerate or the BBFC's desire to
ingratiate itself with local authorities is uncer-
tain. To keep the BBFC's restrictive function in
perspective, in 1913 it viewed 7,510 films, of which
6,861 received a 'U' certificate and 627 an 'A' certificate. Of these only 144 were cut, although how
severely or otherwise is now impossible to discover,
while the remaining 22 were the banned films. The
BBFC report revealed one other 1913 action which
created a precedent after the outbreak of the First
World War. The Home Office had drawn the BBFC's
attention to films depicting riots in South Africa
and to the related publicity material. Although
such 'topical' films did not fall within the BBFC's
authority, it nevertheless took steps to suppress
the publicity material and to arrange a pre-exhibit-
ion private performance to Home and War Office representatives. The precise outcome is unclear, but
contacts with government departments were greatly to
increase during the First World War and to become a
regular feature of BBFC peacetime activities after
November 1918. Already in 1913 BBFC-Home Office
liaison was closer than was apparent in public at the
time. On 19 November the governor of Portland Prison
made representations to the Home Office for a ban on
a film entitled £1,000 Reward because it showed the
bribery of a prison warder and was filmed at Portland
Quarries. As a result of Home Office pressure the
BBFC took up the matter with the producer who removed
the offending material.[11] However, in general the
BBFC still sought a more open involvement with the
Home Office than the latter was willing to tolerate.
When the BBFC 1913 annual report was submitted in
draft to the Home Office on 3 February 1914, the
latter amended sections which pointed to the extent
of its contacts with the BBFC, a statement to the
effect that the Home Office approved of BBFC religious policy being omitted at Home Office instigation.

At this time Redford and Brooke Wilkinson so feared the BBFC's collapse that they unsuccessfully proposed Home Office recommendation to local authorities of the BBFC.[12]
     If during 1914 the producers were intent on wearing down the BBFC's initial firmness, they must have been disappointed. Of twelve BBFC-banned films in the year (See Appendix 3) all but one were banned before the outbreak of war with Germany and none was concerned with the war or national security. By arrangement with the Home Office the BBFC at the outbreak of war undertook the censorship of 'topical' films, which meant responsibility for all film censorship. To judge from the second BBFC annual report, the film industry and possibly the BBFC managed to reverse an initial government decision to prohibit any war films in order to produce propaganda features, although there is no corroboration for this in the Home Office documents. In the event the BBFC was soon called upon to view several flagwavers, most of them from London Films. The first, England Expects (produced by G.L. Tucker), which set the pattern for the image of the savage Hun, was passed uncut as early as 21 August, a mere 17 days after the British declaration of war. During September there followed a number of unquestioningly patriotic offerings of the same ilk, all passed uncut - For the Empire (passed at the BBFC on 5 September), An Englishman's Home (9 September) and England's Call (22 September). These now shameful and over-simplistic efforts to stimulate germanophobia were offset to only a minor extent by more sophisticated simultaneous war films. Most notable of these were Maurice Elvey's Lest We Forget, passed uncut on 17 September, and Cecil Hepworth's Unfit, passed uncut on 10 September. While these, too, were by no means free of excessive nationalism, they concentrated upon individual experiences rather than national enemy stereotypes. Apparently the BBFC saw nothing odious in inculcating wartime jingoism into children, for all these films were given a 'U' certificate!
     However, the bulk of the BBFC's work for 1914 was concerned with films unconnected with the war, even after August. Owing to the failure of British distributors to obtain any European films after the outbreak of war, a decrease not fully compensated for by the increased output of British films because of the war, the BBFC viewed fewer films than in 1913. 5,866 films were passed with a 'U' certificate, 416 with an 'A' - 6,282 of which 148 were cut. The new grounds for bans and cuts show that the BBFC remained

preoccupied with moral and social questions rather than the war. The main additions were funerals and death bed scenes treated with levity; the careers of notorious criminals; the <u>modus operandi</u> of criminals; cruelty to young infants; excessive cruelty and torture to adults; unnecessary exhibitions of feminine underclothing; incidents injurious to the reputation of government departments; suicides, strangulation scenes and massacres; the effects of vitriol throwing; realistic horrors in warfare; incidents to scare the public and produce panic during the war; scenes depicting the movement or dispositions of troops and other incidents calculated to afford information to the enemy; incidents having a tendency to disparage Britain's allies; the white slave traffic; scenes depicting the effects of hereditary disease; stories tinctured with salacious wit; incidents suggestive of incestuous relations; outrages on women; themes relative to 'race suicide'; scenes in disorderly houses. The 1914 report admitted that the BBFC had bowed to government pressure to suppress certain films during the war which had been granted a pre-war BBFC certificate. In this respect the report singled out films disparaging nations now British allies.

The four BBFC censors retained responsibility for viewings, but they consulted the Admiralty and the War Office in doubtful cases. How often such consultation took place will probably never be known, although the BBFC register of banned films shows that during the First World War many films were rejected on security grounds. The viewing of all films for export was an extra burden which came to occupy a large part of the BBFC's time. In the BBFC 1915 report, the last of the war, it was emphasised that acceptable material before the war had now become censorable. Examples were industrial relations (there had been trade union unrest in Clydeside and South Wales during the year); the domestic policies or social customs of Britain's allies; the religious beliefs of Indians; and British maltreatment of Indian natives. However, moral issues dominated the report. New grounds for BBFC objections were profuse bleeding; nude figures; excessively passionate love scenes; bathing scenes passing the limits of propriety; controversial politics; relations of capital and labour; scenes holding up the king's uniform to contempt or ridicule; subjects dealing with India in which British officers are seen in an odious light and attempting to suggest the disloyalty of native states or bringing into disrepute British prestige in the empire; the exploitation of tragic incidents of the war; the drug habit e.g. opium, morphia, cocaine etc.; the premeditated seduction of girls; 'first night' scenes; men and women in bed together; illicit sexual relationships; prostitution and pro-curation; the actual perpetration of criminal assaults on women; and the effect of venereal dis-eases. Moreover, the BBFC frowned upon prolonged fight or struggle scenes because of their presumed harmful influence on children, crime films and films dealing with marital unhappiness or infidelity. All these might be cut and would receive an 'A' certifi-cate even when passed, the BBFC warned, while crime films which specifically showed how criminals planned and carried out their crimes would be banned. In 1915 the BBFC viewed 4,789 films of which 4,395 were awarded a 'U' certificate, 372 an 'A' and 22 were rejected. The dearth of European films continued, which led to a further slight drop in the amount of footage viewed. American features had largely filled the European vacuum, while the decrease in the number of viewed features was caused by their growing length.

Of the 22 banned films eleven suffered this fate for wartime reasons. The grounds for the bans on the other eleven (See Appendix 3) were nudity, over-passionate love scenes, drugs, premeditated seduction of girls, men and women in bed together, prostitutes and pimping, and venereal disease, although it is no longer possible to trace which ground applied to which film. From other isolated examples it is clear that the BBFC's general rules were not always strict-ly adhered to in practice. For example, the award on 5 August 1915 of a 'U' certificate without cuts to the anti-black The Birth of a Nation (Epoch, 1915, dir D.W. Griffith) is not easy to reconcile with the BBFC's new-found sensitivity to racialism within the British empire as well as its aversion to excessive violence. Furthermore, where the BBFC's general rules clashed with wartime propaganda needs, the former were sometimes modified or disregarded. Cecil Hepworth's The Outrage involved a German's death in 1914 at the hands of the son of a girl whom the German had raped in the Franco-German war of 1870-1. The BBFC passed this material uncut on 27 October 1915 but with an 'A' certificate. The BBFC viewed The Outrage against a background of unfounded rumours in Britain that German troops had been mass raping Belgian women, which probably explains the BBFC acceptance of the film despite its general in-clination to stamp out rape as a screen topic. How-ever, a possibly even greater influence on The

Outrage decision was the German execution for spying
two weeks earlier of Edith Cavell, a British nurse in
Belgium who had been shot for helping British prisoners in German-occupied Belgium to escape. Although
in international law Germany had a strong case, Edith
Cavell was widely regarded in Britain as an innocent
victim of German barbarity. Early in November 1915
the crime novelist Edgar Wallace scripted a film submitted to the BBFC as The Martyrdom of Nurse Edith
Cavell. Initially the BBFC rejected it, evidently on
the ground that it exploited a tragic wartime incident for commercial profit, but on 11 November the
BBFC passed it with cuts and a 'U' certificate on
condition that Edith Cavell's name should not appear
on the screen or on posters or other publicity material. When this condition was accepted, the title was
altered to Nurse and Martyr and the film was released
late in 1915. This seems to have been the first
occasion when the BBFC had to consider a film dealing
with a specific First World War event. Doubtless the
BBFC was motivated by a wish not to offend the Cavell
family while simultaneously retaining the film's
propaganda value, but British cinema audiences were
left in no doubt that Nurse and Martyr referred to
Edith Cavell even without any express mention of her
name.
       At this time neither all of the local authorit-
ies nor the Home Office considered BBFC standards
sufficiently stringent. Some authorities had banned
films after the BBFC had allowed them - the subjects
were mostly sexual 'immorality' and bare knuckle
boxing matches - while some chief constables had
blamed films for an increase in juvenile delinquency.
During 1916 considerable pressure for a full-scale
central government censorship emerged from a minority
of local authorities which found a powerful ally in
Sir Herbert Samuel, now Home Secretary. Although a
Liberal within Asquith's wartime coalition, Samuel
favoured a censorship system operating under model
conditions drawn up in the Home Office with a new
censorship body to replace the BBFC. On 14 April
1916 at Samuel's initiative a London conference took
place between the Home Office and representatives
from 20 urban local authorities. Samuel himself
attended and made it plain from the outset that he
wanted a new BBFC with Home Office representatives
and possibly film industry appointees under Home
Office control. If the film producers or distributors bypassed the new BBFC, the individual cinema
would have to inform the local authority concerned
of its intention to screen any such film. The

authority could then proceed against the cinema under
the 1909 Cinematograph Act if it so wished. Samuel
admitted the difficulties of his proposals, but he
questioned whether the resulting problems would be
any greater than allowing the existing position to
continue. This conference's official record reveals
that Samuel was moved totally by social considerations rather than wartime pressures. Not once in the
conference was the war so much as mentioned, but the
fact that legal actions were pending against several
chief constables for their moves against certain
films was emphasised. Only Middlesex County Council
openly objected to Samuel's plan, but several other
authorities agreed only if it was a temporary measure
as a prelude to legislation establishing an official
Home Office censorship.

Although ill and within a few months of death,
Redford two days later rallied to the BBFC's defence.
In a letter to Samuel he put forward a strong argu-
ment for the retention of the status quo. Redford
commented,[13]

> The surmounting of such inevitable
> difficulties, the necessary conciliation
> of interested parties, and the suppress-
> ion or modification of objectionable films,
> often call for considerable tact and diplo-
> macy. Owing to our exceptional position
> with regard to all sections of the trade,
> we have generally been able to effect a
> successful arrangement of any difficulty
> that has arisen. I think it will be
> admitted that such censorship as we
> exercise, qualified and experienced, must
> have an advantage at a time like the
> present, and that any fresh institution
> would be at a disadvantage.

However, Samuel remained unmoved and went on the next
day to outline his scheme to film industry representatives, once more led by Brooke Wilkinson and Hepworth. The film delegation was predictably unenthusiastic. One member told Samuel that the film industry would accept his proposal if the new BBFC's decision was binding on local authorities, but not otherwise, while other members disagreed and all urged
Home Office co-operation with the existing BBFC,
possibly with the addition of Home Office-appointed
staff to confer an official status until legislation
was possible. Samuel did not commit himself to
accept any of the film industry's counter proposals

and perhaps underestimated the extent of the
opposition, for in his circular of 16 May to all
local authorities, when sounding them out on the
possibility of their acceptance without appeal of any
official government BBFC's decisions, he conveyed the
utterly erroneous impression that the film industry
favoured his plan.

This tactical error led the film industry to go
over to the offensive. Another deputation to Samuel
of 22 May expressed much stronger opposition than on
19 April, and a CEA letter of 27 May to Samuel was
strongly worded. However, the film world's sharper
resistance was not Samuel's only problem, for by mid-
July 1916 a diversity of local authority views had
also emerged. Some objected outright to a surrender
of their censorship powers, others were willing to
agree to Home Office policy and some wanted only
legislation to restrict the admission of children to
cinemas.[14] Nevertheless Samuel pressed ahead, the
broad lines of his plan appearing in a private Home
Office memorandum of 23 August 1916. The new BBFC
would consist of a chief censor as well as a number
of assistant censors, of whom at least one would be a
woman. None would have any connection with the film
industry, while in addition there would be an advisory committee appointed by the Home Secretary consis-
ting of local authority representatives, prominent
public figures, authors of standing who had no ties
with the cinema and only one member to represent the
film industry. At least one advisory committee
member would be a woman. The entire scheme was due
to take effect on 1 January 1917.

This policy relegated the film industry to a
very minor place in the censorship structure and
consequently provoked even fiercer resistance. When
a Home Office permanent adviser conferred on 7
September with Brooke Wilkinson, the latter reaffir-
med the film industry's strenuous opposition and
threatened a producers' public campaign against
Samuel's scheme. He counter proposed four film
industry members of the advisory committee rather
than one. At the same time Brooke Wilkinson was
approached about the secretaryship of the new BBFC.
He neither accepted nor declined the projected new
post but was interested enough to enter into a discussion of details about staff. He recommended the
appointment of Blaxland and Husey to the new BBFC
and suggested that the new President should be assisted by four male censors and two female ones. Each
film should be viewed by two male censors and a
woman, their decision being final with the President

consulted only in very borderline cases.[15]   In private the Home Office was prepared to go along with
Brooke Wilkinson's proposals, although it is unclear
whether he was ever expressly informed of this.
     If by appointing Brooke Wilkinson as Secretary
of the new BBFC Samuel hoped to take the sting out of
film world resistance, he was to be disappointed. A
CEA letter of 22 September to the Home Office challenged the legality of some Samuel proposals and
objected to other parts of the plan. In the light of
this letter Samuel on 13 October received yet another
film deputation which expressed its fear that the
small number of local authorities wishing to reserve
for themselves the final censorship decision would be
those with many cinemas, and that the advisory
committee would be packed with members of pro-censorship pressure groups or of religious bodies. The
deputation was also concerned that the advisory
committee would possess extensive powers, while the
delegation's general conclusion was that the Home
Office plans had been drafted with 'too much consideration for the susceptibilities of the local authorities and are calculated to foster their interference
rather than otherwise'.[16]   When on 27 October Samuel
met A.E. Newbould, the CEA chairman, he rejected the
latter's proposal that a new BBFC should be delayed
pending the outcome of a private enquiry by the
National Council of Public Morals into the social
results of film. However, Samuel had been sufficiently impressed by the film world's intense distrust of
some local authorities to ask Newbould for a list of
those the CEA believed were most reluctant to
surrender their censorship powers. He also on 3
November approached the dissenting authorities, asking them to reconsider their position in order to
reduce the strength of the film industry's opposition. As Samuel himself had explained to the film
deputation of 13 October, the industry's assent as
well as that of the local authorities was essential
because the government had committed itself in the
Commons to carry out only uncontroversial legislation
during the war. None the less there is tentative
evidence in a Home Office letter of 1 November to the
Board of Education that in the last analysis Samuel
was considering legislation to implement his proposals against all opposition.[17]
     Redford died on 10 November. The Home Office
documents afford no clue as to how his successor was
selected, but a minute by Harris of 21 December 1921
suggests that Samuel simply approved a film industry
appointment in order not to antagonise it still

further while his plan hung in the balance. Harris
in 1921 was to remark that Redford's decisions had
not been satisfactory, that the BBFC had reformed
itself as the film industry's reply to Samuel's
scheme and that the industry had chosen new BBFC
staff wisely.[18] Since the presidency was the only
change at the BBFC before 1922, it appears that the
new President was the choice of the industry, for
whom Brooke Wilkinson acted as intermediary,[19] rather
than the Home Office. This mantle now fell upon a
Liberal MP, T.P. O'Connor, who was then just turned
68 and still an active politician. Samuel possibly
hoped that a MP would facilitate Home Office policy,
and it might be a sign of BBFC apprehensions at
Samuel's proposals that during 1916 the number of
films banned on non-security grounds reverted to the
1913 high level. However, in the event the BBFC and
the film industry were fortuitously rescued from
Samuel when in December 1916 the Asquith government
fell. As a result Samuel left the Home Office with
film censorship still unreformed, and his successor
in the Lloyd George coalition, Sir George Cave, lost
little time in abandoning the Samuel scheme. However, Cave also urged the authorities to exercise
their powers under the 1909 act against objectionable
films to the full, and the BBFC deemed it prudent
from January 1917 onwards to supply the local authorities with a list of films allowed. Coupled with
the abandonment of the Samuel plan was Cave's decision to declare government approval for the National
Council of Public Morals commission of inquiry which
at once began its work. It sat for six months
during 1917 and heard evidence from among others
O'Connor who explained that the BBFC had drawn up 43
rules which, if infringed, led to cuts or bans. In
substance the 43 rules were a condensed version of
those published in the BBFC annual reports for 1913,
1914 and 1915.[20]
    O'Connor's public position as a MP probably
helped to secure a favourable commission of inquiry
reaction towards the BBFC and the film industry. In
consequence the Samuel proposals were shelved indefinitely, the Home Office implicitly endorsed the
status quo and film censorship ceased to be a public
issue for the remainder of the war. BBFC policies
therefore remained unaltered. Although the American
production companies apparently took it for granted
that the BBFC would not accept certain types of
features, there are indications that in fact the
BBFC was more liberal than the Americans gave it
credit for. For instance, the pacifist classic

Civilisation (Triangle, 1916, dir Thomas Ince), which depicts Jesus as an anti-war agitator, was not submitted to the BBFC, but it was shown in London without a BBFC certificate from October 1917 to February 1918, which brought only a few public protests to the Home Office.[21] However, the BBFC passed another American 1916 pacifist film, Herbert Brenon's War Bride, uncut with a 'U' certificate on 10 August 1916 as The War Bride of Plumville. This remarkable piece centres on a woman who organises a public campaign to persuade women to have no more children until men cease to fight wars. During a war such a theme might be seen as pure pacifist propaganda, but the BBFC was probably influenced in this case by the facts that the film is set in a European country resembling Germany, and that the woman commits suicide once she realises her anti-war efforts have failed and war would always exist. As no figures are available for the number of films which the BBFC passed during the war after 1915, the 23 banned 1917 films (See Appendix 3) cannot be placed in the overall context of BBFC policies.

Despite repeated BBFC bans and cuts on moral grounds and the National Council of Public Morals commission of inquiry's favourable conclusions, some local authorities did not abandon their belief that the BBFC was too lax. These authorities continued to ban BBFC-allowed films, one flagrant example being Shadows on My Life which the BBFC passed uncut on 17 January 1918 as Evelyn Thaw. She was an actress whose activities had attracted adverse publicity, and in March 1918 the CEA urged the BBFC to ban the film and in future to reject films exploiting the careers of 'notorious' personalities. The BBFC was already carrying out such a policy in connection with books which had a bad public reputation, but the decision in favour of Shadows on My Life stood. Nevertheless the BBFC accepted the CEA's general principle for the future. The BBFC banned a mere handful of films in 1918 (See Appendix 3), but this probably reflected, at least in part, the producers' awareness over several years of what the BBFC would stomach under wartime conditions. Features likely to fall foul of BBFC rules, particularly those made abroad, were often simply not submitted. Well-known examples are the D.W. Griffith masterpiece Intolerance (1916), which depicts four episodes of human bigotry including Christ's crucifixion, and Abel Gance's I Accuse (France, 1918), a powerful plea for peace and the first offering in such vein from a belligerent nation produced while the First World War was still in progress.

Only a small proportion of the films viewed at the BBFC in its early years is extant, and thus it is very difficult indeed to discover how flexible or otherwise the censors were in applying the rules in practice over a wide range of genres in peace and war. However, the First World War played a significant and decisive role in the BBFC's establishment as Britain's most important film censorship body even though problems persisted in the BBFC's relations with a small minority of local authorities. By the end of 1919 a majority of these came to accept a BBFC certificate as a sufficient guarantee of a film's suitability for public exhibition. Furthermore, the wartime co-operation between the BBFC, government departments and the government's press censorship apparatus had served to convince the Home Office that with O'Connor and Brooke Wilkinson at the helm the BBFC could be trusted to act in accordance with the broad lines of social convention. It could also preserve its own independence and simultaneously protect the film industry from dissatisfied local authorities and from pressure groups hankering after a stricter censorship system, without becoming involved in party politics. Liaison with government departments grew into a permanent characteristic of the BBFC's work after the First World War, while the BBFC also quietly retained its originally temporary wartime authority to censor 'topical' films whether these were educational documentaries or pressure group propaganda vehicles.

Chapter 2

THE CONSOLIDATION YEARS, 1919-1927

Some of O'Connor's 43 rules of 1917 were originally
intended to last only for the duration of the war,
but by the time the war ended the Bolsheviks had
seized power in Russia, Communist revolutions had
broken out in Germany and the working class comprised
a majority of the British electorate. The Lloyd
George coalition had swept back into office, and
Labour was a stronger force in the Commons than before the war. An upper and middle class fear of the
masses fed upon tension in industrial relations to
perpetuate the notion in these circles that a British
Communist revolution lay just around the corner. As
a result of the political confusion at home and
abroad the BBFC during 1919 quietly retained the temporary wartime rules against conflict in industrial
relations, Britain's poor relations with former
allies, unfavourable views of former allies, Indian
religious beliefs and British maltreatment of
colonial peoples.
     Although the wartime emergency regulations were
soon set aside, the BBFC in 1919 could not function
exactly as in August 1914. Film censorship had become more complex, for although the Americans were
producing fewer features, these were often much
longer than before the war - along the lines of The
Birth of a Nation, Civilisation and Intolerance - and
the BBFC usually viewed them more than once. Moreover, the war had contributed to the cinema's growing
popularity in Britain and converted it beyond question into the chief mass communication medium. A fear
of the masses, the presumed ability of film to
influence them and their newly gained potential
political power was evident in the BBFC 1919 annual
report which stated that crime stories 'make a strong
appeal to the imagination of the public, especially
to the less educated sections (author's italics)'.

To ram home the same point, the BBFC distinguished
the cinema from the theatre in a 1919 letter to
producers and local authorities concerning films
expressly made to influence public opinion.[1]

> The function of the Board is confined to
> the question whether films are suitable
> for exhibition in the usual cinemas, over
> which their jurisdiction and responsibility
> exist. The audience at a cinema is very
> differently constituted from that of a
> theatre, being composed largely of young
> people and family parties, who, more
> often then not, have no knowledge beforehand
> of the programme which is to be put before
> them. This consideration obviously (author's
> italics) imposes on the Board other canons
> of criticism than those which are adequate
> in the censorship of dramatic productions.

In other words films required a stricter censorship than the theatre because the clientele was the
working class. The BBFC report recommended the
exhibition of films trying to sway public opinion in
specially hired premises 'where securities could be
taken for choosing the audience which are impossible
in the ordinary cinema'. Later on the report again
emphasised the difference between cinema and theatre
audiences in order to justify bans on certain subjects to maintain public morality. The report concluded that '...the Board feels it ought to err, if
anything, on the side of restraint rather than slack-
ness'. In avoiding politics the report fostered the
impression that 'propaganda' films dealt only with
moral and social rather than political questions.
However, the report's stated grounds for cuts and
bans reveal that the BFFC was now exercising a
political censorship. Apart from the retention of
the temporary wartime rules, the BBFC had also inserted related new rules. These included the unauthorised use of royal names, public personalities and
well-known members of society; inflammatory political sub-titles; references to controversial domestic
or international politics; scenes calculated to
inflame racial hatred; misrepresentation of police
methods; scenes tending to disparage public characters and public institutions; and trial scenes of
important personages that were sub judice. The
BBFC's 43 rules of 1917 had expanded to 67, and
among the new non-political ones were sub-titles
with swearing; cock fights; criminal poisoning by

dissemination of germs; the 'third degree' American police interrogation method; the branding of animals and men; women fighting with knives; doubtful characters exalted into heroes; disparagement of marriage; excessive revolver shooting; advocacy of 'free love'; holding up as laudable the sacrifice of a woman's virtue; a husband's infidelity as justification of his wife's adultery; equivocal bedroom and bathroom scenes; illegal operations; a chosen immoral life, justified or extenuated; women promiscuously taking up men; dead bodies; 'clutching hands'; and animals gnawing men and children.

The substantial growth in the BBFC's restrictive function shows that the producers were trying to open up new cinematic ground as a result of the war, for the BBFC in 1919 also awarded more 'A' certificates than ever before - 829 compared to 1,454 'U' certificates; 228 films were cut, while a further eleven were banned (See Appendix 3).[2] The eleven reasons for suppression were a notorious drugs case; insistence on coloured racial inferiority (how the BBFC could reconcile this with its earlier decision to pass the anti-black The Birth of a Nation is obscure); predominance of crime and sympathy for the criminal; advocacy of 'free love'; inflammation of racial hatred; advocacy of anti-social and revolutionary doctrines; realistic executions; venereal disease; materialisation of the deity; illegal operations; and seduction or attempted seduction of girls treated without due restraint.

The origin of some of the new BBFC rules can be traced from the titles of the banned films, but other films were stifled without BBFC involvement. With the participation of British troops in anti-Bolshevik foreign intervention in Russia, British producers wished to exploit contemporary events. On the other hand contemporary political films might fall foul of the BBFC or arouse public pressure for a stricter censorship, possibly under state control. To test the social climate for such films, producers sometimes staged preliminary private performances for a selected audience of public personalities, including government ministers and MPs, and reporters from the quality press. One such in February 1919 concerned Russia, the Land of Tomorrow (Gaity, 1919, dir Maurice Sandground), which submerges a dramatic story in a survey of Russian events from the 1905 upheaval to the Bolshevik revolution. The Times questioned the use of film to attack Tsarism, and it was no coincidence that Russia, the Land of Tomorrow was subsequently neither submitted to the BBFC nor shown in public.

The sensitive link between films concerned with the Soviet Union and public order was demonstrated by an incident in Clapham outside the Majestic Picture Palace on 16 September 1919. A film hostile to Russia entitled Bolshevism had been advertised for showing on that date, whereupon the Clapham Independent Labour Party had threatened to disrupt the performance. The Majestic's manager had asked for police protection, while representatives from various ex-servicemen's organisations turned up to help the police. The police and the ex-servicemen repelled several rushes on the cinema by some 300 Independent Labour Party members. Despite the fights outside the cinema and protests about the film from some ejected audience members, the showing of Bolshevism was completed. However, it was apparently not shown again and was never submitted for censorship. While the Clapham affray was an isolated incident, it nevertheless probably conditioned the attitude of both the BBFC and many local authorities to contemporary political films in general and Soviet films in particular for years to come. Moreover, the Amritsar massacre of April 1919, when General Dyer gave an order to fire on an Indian crowd which resulted in 379 deaths, almost certainly accounts for the BBFC's continued unwillingness to see British imperial rule depicted unfavourably. In 1919 the royal family twice appeared in features. The Power of Right, which the BBFC passed uncut on 1 April, showed one scene with the real Prince of Wales, the future Edward VIII, while Queen Mary and the dowager Queen Alexandra appeared in person in Women Who Win (Trans-Atlantic, 1919, dirs Fred Durrant and Percy Nash). King George V's permission was necessary for these royal appearances, which explains the BBFC's new 1919 ban on the unauthorised use of royal names.

In October 1919 the BBFC was bypassed with Mr Wu (Stoll, 1919, dir Maurice Elvey), the first of two silent versions (the second was made in 1927 with Lon Chaney Senior) in which Wu (played by Matheson Lang) is portrayed unfavourably for killing his daughter when she tarnishes the family honour by wishing to marry a Briton. As The Times of 20 October 1919 noted, the film emphasises 'oriental cunning', and it proved to be the forerunner of many inter-war features which stereotyped the Chinese in derogatory racial terms. As such Mr Wu infringed the BBFC rule against the disparagement of Britain's wartime allies, for China in 1917 had declared war on Germany, although she had done no fighting.

However, the release circumstances of Mr Wu reflected
film censorship confusion between the end of the war
and 1921. The difficulty lay with the BBFC's all-
embracing definition of 'propaganda' films as those
intending to influence public opinion, which failed
to distinguish between unworthy and worthy causes.
Where local authorities considered a cause to be
worthy, they wished any film supporting it to be shown
in their areas even if the BBFC refused it a certificate. The most glaring 1919 example was Damaged
Goods (Samuelson, 1919, dir Alexander Butler), based
upon a successful play which served as a warning
against venereal disease to juveniles of both sexes.
The Samuelson company had approached the BBFC about
the possibility of a film on this theme as early as
mid-1917 when Husey had seen the play and informed
the company that no film based upon it would pass the
BBFC without considerable changes to both story and
subject.[3] None the less Samuelson had gone ahead,
and after a private showing in London in mid-December
1919 a few liberal clergymen and MPs endeavoured to
mobilise public support. However, the BBFC refused
to go back on its ban of 21 November. Although
Damaged Goods was supported by many local authorities, it was not shown in public at all.
    By the end of 1919 the BBFC had moved to more
spacious premises at 167-169 Wardour Street. The
move was a reflection of improved finances, for
during the war BBFC fees for viewing film for export
on the government's behalf had exceeded one million
pounds, a huge sum for the time. Growing affluence
brought increased self-confidence, as the BBFC
demonstrated in its treatment of challenges to the
1919 rules during 1920-1. In those two years only
eight films were actually banned (See Appendix 3),
but the number of films cut and the proportion of 'A'
certificates to 'U's mounted dramatically despite a
reduced total annual footage viewed. In 1920 the
percentage of 'A' films was 45.8, in 1921 49.7.
During 1921 no fewer than 433 films were cut, more
than one fifth of the films submitted in the year
(1,960). The grounds for the eight bans were only
six - brothel scenes; a woman surrendering her
virginity for a good purpose; incidents in the life
of a prostitute; horror and torture scenes;
advocacy of 'free love'; and crime and immorality.
However, there were 38 grounds for cuts in 1921
alone. Some of these were industrial relations,
revolutionary propaganda, inflammatory political
sub-titles and British social life held up to
ridicule. Nevertheless, despite the high level of

cuts, the BBFC bent over backwards to cut a film
rather than ban it, for it was during this period
that O'Connor and Brooke Wilkinson instigated the
practice of meeting individual producers and distributors at the BBFC offices to discuss projected films
and changes to completed films. This informal procedure, of which no detailed records survive, seems to
have superseded the regular committee meetings with
representatives of the producers, distributors and
exhibitors.

However, during 1920-1 the BBFC's uneasy relations with local authorities supporting nationally
uncontroversial causes persisted. As a result by-
passing of the BBFC, particularly in London, grew
more frequent. In January 1920 the newly formed
League of Nations Union arranged a twice-daily,
three-week showing at the Albert Hall for Auction of
Souls. This film, produced privately by Colonel W.R.
Selig and based upon a book called Ravished Armenia
as well as upon the report of the League-appointed
Bryce commission, deals in documentary style with the
Turkish massacre of the Armenians in 1915. It stars
Aurora Mardiganian, a young girl who according to the
publicity material for the film had narrowly escaped
death in the massacre and later been sold to a Turk
as a slave. One scene explicitly shows the crucifixion of 14 naked Armenian girls and women. The
purpose of the Albert Hall run was to gain public
support for League protection of persecuted national
minorities, to which end the film had first been
privately shown to a large audience of public figures, including O'Connor, at the Queen's Hall on 29
October 1919. However, the effect at the BBFC had
been rather the opposite, for at the end of December
Husey had informed the Foreign Office that the film's
British agents had rejected cuts, and that in consequence the BBFC would refuse Auction of Souls a certificate.

The Foreign Office feared that the film might
arouse anti-Turkish feeling in Britain and thus
influence the peace talks with the Turks then still
in progress, while Lord Curzon, the Secretary of
State for India, was concerned that anti-Christian
sub-titles might provoke Moslem uprisings in Egypt
and India during the aftermath of the Amritsar
incident. On 5 January 1920 Curzon proposed to the
Foreign Office that the Home Office should ban the
film on the pretext of harm to public morals. As a
result Scotland Yard officers on 14 January visited
the film's agents, presumably to warn that a prosecution might arise if the Albert Hall showing went

ahead. The League of Nations Union had already
protested to the Home Office about this action when
on 17 January Husey, a Home Office adviser and two
Scotland Yard officers viewed the film. The latter
two believed that only the crucifixion scene need be
cut, but after a further viewing by the same four men
two days later it was agreed to ask the producer to
make other cuts as well. The Home Office feared that
if it demanded too many changes, the producers might
refuse to carry out any cuts and risk prosecution,
with no guarantee that the prosecution would succeed,
but eventually the Home Office insisted upon cuts to
five scenes which were agreed to. The Home Secretary, Edward Shortt, who was to become BBFC President
from 1929 to 1935, never saw the film, but in public
he gave permission for the Auction of Souls performance to take place on 20 January as planned, provided
the crucifixion scene was cut and 'christian' was
omitted from the sub-titles.[4]
   The Auction of Souls affair opened the way for
other controversial films to bypass the BBFC. Such
few war films as had been shown in Britain since the
armistice were mostly vengeful, seeking to capitalise
on immediate post-war germanophobia. Anti-war films
were not distributed, but in the wake of Auction of
Souls Abel Gance's distinguished I Accuse was at last
shown in London in May 1920. The film calls into
question the very purpose of the First World War, and
its success at the Philharmonic Hall suggests that
anti-war sentiment in Britain was already gaining
ground, at least among the educated classes, less
than two years after the armistice. However, the
silent version of I Accuse was not submitted to the
BBFC and as a result has never been widely shown.
   After the success of Auction of Souls and I
Accuse distributors planned as standard policy a
trial run in London to test public reaction before
submitting a controversial film to the BBFC. The
Land of Mystery, produced and directed by Harold
Shaw, was in 1920 reportedly the most expensive
British film ever made, but its content was very
recent Russian history when Russia herself remained
convulsed by civil war. The film, which traces the
fall of the Romanov dynasty and the growth of
Bolshevism in uncontroversial factual presentation,
was shown at the Winter Garden Theatre on 1 July 1920
to an invited audience including MPs and members of
the Lords. Their resulting approval caused Shaw to
add footage of rural Russia between the downfall of
Tsarism and the Bolshevik seizure of power before he
put on his two-hour film at the London Pavilion on 19

July. After its initial success he sent The Land of
Mystery on 4 August to the BBFC which, after many
objections, finally passed it with only minor cuts
and an 'A' certificate on 2 November.
     In other respects, however, the BBFC was less
cautious. John Barrymore's stirring performance in
the title role of Dr Jekyll and Mr Hyde transformed
Robert Louis Stevenson's novel into a horror film,
but the BBFC on 25 August 1920 allowed it with an 'A'
certificate and only one sub-title alteration. No
local authority complained, while press comment was
favourable. On 25 November 1920 Gaumont submitted to
the BBFC Li-Hang the Cruel which concerns the callous
Chinaman of the name part who blackmails a European
merchant into giving him permission to marry the
merchant's daughter. When she carries out her
father's wishes but refuses to consummate the
marriage, Li-Hang rapes his own wife when she cannot
submit herself to him. Mindful of Mr Wu a year
earlier and the possible adverse influence of such
films on Anglo-Chinese relations, the BBFC did not
pass Li-Hang the Cruel until 2 March 1921 and then
only on condition that a foreword was added indicat-
ing that Li-Hang was not a typical Chinese. The film
opened in London with minor cuts on 13 March, and the
hostile review in The Times makes it plain that the
rape scene was retained. A more complex case faced
the BBFC with The Branding Iron, a Sam Goldwyn
production of 1920 in which Barbara Castleton is
stripped to the waist and branded on her back. A
branding had already appeared in The Cheat (Paramount, 1915, dir Cecil B. De Mille), but this had run
into difficulties in Britain for political reasons.
When it had been shown briefly in Edinburgh and
London during 1916, Japan had protested about its
anti-Japanese content. The story concerns a wealthy
Japanese (Sessue Hayakawa) who during a quarrel
brands the American married woman he has fallen in
love with on the shoulder with a red hot iron.
According to Brooke Wilkinson on 5 August 1916, the
BBFC had already banned The Cheat, but there is no
record of this in the BBFC records. However, on Home
Office instructions the Metropolitan Police
suppressed The Cheat later in August 1916. De Mille
had remade it in 1919, and it had been shown in
London without submission to the BBFC in February
1920. Japan again protested because although the
wealthy Japanese had been changed to a Burmese, he
was still played by Sessue Hayakawa (a Japanese),
dressed as a Japanese and lived in a Japanese-style
decorated house. A Foreign Office adviser had then

seen the remake and agreed with Japan, the Home
Office once more initiating the suppression of the
film in March 1920.[5] Not until 19 November 1923,
when the 1902 Anglo-Japanese alliance which had
brought Japan into the First World War had ended,
would the BBFC allow the remake of The Cheat with a
minor cut. This reversal of policy was probably
connected with The Branding Iron as well as Anglo-
Japanese relations. On 4 January 1921 the BBFC
passed The Branding Iron with minor cuts which retained at least a part of the branding scene. For
some reason the film was not released in Britain
until March 1922 when its violent end did not arouse
unfavourable press comment.

Such liberal decisions did nothing to dispel the
confused film censorship structure of 1920-1. The
BBFC had clashed with bodies like the church and the
League of Nations Union whose public reputations were
unblemished. Some local authorities and individual
exhibitors wished to show films supported by such
bodies without BBFC approval if necessary, while
other local authorities remained anxious to ban
doubtful films allowed by the BBFC. The legal
position was unclear but was clarified to some extent
through developments in London and Middlesex during
1920-1. Middlesex County Council in 1920 had inserted into its film licensing conditions a clause to the
effect that any exhibited film had to possess a BBFC
certificate. However, when a Twickenham cinema had
shown Auction of Souls, Middlesex County Council had
sued the exhibitor for breach of contract. This case
had gone to the Court of Appeal which had decided
that the new licensing regulation was unreasonable in
that there was no appeal against BBFC rulings. The
court also suggested that the regulation should be
amended in such a way as to allow an exhibitor to
appeal to a local authority against a BBFC ban. This
judgment showed that local authorities possessed the
ultimate legal right to decide whether or not a film
should be allowed in their areas, but at the same
time it did not destroy the accepted authority of the
BBFC. In October 1921 the London County Council
(LCC) notified the BBFC that it would follow the
court's ruling but also restrict the showing of BBFC-
allowed films to adults only, regardless of certificate. This would have barred London children from
cinemas altogether and partly nullified the purpose
of the BBFC as well as reduced film industry profits.
Consequently the LCC decision led to a hastily summ-
oned conference involving the Home Office, the LCC,
the various sections of the film industry and the

BBFC. At length in December 1921 the LCC agreed to
permit only BBFC-passed films unless these were sub-
versive of public morality. Only children of 16 and
over could see 'A' films, while the under-16s had
always to be accompanied by a parent or legal guardian. This system came into operation in London on 1
July 1922 and was so successful that a year later the
Home Office was to advise all local authorities to
follow London's lead. Most were to do so by the end
of 1924, which brought a large measure of uniformity
to British film censorship for the first time.

However, controversy over film censorship was
never far from the surface of British public life
from 1921 to 1924. In February 1921 press criticism
of the BBFC for having passed The House of Children
gave rise to renewed press advocacy of a state censorship. Parliamentary questions on the subject were
tabled for Shortt to answer in the Commons on 23 and
28 February, but by now the Home Office had become
convinced of the BBFC's indispensability. Harris on
21 February wrote that the failure of the 1916 Samuel
proposals had been a 'blessing in disguise'.[6] Another Home Office view of 29 July 1921 was that 'complaints as to films made by the public...afford little
ground for now doubting the adequacy of the trade
censorship'.[7] But before the year was out a fresh
controversy was in the making. The Times of 23
November 1921 published a letter from Major-General
Sir Stanley Von Donop protesting against a British
film entitled The Betrayal of Lord Kitchener (Screen-
plays, 1921, dir Percy Nash, alternatively known as
The Kitchener Film or How Lord Kitchener was Bet-
rayed). The basis of Von Donop's protest was that
the film was inaccurate in its contention that a
German female spy had learned from a War Office staff
member about Minister of War Kitchener's impending
secret trip to Russia in June 1916 and had informed
Berlin, with the result that a U-boat had torpedoed
HMS Hampshire and Kitchener had been killed. The
film touched upon and revived a wartime controversy
about Kitchener's death, and the day after the publication of Von Donop's letter the LCC announced a
ban on the film. In the light of the adverse publicity it was not submitted to the BBFC until 10
April 1922, when O'Connor viewed it with Admiralty,
Air Ministry, Home Office, Imperial War Museum and
War Office staff. Three days later O'Connor banned
it, but in November 1922 it opened at the Leicester
Square Cinema, whereupon the LCC instituted legal
proceedings. The court granted an interim injunction
against further showings, and the licensee

subsequently conceded the case. The Betrayal of Lord Kitchener was also banned in France and the United States as a result of British representations.[8]

The suppression of The Betrayal of Lord Kitchener at home and abroad showed how a determined and influential minority could place the BBFC under pressure before it had a chance to arrive at an independent decision. The Von Donop-instigated early press campaign against the film evidently reinforced the Home Office's satisfaction with the status quo. On 21 December 1921 Harris, who by now was a leading Home Office permanent official and the most experienced in film censorship, observed,[9]

> ...the Board has secured for itself an
> independent position; the present
> members would not, I think, tolerate any
> interference with the exercise of their
> judgment, and it is only fair to the
> trade to add that they (sic) seem to have
> given their Board a free hand. If ever
> the position of the Board were altered it
> would become necessary to consider the
> question of appointing an official Board.

This comment was telling testimony on the work of O'Connor and Brooke Wilkinson since 1916.

Among the eight BBFC-rejected films of 1922 (See Appendix 3) was Nosferatu (Germany, 1922, dir Friedrich Murnau), submitted as Dracula, but this decision attracted no public attention, whereas the ban on Cocaine (Astra, 1922, dir Jack Graham Cutts) caused much friction between its producer, Herbert Wilcox, and the BBFC. From September 1921 to April 1922 Hollywood's reputed off-screen debauchery had centred on Roscoe 'Fatty' Arbuckle who was charged with the murder of a girl at a party. In fact Arbuckle was innocent, but in the United States even after his acquittal he became the victim of public anti-Hollywood hysteria. As a result the BBFC became even more cautious than hitherto over drugs. O'Connor viewed Cocaine on 9 May 1922 and on Home Office advice banned it three days later.[10] This decision annoyed Wilcox because of the high production costs when the British film industry needed maximum encouragement to fight American competition and because Wilcox himself had gone out of his way to make Cocaine acceptable to the BBFC. Wilcox refused to accept the BBFC ban, but his efforts in London to show Cocaine, which delivers a clear warning against drugs but depicts much night club life and the

effects of cocaine, were thwarted by LCC support of
the BBFC ban. However, Manchester took a different
view, Cocaine being shown at the Gaiety Picture House
in May 1922 when it attracted large audiences.
O'Connor on 15 May asked Shortt to place pressure on
Manchester to rescind the decision. Since the Home
Office feared that the existing censorship would
break down through Manchester's decision, Shortt on
23 May wrote to the Lord Mayor of Manchester but
without success. Cardiff followed Manchester's
example and came under identical Home Office pressure. After an initial refusal to give way, Cardiff
banned Cocaine on 31 May following a Chinese protest
to the Home Office about an advertising poster in
Cardiff which showed a leering Chinaman![11] But the
continuing success of the film in Manchester virtually compelled O'Connor to reconsider the BBFC ban, a
full version with some sub-title alterations being
passed on 19 June 1922 under the title of While
London Sleeps. An exactly opposite fate awaited
Foolish Wives (Universal, 1921, dir Erich Von
Stroheim), which was submitted to the BBFC in eleven
parts during August 1922 and cut only in the eleventh
part. This story of a bogus aristocrat who seduces
and then blackmails rich women in Monte Carlo opened
in London in September. There it ran for several
weeks, but on 16 November Manchester banned it, a
curious decision in the light of Cocaine!
    Cocaine and Foolish Wives showed that even by
the end of 1922, despite the LCC's October 1921 lead
in the direction of consistency, the censorship situation still lacked uniformity. However, the percentage of 'A' certificates in the BBFC's 1922 total
passes dropped to 26.6 (1,546 'U's, 560 'A's) and in
1923 to 13.3 (1,659 'U's, 254 'A's). This trend, in
marked contrast to 1920-1, lasted until the emergence
of sound (1924 20.7 per cent; 1925 18.6; 1926 19.4;
1927 18.9; 1928 17.3 and 1929 21.9) and was a tribute to previous BBFC firmness. But at the same time
these statistics, coupled with the large number of
BBFC cuts throughout the 1920s, disclose that
American and British film-makers never ceased to try
to erode the BBFC rules. 1922 also saw important
changes in BBFC personnel. The two unknown censors
with the initials CCR and OC both ended their service, one through death. As their replacements
O'Connor appointed the first lady censor, Redford's
widow, and Colonel J.C. Hanna DSO, who was destined
in 1930 to succeed Husey as chief censor and play a
leading part in BBFC affairs until 1946.
    Towards the end of 1922, when the general

censorship position remained unstable, O'Connor
initiated the BBFC's first public relations exercise.
This took the form of a pamphlet O'Connor himself
wrote, The Principles of Film Censorship, which the
BBFC published in January 1923 and reprinted immediately after his death in November 1929. In the
pamphlet O'Connor described how the BBFC functioned
and defended both its rules and general policy,
including the anonymity of the censors, as well as
the wider film censorship status quo. He advocated
deeper collaboration between the BBFC and the local
authorities and remarked,

> I have immense faith in the even yet
> unexplored potentialities of the film
> ...for the moment responsible for the
> guardianship of the cinema industry,I
> feel that I have a great duty...to
> safeguard not merely the decency of the
> film, but also its liberty.

This was not the language of a government hack,
and it was a measure of the BBFC's progress in ten
years that O'Connor did not consult the Home Office
beforehand as Redford had done over the BBFC 1913
annual report. On 30 April 1923, on the eve of a
Home Office film censorship conference with the local
authorities,Harris recognised this progress when he
observed,[12]

> The chief examiner - Mr Husey - is not a
> man who would continue to hold office if
> there was any suspicion of wire-pulling.
> One of the great advantages the Board
> possesses is that they (sic) can often
> persuade members of the trade by private
> negotiation to alter films...I doubt if an
> official Board would retain the same
> influence, and it might easily happen that
> the trade would be tempted to fight the
> decisions of an official Board to the ut-
> most. Another advantage is that the Home
> Office is relieved of a direct responsibil-
> ity which it will have to accept if the
> Board were official, and it must be remem-
> bered that criticism would come not only
> from the public in different parts of the
> country, but from aggrieved members of the
> trade who would not be very scrupulous in
> their methods.

Clearly the film industry's strong stand against
Samuel in 1916 had made a lasting impression in
Whitehall. It was thus not surprising that at the
conference of 3 May the Home Office supported the LCC
and Middlesex County Council in their expressed satisfaction with the BBFC against those authorities,
mostly urban, pressing for a more official body than
the BBFC, unfinanced by the film industry in any way.
On 12 May in a speech at Central Hall, Westminster,
O'Connor took up much the same themes as in his
pamphlet. It was testimony to his foresight and
dedication that he spared so much time from his parliamentary activities for a post which carried no
public prestige, while his readiness to air film
censorship issues in public strengthened the Home
Office in its dealings with those authorities seeking
an official censorship.
      However, while the Home Office was mulling over
its next move towards uniformity, the BBFC in mid-May
1923 was called upon to deal with Married Love. This
film was based upon Dr Marie Stopes's book of the
same name which had advocated birth control within
marriage under cover of a dramatic story, and she
herself had written the script. O'Connor viewed it
with Harris and LCC members. O'Connor and Harris
favoured an outright ban, but the LCC representatives
differed. If the BBFC banned but LCC allowed Married
Love, other local authorities would probably follow
the LCC and the Home Office efforts to bring about
censorship uniformity might be frustrated. Under
such circumstances O'Connor became anxious to avoid a
ban. With LCC agreement the BBFC in June 1923 passed
the film with substantial cuts eliminating the under-
lying birth control material and a new title of
Maisie's Marriage as well as the removal of Marie
Stopes's book and name from the credits.[13] An
awkward problem was circumvented, and on 6 July 1923
the way was at last clear for a Home Office circular
urging all local authorities not to pass BBFC-rejected films and to follow the LCC admission system of
1922. Most authorities came into line by December
1924.
      1923 proved to be a relatively humdrum year for
routine censorship. Of the ten BBFC-banned films
(See Appendix 3) only Boston Blackie retains any
special significance. He was an American confidence
trickster who has to solve crimes to divert police
attention from his own criminal activities. In 1941-
9 the character (Chester Morris) appeared in thirteen
Columbia B-features which raised no censorship problems. From this one can surmise that in 1923 Boston

Blackie fell prey to the BBFC's insistence that a criminal should not be permitted to have his crime undiscovered by the law. During the year 227 films were cut. Among the innovations for bans and cuts were themes impugning the honour of the medical profession; painful scenes of lunacy; medical subjects unsuitable for general exhibition; scenes of Suttee (the practice by which a Hindu widow in India was placed in her husband's funeral pyre); extenuation of crime on grounds of ostensible good motives; misrepresentation of prison life, and the holding up of constituted authorities generally to odium; knuckle fights with intent to bodily injury; glove fights carried to the point of brutality; fights between women; and methods of forgery and blackmail which could be copied.

On 7 February 1923 the BBFC passed uncut The Golem (Germany, 1920, dirs Paul Wegener and Carl Böse), the story of a 16th century Jewish rabbi in Prague who builds a clay figure to protect the city's Jews from a pogrom, which was influential on Hollywood sound horror films following the success in 1931 of Frankenstein (Universal, dir James Whale). Like The Golem, The Wandering Jew (Stoll, 1923, dir Maurice Elvey), the story of a Jew condemned to eternal life (Matheson Lang) after death at the hands of the Spanish Inquisition, might have stimulated anti-Semitism, but nevertheless the BBFC allowed it in May 1923. Moreover, despite the preoccupation of Dr Mabuse (Germany, 1922, dir Fritz Lang) with a raving lunatic criminal mastermind, the BBFC passed it on 10 January 1923 in its original four-hour long two parts which received a London opening in March. Such cautiously liberal decisions probably took into account that foreign films other than American were unlikely for commercial reasons to receive a general release, for they were usually restricted to specialist cinemas in the large city centres. Nevertheless some British producers continued to bypass the BBFC while they still had a chance to do so, for by 1923 the British film industry was making fewer than 50 films a year and was showing signs of desperation in attempting to ward off American competition. Possibly the best example was Dr Fu Manchu (Stoll, 1923, dir Fred Paul), the western-educated Chinese master criminal created in 1911 by Sax Rohmer as the Yellow Peril incarnate in one man. The film, 15 distinct episodes with H. Agar-Lyons in the title role, followed the racialist trail already blazed by Mr Wu and Li-Hang the Cruel and opened in London in May 1923 without submission to the BBFC.

At first a more stable political climate at home and abroad in the mid-1920s made no impact on British film censorship, for in content the staple diet of 1924-5 films remained much the same as earlier in the decade. Of the 15 films which the BBFC banned during those two years (See Appendix 3) only one - Human Wreckage (USA, 1923, dir John Griffith Wray) - possesses any significance in cinema history. In January 1923 top box office star Wallace Reid had died of drugs. As a result his widow, Dorothy Davenport, had sponsored Human Wreckage and starred in it with Bessie Love. To overcome censorship difficulties, Mrs Reid had given the film a foreword which began, 'Dope is the gravest menace which today confronts the United States.'[14] However, the film itself (now lost) contained a scene in which Bessie Love prepares to inject herself with morphine, while in 1922 the same moral veneer had failed to save Cocaine from the BBFC's initial displeasure. The BBFC banned Human Wreckage in January 1924, but it appears that Mrs Reid would not give in without a struggle. She evidently sent a representative to Britain to arrange a private showing for public celebrities to put the BBFC under pressure to reconsider its decision, as Wilcox had done successfully with Cocaine. Brooke Wilkinson on 6 March 1924 wrote to the Home Office to warn of what was afoot and condemned Human Wreckage in strong terms.[15]

> There have been few, if any films, submitted to the Board since its inception which the examiners look upon as more dangerous than this film 'Human Wreckage', and we see no possibility of altering it so as to make it suitable for public exhibition in this country.

The eventual outcome is unclear, but the BBFC did not lift its ban.

The new BBFC grounds for cuts and bans in 1924-5 were offensive and unseemly scenes in places of worship; scenes of the Last Judgment; bringing discredit on British uniforms; British officers and officials in India and elsewhere shown in invidious circumstances; misuse of titles actually borne by living persons; libels on the British nursing profession; Bolshevik propaganda; incitement to class hatred; grossly vulgar and offensive travesties of the First World War; scenes of orgy and dissolute revelry; serious crimes lending themselves to imitation; methods of attempted suicide capable

of imitation; oppressive treatment of natives;
scenes suggestive of indulgence of vice; immorality
and debauchery; attempts at procuration; depiction
of the lives of immoral women; American 'road house'
scenes; complacent acquiescence of a husband in his
wife's infidelity; and advocacy of contraception.
This list was a logical extension of the BBFC's
openly stated general policy since 1913, although the
inclusion of Bolshevik propaganda and incitement to
class hatred was the first overt admission that the
BBFC was discriminating against a particular
political party.

The BBFC's treatment of Cecil B. De Mille and
Erich Von Stroheim during the first half of the 1920s
is illuminating. Manslaughter (Paramount, 1922, dir
Cecil B. de Mille), now a cinematic curiosity,
centres upon a crusading district attorney who draws
parallels between Roman orgies and wild parties in
the contemporary United States, then in the early
stages of prohibition. De Mille used his mastery of
spectacle to emphasise the supposed similarity, with
the result that the BBFC on 22 November 1922 had cut
Manslaughter by 1,000 feet, about 17 minutes running
time and over 10 per cent of its total length.
This represented a particularly savage cut for the
time, and the theme of De Mille's next film, The Ten
Commandments (Paramount-Famous Players/Lasky, 1923),
must have aroused the BBFC's apprehensions in the
context of its religious policy. The film is really
one of two unconnected halves, the first of which
deals with Moses's leadership of the Israelites to
the promised land of modern San Francisco. This was
prickly stuff to place before a BBFC riddled with
anti-Americanism, yet the film was passed on 22
February 1924 with cuts to only one scene. Von
Stroheim's films, too, were not unduly mutilated.
For example, Blind Husbands (Universal, 1919), the
story of an Austrian officer who seduces a wealthy
American's wife which is a barbed satire on contemporary sexual conventions, had been passed on 11 June
1920 with only minor cuts.

The Film Society, founded by London middle and
upper class intellectuals as an outlet for films
likely to incur the displeasure of the BBFC or local
authorities, was established in 1925. It was a club
which charged a high annual membership subscription
and hired premises for special performances, usually
on a Sunday. It was also a limited company to which
the LCC granted licences for its showings because it
had taken precautions to keep working class members
to a minimum. The Film Society placed on a more

35

formal basis the previous tendency of producers to show risky films in London at celebrated venues and thus to evade censorship. In 1925 the Film Society possessed no political undertones, but shortly after its formation the first Soviet films reached Britain and were shown at the Film Society over the next five years. By contrast the initial fate in Britain during 1925 of The Phantom of the Opera (Universal, 1924, dir Rupert Julian) was unique. This now acclaimed horror classic starring Lon Chaney Senior first appeared in the United States during the first half of 1925 and in consequence was the recipient of adverse publicity in Britain before the film actually arrived there. As a result the CEA took a public stand against it, and in August Universal withdrew it from Britain without a public performance but five years later added a sound track, the BBFC passing this version uncut on 7 July 1930. What the BBFC's decision in 1925 would have been can only be conjectured.

Politics in 1925 largely centred upon British negotiations with Belgium, France, Germany and Italy for the Locarno treaties, signed in October. Just as these were close to completion Captain J. Noel planned to show Red Russia in London for an eight-week season beginning on 5 October. It covers the Bolshevik revolution of 1917 and had been filmed in 1921, since when footage dealing with post-1917 Russian conditions had been added. Noel's motive was probably to stimulate anti-Soviet feeling to render the Anglo-German reconciliation symbolised by Locarno more palatable to British public opinion, for Red Russia in November 1921 had provoked Communist disturbances in Amsterdam and Bordeaux and the overt anti-Soviet content conflicted with the BBFC's policy of no political controversy. When Red Russia was submitted to the BBFC on 24 September 1925, it predictably ran into trouble and its opening date had to be put back. Eventually it opened on 20 October, over two weeks late, after the BBFC had passed it on the 12th. However, BBFC cuts amounted to 4,100 feet, a colossal reduction for a silent film.

Red Russia ushered in a period when both domestic and international politics came to intrude more and more on the BBFC's work. The first of the American anti-war features, The Big Parade (MGM, 1925, dir King Vidor), opened in Britain in May 1926. It describes the Western Front experiences of a young American patriotic volunteer (John Gilbert) who once in France becomes bent on personal survival but is none the less wounded and has a leg amputated. This

story fitted in with the 'forgive and forget' mood
of Locarno, which is evidenced by the film's 24-week
run in London. The Big Parade posed no special
problems for the BBFC because the anti-war theme was
subdued and sober as well as uncontroversial,
although the sub-titles contain the word 'b------s'
when Gilbert shouts at the Germans who have just
killed his friend. What Price Glory? (Fox, 1926, dir
Raoul Walsh), which opened in Britain in March 1927,
is much more heavy handed in its pacifist approach
and uses the play's bad language which an audience
could identify through the actors' lip movements.
Nevertheless the BBFC passed it on 28 February 1927
with only minor cuts and some sub-title alterations.
However, if anti-war sentiment was unexceptionable
British politics in 1926-7, the same could not be
said for industrial relations. The British proper-
tied classes' fear of revolution, temporarily buried
in the decisive Conservative election victory of
October 1924 after the short-lived first minority
Labour government, was fully revived in the unprecedented nine-day general strike of May 1926. Despite
the swift collapse of the strike, the general political climate thus created made for an extremely
unpropitious appearance in Britain of Potemkin (USSR,
1925, dir Sergei Eisenstein). Now known as Battleship Potemkin, this homage to the Bolshevik revolution culminates in the spectacular Odessa Steps
massacre sequence when the Tsarist army shoots down
innocent civilians. Eisenstein's narrative montage
is so unambiguously pro-revolutionary and memories of
the general strike were so recent that the BBFC might
have undone all of its previous work if the film had
been allowed. After BBFC consultation with the Home
Secretary, Sir William Joynson-Hicks,[16] who was
hostile to the cinema in general, Battleship Potemkin
was banned on 30 September 1926, a decision not
reversed at the BBFC until 1954.
    By 1926 post-war resentment at the American
cinematic hegemony in Britain was penetrating into
politics. The BBFC 1925 report had commented adver-
sely on the growing use of non-British (i.e.
American, although the United States was not named)
terms and idioms in sub-titles. O'Connor had already
written to the producers asking them to edit sub-
titles 'to bring them more in accordance with the
English language'. He also drew attention to the
danger of American cultural penetration through the
cinema in a speech at Greenwich on 30 April 1926.
Moreover, the subject of American films not only in
Britain but also throughout the empire was raised at

the 1926 Imperial Conference where it was agreed that
more British films were desirable to counteract a
possible American monopoly. In this context Stanley
Baldwin's Tory government was given a salutary
reminder in November 1926 of highly placed British
hostility to American films. One such was The
Unknown Soldier (1926, dir Renaud Hoffmann), the
story of a soldier who returns home to the United
States after some years at the Western Front to a
wife who had never accepted that he had been killed.
This film was due to be premiered in Britain during
the armistice week of November 1926. On 8 November,
Joynson-Hicks received representatives of ten right-
wing societies, including the British Fascists,
following a British Women's Patriotic League appeal
direct to Baldwin for the suppression or postponement
of the film on the ground that the unknown soldier
was American. This conflicted with the widely held
notion in Britain that the unknown soldier was solely
a British invention deriving from the placement of
his grave at Westminster Abbey in 1920. Joynson-
Hicks pointed out to the societies that he had no
power to ban films, only the BBFC had. Thereupon the
societies took exception to the entire censorship
system and pressed for the establishment of a govern-
ment-appointed BBFC to be financed by the Treasury.
The societies then switched their attack onto the
floor of the Commons. Sir William Davison, the
Conservative MP for South Kensington, asked on 10
November whether the Home Office would ban The
Unknown Soldier. He was told that the BBFC had
already passed it, it had been shown in public and
the Home Office would take no action. On 11 January
1927 O'Connor himself met a deputation from the ten
societies in the new BBFC offices at 80-82 Wardour
Street, occupied at the end of 1925. The societies
suggested that the BBFC was allowing many undesirable
films because of its financial dependence on the film
industry. O'Connor refuted this charge, and in yet
another defence of the status quo he emphasised that
none of the BBFC staff was connected with the film
industry in any way. Right-wing pressure for direct
government film censorship persisted on and off until
the early 1930s, without success, but The Unknown
Soldier episode provided an impetus to the political
advantages of a revived British film industry. The
result, coupled with the discussion at the 1926
Imperial Conference, was the Cinematograph Films Act
of March 1927 which laid down a quota system for the
showing of British films in British cinemas. These
were now compelled by law, with effect from 1 January

1928, to exhibit a certain percentage of British films, rising to 7½ per cent by March 1929 and 20 per cent by 1938. This act laid the basis for an increased British output as the producers concentrated on the rapid making of low budget features caustically known in the film world as 'quota quickies'. These were more notable for quantity than quality, however, and did little to reduce the popularity of American films with British audiences.

In other respects 1926-7 was relatively routine, although there were several minor developments. In 1926 the BBFC annual report codified the grounds for bans and cuts (See Appendix 1). No new grounds of principle were introduced, but in his letter to producers of 17 November 1926 O'Connor confirmed that since bare knuckle organised fights were now illegal in Britain, these would not be allowed, whereas in contrast to the BBFC's early days glove fights would be allowed provided they were not brutal. By then almost all the local authorities had fallen into line behind the 1923 Home Office recommendations. Some were even entering into direct contact with the BBFC when they entertained qualms regarding BBFC decisions, while O'Connor proved increasingly prepared to receive deputations from pressure groups such as The National Association of Head Teachers and the London Public Morality Council (LPMC). His professional sense of public relations in the slowly emerging age of the masses was a great asset in gaining for the BBFC a wider degree of government, local authority and public acceptance by the end of 1927. Nor did he shrink from using his parliamentary position on behalf of the BBFC when in the Commons on 10 November 1926 he had defended the BBFC decision to allow The Unknown Soldier against the attacks of Sir William Davison.

During 1926-7 the BBFC banned 15 films (See Appendix 3). Only one, Salvation Jane, broke new ground in reasons for suppression because it seems to have been the first to attack the Salvation Army. Among the allowed features was Metropolis (Germany, 1926, dir Fritz Lang), a futuristic fantasy of city workers incited to an uprising by a crazy inventor in 2000 AD which is capable of a pro-working class, pro-socialist and pro-revolutionary interpretation. The Prince of Adventurers was a biography of the famous womaniser Casanova which the BBFC first viewed on 15 May 1927. Extensive cuts were demanded, and O'Connor personally viewed the amended version on 7 June. As a result there were further cuts before the film was passed three days later. Altogether

the footage was reduced from 12,875 to 10,000, more
than 45 minutes running time. The Greta Garbo-John
Gilbert star vehicle Flesh and the Devil (MGM, 1926,
dir Clarence Brown) was embellished with much physical eroticism by contemporary standards. The BBFC
viewed it initially on 17 January 1927 but did not
finally allow it until 5 October, an unusually long
lapse for the 1920s. In the process of amendment the
footage dwindled from 8,700 to 7,100. However, the
most remarkable fact about the last two films is
that they were passed at all. This is further
evidence that the BBFC did its utmost to allow films
and decided upon bans only in the very last resort.
It also indicates that by 1926 the BBFC felt itself
to be sufficiently well established to risk allowing
controversial films. None of the films passed in
1926-7 raised any serious objections from the public
at large, in itself a tribute to the skill with which
O'Connor and Brooke Wilkinson had steered the BBFC
through a potential political and social minefield
since 1919.

However, fresh storm clouds were gathering late
in 1927 when King of Kings (Pathé, 1927, dir Cecil B.
de Mille) was sent to Britain after a recent striking
success in the United States. This well-known life
of Jesus (H.B. Warner) is reverential, but Mary
Magdalene (Jacqueline Logan) is portrayed as a
prostitute who has had an affair with Judas Iscariot
(Joseph Schildkraut) and there is a prolonged
emphasis on Christ's crucifixion and that of two
thieves who are crucified with Him while all three
are actually nailed to the cross. Pathé did not even
submit the film to the BBFC but instead arranged
private showings for British churchmen of every denomination as well as for the LCC and Middlesex County
Council on 26 October 1927. Both councils decided to
allow it, a major factor in the outcome being the
councils' knowledge that a majority of churchmen of
all denominations actively supported public exhibition. That the dissenting church views were at least
partly rooted in anti-Americanism is clear from a
clergyman's letter published in The Times of 17
November 1927. This stated that the approval of
American religious organisations for King of Kings
meant very little as a reason for showing it in
Britain since 'the standard of good taste in America
is in certain respects different from that accepted
in this country'. Such efforts failed to rally public opinion against the film which duly opened on 14
December 1927 in London. Its success there led other
local authorities to pass it, which they could do

without infringing the 1923 Home Office guidelines
because the BBFC had not been afforded an opportunity
to pronounce a ban. <u>King of Kings</u> thus set a precedent which was very soon to be copied, threatening to
upset the uniformity which had existed in film
censorship since the end of 1924.

However, this lay in the near future. By the
end of 1927 O'Connor and Brooke Wilkinson had every
reason to be content with the BBFC's progress. For
the most part the local authorities had come to
accept the BBFC as the chief body for film censorship. The Home Office was sufficiently satisfied
with the BBFC to resist political pressures for
reform, while the producers were the beneficiaries of
liberal BBFC decisions as measured against the openly
stated BBFC rules as a mirror of accepted middle and
upper class social values. These achievements were
considerable when the cinema's development in
Britain remained in comparative infancy and patronis-
ing antagonism to film as a mass communication medium
was still rampant among the traditional governing
class.

Chapter 3

'DAWN' AND THE TALKIES, 1928-1939

In October 1927 filming began in Belgium on <u>Dawn</u>
(British Dominions Films, 1927-8, dir Herbert
Wilcox), an account of Edith Cavell's trial and
execution which produced the fiercest censorship
clash of the entire inter-war period. The German
Foreign Office took alarm, presumably because such a
film might revive wartime germanophobia in Britain
and damage the Locarno fabric of Anglo-German relations. Unsuccessful German pressure on the Foreign
Office for the suppression of <u>Dawn</u>, coming from the
highest level and personally involving German Foreign
Minister Gustav Stresemann, eventually led the
Foreign Secretary, Sir Austen Chamberlain, to consult
the Cabinet in January 1928. As a result he was
authorised to approach O'Connor, previous pressure on
Wilcox from the German embassy in London and the
Foreign Office having met with no response, but in
the following month the pressure from Berlin and
Chamberlain's talk with O'Connor became public knowledge. Despite a subsequently announced BBFC ban on
<u>Dawn</u>, Wilcox successfully applied to the LCC to allow
it early in April 1928 and other local authorities
gradually followed the LCC's example during 1928-9.
The author has related the full story of <u>Dawn</u> elsewhere,[1] and here it is necessary only to consider its
effects. First, Wilcox had driven a coach and horses
through the Home Office-inspired censorship uniformity of 1923-4. Second, he had exposed the extent of
the BBFC's political function through the parliamentary questions of February and March 1928 put by
liberal and left-wing allies in the Commons. Third,
whereas Pathé had merely circumvented the BBFC with
<u>King of Kings</u> at the end of 1927, Wilcox had openly
and decisively defeated not only the BBFC but also
the combined pressure of the Foreign and Home
Offices. His overt triumph would have been all the

42

greater if Cabinet involvement had been known at the
time. Both the right-wing and left-wing critics of
the BBFC and of the film censorship system were
supplied with much ammunition for reforming pressures. The Home Office was caught in the ensuing
crossfire of 1928-31 (described in more detail
further in this chapter), which at length produced
the compromise and largely ineffectual Film Censorship Consultative Committee of November 1931.

The censorship repercussions of the Dawn incident might have been much wider if its piecemeal
circulation in Britain had not coincided with the
advent of sound. The Jazz Singer (Warner Brothers,
1927, dir Alan Crosland) was released in London in
September 1928 as the first film with sound, while
The Terror (Warner, 1928, dir Roy del Ruth) followed
in the next month as the first all-sound feature to
be shown in Britain. The increased use of sound over
the next few months introduced problems for the BBFC,
and the 1928 annual report provides an insight into
the confusion which the talkies first brought before
they became the rule rather than the exception. The
report noted that sound had taken deep root before
the end of the year, and that the producers had
agreed to submit scripts with completed sound films
where spoken dialogue rather than just music and song
was involved. There had been no technical difficulty
in carrying out cuts to silent films, but cuts in
sound films upset the continuity of reels, with the
result that the sound version of a film might be
banned whereas the silent version might be allowed.
In some cases the silent and sound versions of a film
might receive different certificates.[2]

Apart from the last consideration the emergence
of sound does not appear to have unduly influenced
the BBFC's 1928 decisions. Only a slightly reduced
total footage was viewed compared to the previous few
years, while the number of banned films for the year
was only nine (See Appendix 3) compared to nine for
1927 and six for 1926. Of the nine banned 1928 films
the most significant other than Dawn was Mother
(USSR, 1926, dir Vsevolod Pudovkin), a pro-Bolshevik
classic in which a mother in Tsarist Russia betrays
her son to the police for revolutionary activity but
then comes to see the error of her ways. Submitted
by the left-wing partnership of Ivor Montagu and
Adrian Brunel, Mother was banned at the BBFC on 6
December 1928, but pro-Bolshevik propaganda did not
figure among the grounds listed in the 1928 report
for bans, probably because Joynson-Hicks had admitted
in the Commons on 8 March 1928 that he had been a

party to the 1926 BBFC ban on <u>Battleship Potemkin</u>.
     Just as the number of 1928 banned films was on a
par with 1926 and 1927, so was the number of cut
films - 337 in 1926, for example, and 305 in 1928.
The 77 reasons for cuts in 1928 mostly retraced well
trodden ground. However, among the new religious
grounds was consecration and administration of the
eucharist; new political grounds were references to
the Prince of Wales and 'libellous reflections' on
royal dynasties; new military grounds included
conflicts between the armed forces of a state and its
populace as well as reflection on the wife of a responsible British official stationed in the east. In
1926 the administration of justice had been included
under a general social heading, whereas in 1928 it
was listed separately and embraced police firing
upon a defenceless populace, fights between police
and organised criminal gangs, and persecution of
ex-convicts by detectives. New social grounds
appeared as references (not necessarily derogatory!)
to well-known and public characters, reflections on
the medical profession, intimate biological studies
unsuitable for general exhibition, contract and
companionate marriages, accouchement and puerperal
pains, a son in love with his father's mistress, an
employee selling his wife to an employer to cover
defalcations, pernicious scenes in the underworld of
large cities, and lascivious embraces. The cruelty
heading was extended to cover bull fights, scenes of
martyrdom exploiting the agony of the victim, and
carnage. An innovation in the crime list was delib-
erate preparation for suicide (then a criminal
offence).
     The events surrounding <u>King of Kings</u> and <u>Dawn</u>,
coupled with the growing popularity of sound, had by
the end of 1928 revived the BBFC's uneasy relations
with some local authorities when these had become
more stable on the basis of the 1923 Home Office
circular. The impact of the talkies had thus far
been only marginal, but from 1929 to 1931 talking
films slowly supplanted the silents as the staple
diet of British cinemas and as a result both the
number of cinemas and the average weekly attendance
rose. The precise extent of the attendance increase
is hard to measure owing to unreliable statistics for
the silent period. According to the 1917 Cinema
Commission report, the average weekly attendance was
already over 20 millions, possibly the same as for
the mid-1930s and only fractionally below the high
figure for the late 1930s.[3] However, if the increased popularity during the 1930s was perhaps not so

dramatic as was once believed, it is nevertheless
clear that sound entrenched the social importance of
the cinema in Britain, and that out of a total population of just over 45 millions approximately a
half of the adults attended the cinema at least once
a week by September 1939.

The sound revolution brought about a change in
the film programme structure outside the large city
centres where the one-feature show was mostly retained in quality cinemas. Elsewhere in the early 1930s
the main feature usually ran for 70 to 80 minutes,
but as the quality of sound as well as of other film-
making techniques improved over the decade, the
length of the main feature rose to between 90 minutes
and two hours. After 1932 Hollywood's increased output and the British 1927 quota system facilitated the
growth of B-features, usually just over one hour
long. Sandwiched between the two features were
cartoons, trailers of forthcoming films, newsreels,
advertisements and topical interest films. The
entire show lasted somewhere in the region of three
hours. Children were frequent attenders, and after
1937 special cinema clubs for children were established by the main circuits. These involved
Saturday morning performances of about two hours, the
high spots being a lively but poor quality B-feature
and the episode of a serial which normally extended
to a dozen or so episodes. The mushrooming of
programmes produced yet more work for the BBFC since
all film except newsreel was censorable - even the
cartoons, trailers, advertising films and serials.
In fact cartoons and serials were subjected to some
of the most stringent censorship because they were
specifically made to appeal to children, and what
children should or should not be permitted to see
was a source of incessant public controversy throughout the 1930s. The BBFC gave even Walt Disney's
Snow White and the Seven Dwarfs an 'A' certificate!
At a Public Morality Council conference of 16
February 1937 the proceedings were almost entirely
taken up with the problems arising from the cinema
attendance of children, and even Mickey Mouse
cartoons were attacked for being 'scary'.[4]

The serials comprised a headache for the BBFC
in another respect, for they often showed animals in
adventure stories and westerns. On paper it had
always been BBFC policy to ban cruelty to animals,
but for most of the silent era only wild animals had
been screened. Then no fighting between animals had
been allowed outside natural history films, while the
BBFC had also come down against any depiction of a

hunting 'kill'. Even this did not satisfy some
animal lovers, and from 1926 O'Connor had had to fend
off pressure for a stricter policy from animal protection societies. However, new cinema ground had been
been broken with Chang (Paramount, 1927, dirs Merian
Cooper and Ernest Schoedsack), the tale of a Lao
tribesman and his struggle against the jungle which
was filmed in northern Thailand. In the scenes
showing harm to animals use had been made of stuffed
animals for the first time, but this had been kept
from the public which assumed that real cruelty had
occurred. Shortly afterwards Hollywood turned more
and more to trained animals like the famous Alsatian
Rin Tin Tin, who had made his first screen appearance
in 1923, while Trader Horn (MGM, 1931, dir W.S. Van
Dyke) triggered off a series of jungle melodramas,
most notably the Tarzan films of Johnny Weissmuller
which began in 1932 and retained their popularity
throughout the 1930s. Trader Horn contains what is
probably the best wild life footage of the 1930s
including a fight between a leopard and a hyena pack,
the shooting of a wounded rhinoceros and a lion's
death throes after a spear had been thrown into its
neck. Some of this material was undoubtedly deleted,
for in February 1931 the BBFC insisted on much modification and then many cuts, but even so many
animal lovers were disturbed. The precedent of
Trader Horn was to spread to other genres, cruelty
to animals in a Roman arena appearing in the
religious epic The Sign of the Cross (Paramount,
1932, dir Cecil B. De Mille). The BBFC cut this
extensively in January 1933, but it contains other
content which was censorable and it is clear from
contemporary reviews that at least some of the shots
showing cruelty to animals were allowed. Suspect-
ing, probably correctly, that in such films real
cruelty had been practised on animals for cinematic
effect, British animal protection organisations were
soon up in arms. As a result the BBFC was compelled
to review the subject, but at length it simply re-
affirmed its previous policy, adding only that
scenes likely to have entailed real cruelty to
animals would not be passed. This failed to mollify
the animal protectionists and their influential
supporters in the Commons who early in 1934 tabled a
Cinematograph Films (Animals) bill. On that occasion
the bill was unsuccessful, but in the aftermath of
the first of the Saturday morning children's clubs
Parliament in 1937 passed the Cinematograph (Animals)
Act. This prohibited the showing of cruelty to
animals on the screen, which virtually robbed the

BBFC of any discretion in the matter, and remains in force today.[5]
To take account of the new developments arising from the talkies, the Home Office as early as 16 December 1929 issued a fresh set of model licensing conditions to the 764 licensing authorities. In February 1931 the Home Office followed this up with a questionnaire to all the authorities to discover how far the new model conditions had been complied with. Only 41 authorities failed to respond, most of which had no cinemas. Of the remaining 723 there were 120 without a cinema and 97 with only one. The response from the County and Municipal Boroughs, where the vast majority of the cinemas was situated, was close to 100 per cent, and the resulting information provides the most comprehensive picture to emerge so far of cinemagoing conditions and censorship arrangements throughout England and Wales during the early sound years. Thus the results of the questionnaire are summarised here in detail.
The 1929 Home Office circular recommended seven model conditions. These were (a) that no films injurious to morality or inciting crime should be shown - this was observed by 511 or 84.7 per cent of those authorities which had replied, (b) that no film which the BBFC had not passed should be shown - this was observed by 445 or 73.8 per cent, (c) that children should not be admitted to 'A' films unless accompanied by a bona fide parent or guardian - this was observed by 396 or 65.7 per cent, (d) that the BBFC certificate should be shown on the screen for at least ten seconds at the beginning of the film - this was observed by 267 or 44.3 per cent, (e) that the certificate as indicated by 'A' or 'U' should be shown at least 1½ inches high in advertising outside cinemas - this was observed by 246 or 40.8 per cent, (f) that there should be no immoral advertising outside cinemas - this was observed by 479 or 79.4 per cent, and (g) that there should be complete lighting in cinemas at all times when open to the public - this, an attempt to stamp out kissing and other forms of affection between couples, was observed by 484 or 80.3 per cent.
It was significant that those model conditions touching upon law and order or morality - (a), (f) and (g) - were the most widely enforced. However, only 228 authorities had tried to observe all seven conditions, while 73 observed none at all. 382 had enforced five or more, 113 two or less. Local reactions were very varied, but this was less the case with particular feature films. Since February 1928

only 21 of the 603 authorities had received a complaint about any film; 38 films were concerned, but
more than one complaint had been registered against
only five films. In the same three years 229 authorities had received 405 applications to allow films
that the BBFC had banned or not viewed, but a mere 22
films were involved. However, many of the 405 applications related to King of Kings and Dawn as well
as other silent films. The statistics also showed
that any film which the BBFC, the LCC and Middlesex
and Surrey County Councils had all rejected stood
little chance of a showing elsewhere. No fewer than
586 authorities had neither suppressed nor cut any
film allowed by the BBFC since February 1928, but
eight others between them had banned 27 films which
the BBFC had passed, almost all of them dealing with
sex matters or social hygiene. Various authorities
had cut nine other BBFC-allowed films. From 1922 to
1930 the BBFC had viewed these 36 films from a total
of some 15,000. Liverpool and Newbury prohibited
children from seeing 'A' films under any circumstances, while Bath carried out its own censorship indep-
endently of the BBFC and had ignored BBFC approaches
to resolve differences. Only four authorities
favoured an official government censorship, the LCC
and the vast majority of the rest expressing satisfaction with the BBFC.[6] The answers to the Home
Office questionnaire reveal a high degree of censorship uniformity throughout England and Wales, which
was probably the case for the remainder of the 1930s
despite isolated pockets of local authority resistance, mostly from 1932 to 1935.

The Baldwin administration of 1924-9 had supported the status quo and upheld it without undue
difficulty, but Ramsay MacDonald's second minority
Labour government inherited the main thrust of King
of Kings, Dawn and the advent of the talkies. Some
minor local authorities, supported by a few vocal
pressure groups, pressed again for a stricter censorship under government control as sound brought about
the construction of new or enlarged cinemas, chiefly
in urban areas hit by rising unemployment in the
early 1930s in the wake of the October 1929 Wall
Street crash in the United States. However, the few
but vociferous local authorities and their right-wing
pressure group allies encountered energetic opposition from the BBFC, all branches of the film industry
and left-wing pressure groups often supported by
intellectuals who sought a weaker or more liberal
censorship system. The upshot was a battle to win
over Labour Home Secretary J.R. Clynes as well as

public opinion.

As part of this clash the Communist producer-director, Ivor Montagu, whose 1920s activities had fallen foul of the BBFC on several occasions and were to do so again, wrote a pamphlet in 1929 entitled The Political Censorship of Films. Therein Montagu contended, with what accuracy may never be determined, that the BBFC had initially banned Mother because it depicts a strike and shows state forces firing upon civilians. When he and Brunel protested that the BBFC had passed American films with a sympathetic portrayal of the Bolshevik revolution, the BBFC had shifted its ground to an objection to the general 'tenor' of Mother. When further challenged, O'Connor had agreed, apparently in writing, that the BBFC had suppressed the film because it might offend the Baldwin government and influential sections of the British public. Side by side with Montagu's vain efforts to persuade O'Connor to lift the ban on Mother went a repetition of Wilcox's Dawn tactics over Battleship Potemkin. This was shown privately to the LCC and Middlesex County Council, but on this occasion both backed the BBFC ban. After this setback Montagu intended to apply to other local authorities, but according to him before this could be arranged the British distributors received a visit from Scotland Yard in February 1929, whereupon they refused to supply prints even for private showings without Joynson-Hicks's express permission. This was not forthcoming, which was scarcely surprising in the light of more frequent performances of Soviet films at the Film Society.

In the midst of the looming conflict over the BBFC's political function O'Connor died in November 1929. His achievements for the BBFC can hardly be exaggerated. He had skilfully steered it through a political minefield during a difficult period of rapid social and technological change and only once seriously put a foot wrong, when he had unwisely bowed to the Foreign Office pressure over Dawn. At the close of his presidency the BBFC was more firmly established than when he took up the appointment in 1916. If the BBFC's standing was again at risk by the time of his death, this was due more to talking films than to any failure of his policies. He was succeeded by Edward Shortt, an ex-politician with no film industry knowledge who as Home Secretary in the Lloyd George coalition had been embroiled in the 1920 Auction of Souls controversy.[7] Although conscientious as BBFC President for the six years of life left to him, he was more of a bureaucrat in

mentality and more reactionary in general outlook
than O'Connor. He was over-inclined to bend to Home
Office views and was partly in sympathy with the
BBFC's right-wing critics. He also lacked O'Connor's
flair for public relations. The result of all these
factors was that during his brief presidency the
BBFC gave ground to outside pressures more readily
than under his predecessor.

Clynes and the Home Office civil servants were
reluctant to change the censorship status quo, not
least because the government might lose some of the
increasingly lucrative cinema revenue from entertainments tax if censorship became more stringent and too
open. On the other hand Clynes could not totally
ignore the mounting political pressure from the
right. As a result BBFC-local authority talks under
Home Office auspices took place and had reached an
advanced stage by August 1931 when the Labour government fell. MacDonald's National government rounded
off what Clynes had begun by the formation three
months later of the Film Censorship Consultative
Committee. This originally consisted of two LCC
representatives and four each from the County
Councils Association and the Association of Municipal
Authorities. Two more members from the Birmingham
and Liverpool magistrates were added during 1932. In
theory the new committee's function was a liaison
with the BBFC to create censorship consistency based
upon the 1923 and 1929 Home Office circulars to the
local authorities. However, the committee's powers
in relation to the BBFC, the Home Office and the
local authorities themselves were not clearly defin-
ed, the entire plan representing a cosmetic political
compromise between the defenders of the pre-1931
position and the advocates of a stronger, government-
controlled censorship. The committee became virtually defunct by the end of 1932, but its very
continued existence, however perfunctory its
activity, served as a constant reminder to the BBFC
that it might be subjected to a more rigorous supervision if too many of its rulings provoked government
or local authority displeasure or public controversy.
The BBFC's right-wing critics found the committee a
great disappointment, as a deputation of 15 January
1935 told Prime Minister MacDonald and Home Secretary
Sir John Gilmour. This deputation pressed for a
government commission on film censorship but found
MacDonald and Gilmour unreceptive, the latter stating
that the BBFC had been 'pretty severe and increasingly so'.[8] The Cinema Advisory Council replaced the
Film Censorship Consultative Committee in 1938 when

government preparations for a wartime film censorship - discussed at length in Chapter Five - were simultaneously and secretly set in motion.

In the Film Censorship Consultative Committee's formation the Home Office had paid scant regard to left-wing pressure for a more liberal censorship, and left-wing representations to the LCC over private film societies brought a similar lack of response. The Film Society's post-1928 tendency to show BBFC-banned films, especially Battleship Potemkin and Mother, had led to the establishment of other London film societies, some of which were working class. The Conservative LCC extended less tolerance to the latter than to the upper and middle class Film Society, but after having given permission to The Film Society to screen Mother and then refusing it to The Masses Stage and Film Guild, the LCC found itself on the receiving end of protests. Accordingly in 1930 it decided to alter its film society regulations to forbid all societies to show any film which the BBFC had banned. However, Montagu, backed by some 40 left-wing Conservative, Liberal and Labour MPs as well as by public personalities like Lady Cynthia Mosley, approached the LCC in February 1930 for a freer London film censorship system.[9]

This action was taken to try to counteract the influence of events arising from The Film Society's decision of 3 February 1929 to show Pudovkin's The End of St Petersburg. This performance had attracted the hostility of right-wing Conservative MPs because the words 'all power to the Soviets' figure in the sub-titles. Four days after the performance Joynson-Hicks faced questions from his own side of the Commons. He had refused to intervene, but the Home Office had then asked the LCC to consider whether The End of St Petersburg might lead to public disorder and whether it complied with the LCC's licence conditions to The Film Society. This thinly-veiled invitation to suppress the film was in the end rejected by the LCC. No action was taken against The Film Society over the film, which the BBFC passed in December 1929 with only paltry cuts. However, the Home Office pressure caused the LCC to review its general rules covering private film societies and in the process ignore left-wing pressure in the opposite direction. From 1930 the film societies could show only films which the BBFC had either passed or not viewed. Moreover, a minimum annual subscription of ten shillings was laid down. This was a considerable sum for the 1930s, the stipulation of such a high figure constituting an attempt to abort the working

class societies. But the establishment of these
continued despite such obstacles, not only in London,
although some were subject to local authority har-
assment as the general political temperature rose
under the impact of persistent unemployment and a
lack of British resistance to Italo-German forward
policies after 1935. By 1938 there were approximately 100 film societies in England and Wales, London
working class societies meeting less official
obstruction after Labour gained control of the LCC
in March 1934.

Upon his appointment as BBFC President in
November 1929 Shortt confessed to a personal dislike
of sound films.[10] This might partly explain the very
high number of banned films during his six years of
office, although the failure of American censorship
in the early sound years discussed in Chapter Six
also played a part. From 1930-5 inclusive the BBFC
banned no fewer than 120 movies (eleven in 1930, 32
in 1931, 19 in 1932, 21 in 1933, 23 in 1934 and 14 in
1935),[11] whereas in 1929 the figure had been a mere
seven. Under Shortt's successor, Lord Tyrrell of
Avon, appointed in November 1935, the pre-war figures
were seven in 1936, seven in 1937, two in 1938 and
one in 1939 (See Appendix 3). Furthermore, in 1932
there were 382 cut films, the highest on record for
a single year. Hanna's appointment as chief censor
to replace Husey, who died in March 1930, a few
months after Shortt's own appointment, together with
changes in American censorship arrangements, probably
contributed to an important development late in that
year which enables us to form a clearer picture of
BBFC attitudes during the 1930s and 1940s than before
or since. This was the decision to invite producers
to submit scenarios to the BBFC prior to production
rather than rely upon informal discussions. The
first scenario appeared in November 1930, after which
many scenarios were submitted throughout the 1930s
until the late 1940s when the system was discontin-
ued. The vast majority of these scenarios survive,
and therein is much information relating to projected
American and British features which the BBFC discouraged as well as about the modifications to some films
in response to BBFC pressure. This source, when
combined with the detailed BBFC records, provides
the major basis for any reconstruction of the BBFC's
work from 1930 to 1949. Nevertheless such evidence
has its limitations, for a production company's
decision not to go ahead with a film after a scenario
submission to the BBFC might have been due to factors
totally unconnected with censorship.

The ostensible reason for the pre-production
scenarios was technical, for even before the talkies
there had been a pronounced tendency for the BBFC to
impose larger cuts than in the early 1920s, much to
the annoyance of the affected producers who naturally
resented the financial loss incurred. However, extensive cuts to silent films could be carried out
without mutilating the subtitled dialogue, whereas
similar cuts to sound films could not. The BBFC's
scenario system was thus an innovation to prevent
producers shooting censorable material as much as
possible and to reduce costs just when the British
film industry was showing signs of a revival based
upon the 1927 quota requirements. None the less,
however strong the financial and technical incent-
ives for pre-production censorship and however much
it copied American censorship procedure, the under-
lying motive in 1930 was probably film world expediency. It certainly became so shortly afterwards,
for at the time the BBFC was conducting an important
part of the running battle against the pressures for
a more rigorous, official censorship structure which
ultimately led to the creation of the Film Censorship
Consultative Committee. The BBFC's chief ally in
this conflict was the film industry itself. Under
the pre-production scenario system the BBFC and the
producers could negotiate without outside influences
being brought to bear, while the BBFC could exercise
its political censorship more freely out of the
public eye than was possible when completed films
like Dawn had to be cut or banned.
Not all of the producers by any means co-operat-
ed with the BBFC, for throughout the 1930s only about
one third of British films had a pre-production
scenario. Moreover, the number of American films
with a pre-production scenario was negligible, so
that the scenarios' importance can be exaggerated in
relation to the films which the BBFC passed without
a scenario. Hanna himself dealt with all the
scenarios until April 1934 when Shortt's daughter,
who became Mrs N. Crouzet and was to remain with the
BBFC until just after the Second World War, was
appointed to assist him. If the coming of the
talkies required more work and longer hours at the
BBFC, then the staff doubtless found ample compensat-
ion in the move from Wardour Street to the near
palatial splendour of the Georgian Carlisle House in
Soho's Carlisle Street during the autumn of 1936
until the Luftwaffe totally destroyed it on the night
of 10-11 May 1941. The increase in the censors' work
load was greater than can be measured by the amount

of footage and the number of films viewed, for a
sound film had often to be viewed more than once,
sometimes several times, to discover whether required
cuts were technically feasible. If not, further cuts
might be wanted, which might necessitate yet another
viewing. In the process of all this Shortt was
called upon for viewing more often than O'Connor had
ever been, while he also acted as the BBFC's chief
spokesman on the Film Censorship Consultative
Committee and attended the conferences of other
public organisations.

The attacks of left-wingers, liberals and
intellectuals on the BBFC were gathering momentum
even before Shortt's death. For instance, in 1934
Dorothy Knowles in her book The Censor, the Drama and
the Film carried on where Montagu's pamphlet of 1929
had left off in drawing unfavourable attention to the
BBFC's continued political censorship and liaison
between governments over films. However, the assault
from the centre and the left grew sharper when
Tyrrell became BBFC President. He was a former
professional diplomat who in 1925 had risen to be
Permanent Under-Secretary at the Foreign Office, a
post he had held at the time of the Dawn affair
before moving on a few months later to the ambassad-
orship in Paris. He was more sympathetic than Shortt
to sound and in 1935 was himself a regular, once-a-
week cinemagoer,[12] but he could never cast aside the
influence of his long bureaucratic and diplomatic
career as the European international situation deg-
enerated into serious tension and eventually war.
His steadfast adherence to 'no political controversy'
in films, first openly stated in 1936, earned the
BBFC criticism from such literary figures as Graham
Greene, J.B. Priestley, George Bernard Shaw and H.G.
Wells between 1935 and 1937 as Italy swallowed up
Ethiopia and the Spanish Civil War generated much
passion in Britain. But the 'no political controversy' policy came under even greater fire during
1937-8 in the light of Japanese barbarity in China
and German expansion into Austria and Czechoslovakia.
By the end of 1938 the BBFC's political stance had
become virtually untenable. During the Czechoslovak
crisis of 1938 it had been disclosed in public that
the government of Neville Chamberlain had made representations to the United States government for the
latter to apply pressure on Paramount over its anti-
government newsreel presentation of the crisis. As
a result a particularly persistent Liberal MP,
Geoffrey Le Mander, on 7 December 1938 initiated a
Commons debate on freedom of speech and expressly

attacked the BBFC for its political censorship.
After this debate the BBFC to some extent relaxed
its previously antipathetic attitude to films with
a contemporary political and social propaganda
flavour. It is possible that the government liaison
over wartime censorship arrangements with the BBFC,
begun in September 1938 two weeks before the Munich
agreement, facilitated this relaxation.

Chapter 4

THE TALKIES: SOME FILMS, GENRES AND THEMES, 1929-1939

Horror

Horror films had raised scarcely a ripple of BBFC
concern during the 1920s. The 1922 ban on Nosferatu
(p.29), which was first shown in Britain at The Film
Society on 16 December 1928, was an isolated case,
and horror films did not receive even a mention in a
BBFC annual report before 1932. The Phantom of the
Opera had also been suppressed in Britain in 1925
(p.36), but this had come about without BBFC involvement. The English language horror films of the late
1920s had invariably been mixed with, and subordina-
ted to, comedy or thriller elements and consequently
had encountered no real BBFC displeasure. For
example, The Cat and the Canary (Universal, 1927, dir
Paul Leni) had suffered only minor cuts, while The
Terror and a silent version of Sweeney Todd, the
demon barber of Fleet Street, had passed virtually
unscathed during 1928. Moreover, much the same
gentle treatment had been meted out to the German
silent horror classics when these had reached
Britain. The Hands of Orlac (1926, dir Robert
Wiene) had been passed uncut on 6 September 1928, and
although the same director's famed The Cabinet of Dr
Caligari (1919) had met with stiffer BBFC resistance,
it had eventually been awarded a certificate with
extensive cuts on 12 July 1929 after an original
submission in October 1928. 1930 saw The Cat Creeps
(1930, dir Rupert Julian), a sound remake of The Cat
and the Canary passed uncut on 3 November 1930; and
a sound version of The Phantom of the Opera. Both
were shown to British audiences with little or no
mutilation, the BBFC even granting the latter a 'U'
certificate!
        It was thus largely in line with precedent when
on 16 February 1931 the BBFC allowed uncut Dracula

(Universal, 1930, dir Tod Browning), which starred
Bela Lugosi as the now legendary vampire count. However, the footage recorded in the BBFC register
indicates that the submitted print was about seven
minutes short of the full version, so that the
British distributors probably took into account the
1922 BBFC ban on Nosferatu. On 24 December 1931 the
BBFC allowed Frankenstein with an 'A' certificate,
but once again the BBFC registered footage demonstrates a submitted version some four minutes shorter
than the original. Even then the BBFC imposed a
further three minutes of cuts following two resub-
missions. The box office success of both Dracula and
Frankenstein, the former owing more to the eerie
presence of Lugosi than intrinsic merit and the
latter possessing an impact that has stood the test
of time due to Boris Karloff's impeccable, remarkable
and sympathetic portrayal of the famous monster of
Baron Frankenstein, gave great impetus to the horror
genre and kept the BBFC alert on this score for the
rest of the 1930s. Most of the 1930s horror productions were American and scenarios were seldom submitted to the BBFC, so that now it is all but impossible to discover precisely what cuts were carried out
and why. Moreover, horror often came to be linked
with the supernatural, murder and sex, while plain
undiluted horror itself fell into different visual
categories. For these reasons the BBFC did not find
it easy to determine what constituted a horror film.
     At the third meeting of the Film Censorship
Consultative Committee on 4 April 1932 it discussed
protests to the Home Office over Frankenstein by one
MP and a child protection society. The film was due
for its general release in the following month, the
LCC and Manchester having already announced a total
ban on the attendance of children despite the 'A'
certificate. The committee decided to take up the
matter with the CEA which as a result sent a circular
to its members urging that the film should be public-
ised outside cinemas as unsuitable for children.
This arrangement seems to have been fulfilled when
Frankenstein went on general release, but the LCC and
Surrey County Council subsequently complained to the
committee about the film, while in October 1932 the
Middlesex County Council as well as the Public Morality Council asked the committee to consider the
introduction of a third certificate solely for horror
films.[1] This was the first move towards the advisory
'H' certificate of May 1933. By October 1932 the
BBFC had been called upon to deal with several other
notable horror films, which explains why local

authority concern over the genre had gathered force.
   In the previous February the BBFC had passed Dr
Jekyll and Mr Hyde (Paramount, 1931, dir Rouben
Mamoulian) but only after reducing it by 731 feet,
almost certainly because the story had been given a
highly sexual emphasis that was absent from the 1920
silent version. Then in March 1932 Murders in the
Rue Morgue (Universal, 1932, dir Robert Florey), the
story of a trained ape's appetite for murder, was
cut by 352 feet. In July Freaks (MGM, 1932, dir Tod
Browning), a circus tale of murder and then revenge
on the murderess by the murdered midget's deformed
friends, was refused a certificate altogether, a
decision unreversed until the mid-1960s. Doctor X -
for Xavier - (Warner, 1932, dir Michael Curtiz) in
August was cut by 205 feet even though a print short-
ened by six minutes had been submitted to the BBFC.
However, even with additional BBFC cuts, this story
of a reporter (Lee Tracy) who investigates a series
of murders perpetrated under a full moon and ultimately suspects one of the staff at a medical research
college still packs a strong punch and contains much
borderline content by the then BBFC paper standards.
For example, two of the victims are described as 'a
dope fiend' and 'a woman of the streets'. Dr
Xavier's daughter (Fay Wray), when used as a potential victim in an experiment to find the killer,
appears dressed only in a nightdress when tied to a
hospital bed. Dr Wells (Preston Foster), the armed
scientist-killer, uses synthetic flesh and is hideo-
usly made up to bear a close resemblance to the
monster in Frankenstein, while the climax sees the
reporter plunge a lighted oil lamp full into Wells's
synthetic flesh face. In September White Zombie
(Halperin, 1932, dir Victor Halperin), a creepy
Gothic-style study of zombies in Haiti, received
only minor cuts, but in the following month The Most
Dangerous Game (RKO, 1932, dirs Ernest Schoedsack and
Irving Pichel - British title The Hounds of Zaroff),
the tale of a mad wealthy hunter (Leslie Banks) who
traps people onto his island in order to hunt them
down, was cut by 78 feet.
   The spate of horror films submitted to the BBFC
continued unabated during the early part of 1933 to
make the introduction of the projected 'H' certificate a matter of urgency. Some films were even held
up after receiving BBFC approval so that they could
be notified to the local authorities as 'H' films
before their general release. The Mummy (Universal,
1932, dir Karl Freund) was passed uncut on 6 January
1933 and retained its 'A' certificate. On the other

hand Vampyr (France-Germany, 1931, dir Karl Dreyer)
was passed uncut on 31 January 1933 but then kept
back as a 'H' certificated film, while The Vampire
Bat (Majestic, 1933, dir Frank Strayer) was cut by 99
feet yet retained its 'H' certificate in March 1933.
In the same month the celebrated Mystery of the Wax
Museum (Warner, 1933, dir Michael Curtiz) was cut by
55 feet and certificated 'A', while Island of Lost
Souls (Paramount, 1932, dir Eric Kenton) was rejected
outright. This latter ruling involving vivisection
is almost beyond belief when compared to the leniency
accorded to the classic King Kong (RKO, 1933, dirs
Merian Cooper and Ernest Schoedsack) in April 1933
when it was cut by a mere 68 feet and awarded an 'A'
certificate rather than a 'H'! To modern film fans
these decisions smack of pedantic inconsistency, but
they probably reflect rather a mixture of confusion
and possible fear of an adverse Film Censorship
Consultative Committee reaction at the BBFC. The
1932 annual report made it clear that it was in the
committee that the concern over horror films had
originated, and that the BBFC would simply notify
local authorities of the horror films it considered
unsuitable for children. However, even when the 'H'
certificate system was firmly established, the inconsistency in BBFC decisions remained throughout the
1930s. Few in the 1980s would accept that The
Invisible Man (Universal, 1933, dir James Whale),
passed uncut on 20 November 1933, and the Ritz
Brothers horror comedy The Gorilla (TCF, 1939, dir
Allan Dwan, passed uncut on 5 June 1939), to mention
two random 'H' certificate examples, are more scary
than either The Will of Doctor Mabuse (Germany, 1932,
dir Fritz Lang), the study of an insane criminal who
masterminds the takeover of his country while in
jail, passed with slight cuts on 15 June 1936 and an
'A' certificate or The Walking Dead (Warner, 1936,
dir Michael Curtiz), 'A' certificated on 20 April
1936 with a cut of 101 feet. Furthermore, the
inclusion of the anti-war I Accuse (France, 1937, dir
Abel Gance) on the list of 'H' films on 12 April 1938
tentatively suggests that the BBFC did not always use
the 'H' system for the reason it had been established. However, after 1933 the BBFC did not actually
reject a single horror film, which would have been
the likely fate of all the 31 'H' films of 1933-9
(See Appendix 2) if the 'H' certificate idea, for
all its manifest defects, had not been devised.

Nudity and Sex

Nudity was one of the only two grounds on which
the BBFC at its creation in 1913 automatically rejected a scene, although this had not been expressly
stated in the early annual reports until 1915. However, the first BBFC annual report for 1913 had
specifically included four items relating to sex
among the 22 reasons why films had been cut. These
four were: indelicate sexual situations; scenes
suggestive of immorality; scenes accentuating
delicate marital relations; and cruelty to women.
The 1914 report had added the white slave traffic;
outrages on women; confinements; and scenes laid
in disorderly houses. 1915 had witnessed further
additions - torture of women; unnecessary exhibition
of feminine underclothing; nude figures;
excessively passionate love scenes; bathing scenes
passing the limits of propriety (mixed bathing was
not then socially acceptable); the premeditated
seduction of women; 'first night' scenes; men and
women in bed together; and venereal disease. The
later BBFC annual reports in the pre-sound period
had shown a steady accretion of yet more sexual
grounds to which exception had been taken. These had
included: making young girls drunk; women fighting, especially with knives; disparagement of
marriage; advocacy of contraception and free love;
sacrifice of a woman's virtue depicted laudably; a
husband's infidelity as justification for his wife's
adultery; equivocal bathroom and bedroom scenes;
prostitution and pimping; women promiscuously taking
up men; holding hands; incest; unbridled and
illicit passions; puerperal pains; lives of immoral
women; sex orgies; libels on nurses; sensuous
exposure of girls' legs; suggestive dancing; a
husband's acceptance of his wife's infidelity;
lecherous old men; indecent innuendoes; female
vamps; collusive divorce; abortions; companionate
marriage; and liaisons between coloured (i.e. black)
men and white women (but not between white men and
coloured women - this sexist distinction arose from
a widespread British contemporary belief that black
men were more biologically capable than white men of
sexually satisfying a white woman!).
      This catalogue was so all-embracing that, had it
been applied literally, no sexual material of any
consequence would ever have been seen in British
cinemas by the late 1920s. Yet the very comprehen-
siveness of the list, reflecting what had been cut
from submitted films, demonstrates that film

producers had been trying incessantly to bring about
a more liberal attitude to screen sexuality at the
BBFC and had not been deterred by consistent rever-
ses. A brief survey of sexual content which the
BBFC had let through before the talkies emphasises
the constant difficulties facing the censors in their
efforts to strike a balance between their theoretical
guidelines and the demands of film-makers, which
always grew bolder whenever box office receipts fell.
    The first film with female nudity seems to have
been Daughter of the Gods (1913) in which 25-year-old
Australian swimming star Annette Kellerman appeared
stark naked, but this was not submitted to the BBFC,
although its production possibly accounted for the
BBFC's secret rejection of nudity in its first
operating year. Nevertheless nudity had been
strongly implied if not actually seen in bathing
sequences from Cecil B. de Mille's Male and Female
(1919) and D.W. Griffith's Orphans of the Storm
(1921), while bare breasted women had appeared in Ben
Hur (MGM, 1925, dir Fred Niblo). Moreover, the
figure of the vamp in the person of Theda Bara had
first arrived on the screen as early as 1916, and
although the BBFC had rejected her first major film,
A Fool There Was (William Fox, 1916, dir Frank
Powell), the remainder had all been allowed until her
popularity had waned by 1919. During the 1920s the
vamp character had given way to the sexually aware
heroine as epitomised by first Pola Negri, then Clara
Bow and Lya De Putti, and latterly Greta Garbo. The
BBFC had passed all their films even though the
openly erotic content was often toned down.
    The BBFC was thus not in the strongest of
positions to clamp down entirely on sexual content
during the early talkie period as film industry
pressures again built up for a more overt treatment
of sex, particularly in displaying the female body.
As before and since, the problem for the censors was
where exactly to draw the line once the principle
had been conceded. In Trader Horn, submitted to the
BBFC early in 1931, the native African black women
are all shown with breasts uncovered, whereas a white
woman has her breasts hidden despite the fact that
she had been captured as a child and brought up as a
native woman within the tribe! However, sex had not
figured prominently in the 1929 and 1930 BBFC annual
reports, and it was not until 1931 that the annual
report called attention to a marked increase in the
number of films with sexual content. This was a
tendency Shortt deplored. He warned that the BBFC
'has always taken exception to stories in which the

main theme is either lust or the development of
erotic passions', and that 'more drastic action will
have to be taken with regard to such films in the
future'. The same report later stated,

> There are certainly some producers who
> delight to show the female form divine
> in a state of attractive undress...The
> objectionable aspect is the tendency,
> on every conceivable occasion, to drag
> in scenes of undressing, bathroom scenes
> and the exhibition of feminine under-
> clothing which are quite unnecessary from
> the point of view of telling the story.
> They are solely introduced for the
> purpose of giving the film...'a spicy
> flavour'. The cumulative effect of a
> repetition of such scenes as can be
> described as 'suggestive' is very harmful,
> although isolated instances may do no harm
> and call for no comment.

The 1932 report remarked that there had been a
'substantial decrease' in the number of 'sex' films
submitted, but in reality the worst was yet to come
for the BBFC in this respect, not so much in
quantity as in daring. Indeed the signs were already
present before the end of 1932 despite the optimistic
tone of the annual report, for Greta Garbo's mantle
as the screen's leading femme fatale was fast passing
to Marlene Dietrich and Jean Harlow. In this image
the former's Blonde Venus (Paramount, 1932, dir Josef
Von Sternberg) and the latter's Red Dust (MGM, 1932,
dir Victor Fleming), which provided Harlow with the
role of a prostitute in all but name, both suffered
extensive cuts in November 1932. Furthermore, La
Chienne (France, 1931, dir Jean Renoir), in which a
prostitute (Janie Marèze) is a central character in
the plot, was rejected outright in June 1932. Even
the singer Jeanette MacDonald is twice reduced to her
undies in the musical Love Me Tonight (Paramount,
1932, dir Rouben Mamoulian), a light entertainment
feature which took more than five weeks to pass
scrutiny and underwent a personal viewing from Shortt
before the BBFC allowed it. The film was cut in
several places, it being more than likely that the
scenes with the underclad Miss MacDonald were erased.
    However, the biggest sex headache for the BBFC,
in the shape (literally) of Mae West, was yet to
come when She Done Him Wrong (Paramount, 1933, dir
Lowell Sherman) was submitted in March 1933. Based

upon her own play Diamond Lil, which had once landed
her in jail for a brief spell, the film positively
bristled with sexual double meanings and was outrag-
eous when judged by the surface British sexual conventions of the time. Even when the dialogue is unexceptionable, which is never for any length of time,
Mae West's brash manner and sexually provocative body
manoeuvres are ever present, and even in truncated
form She Done Him Wrong is far and away the sexiest
film of the 1930s. It is probable, to judge from the
registered footage in the BBFC records, that the
version submitted was some eight minutes shorter than
that already shown in the United States. Nevertheless the BBFC imposed further cuts amounting to 574
feet or six minutes running time, which seems to be
the surviving print in the National Film Archive.
But even this badly mutilated version contains much
forward dialogue and thus affords some clue as to the
sexuality of the cut content. Set in the 1890s, the
film has Mae West playing a San Francisco saloon
keeper who indulges in crime but falls in love with
the cop (Cary Grant) posing as a do-good reformer to
expose her. In her opening scene she at once creates
a sexual flavour when she alights from a carriage
when another woman tells her how pretty she looks.
She replies that she is the prettiest girl who ever
walked the streets. Talking to an unmarried girl
who has just tried to commit suicide because of a
failing love affair, Mae is asked by the girl how
she knew a man was involved. Her answer is, 'It
always takes two to get one into trouble (i.e.
pregnant)'. She invites a man to 'come up and see me
anytime'. He responds, 'When I come I hope you'll be
alone' and receives the reply, 'So do I'. Finally,
when Cary Grant arrests her and places her in handcuffs, she enquires, 'Are they necessary? I wasn't
born with them'. Grant suggests that many men would
have been safer if she had been born with them, at
which Mae wisecracks, 'Oh, I don't know. Hands ain't
everything'. The BBFC removed many of her sexiest
utterances but at the same time still managed to let
through what has become some of her most memorable
material.
    The success of She Done Him Wrong evidently
brought about a crackdown on sex in films at the BBFC
during the following months. Baby Face (Warner,
1933, dir Alfred Green), the story of an ambitious
working girl (Barbara Stanwyck) who offers sexual
favours to men, first to obtain a job and then to
gain promotion in the company, appeared at the BBFC
in April 1933. It remained there under scrutiny for

three months and was eventually cut by 757 feet, more
than 12 per cent of its total running time.
Early in October 1933 Red-Headed Woman (MGM, 1933,
dir Jack Conway), a Jean Harlow star vehicle in which
she plays an uncouth working girl who deliberately
breaks up the engagement of her boss (Chester Morris)
so that she herself can marry him for social advance-
ment, was rejected altogether, not to be awarded a
certificate until 1965. By comparison the BBFC
treated I'm No Angel (Paramount, 1933, dir Wesley
Ruggles) and Bombshell (MGM, 1933, dir Victor Fleming, known in Britain as Blonde Bombshell) very
leniently at the tail end of the year. In the latter
case this is not entirely surprising, for Harlow is
simply a liberated female film star seeking a new
image and as a result her sexual attributes are
played down in favour of frequent wisecracks. The
film was passed in full, but even Mae West suffered
only one dialogue cut in the sex romp of I'm No Angel
in spite of many suggestive remarks along the general
lines of She Done Him Wrong. A few random examples
will suffice. When alone in her room with Cary
Grant, she tells him, 'When I'm good I'm very good,
but when I'm bad I'm better'. As her maid expresses
the view that Mae is a one-man woman, she comments,
'Yeah, one man at a time'. After a court case a
woman reporter asks her why during the case she had
introduced in evidence the men in her life. Mae
replies, 'It's not the men in your life that count,
but the life in your men'. In retrospect it was much
to the BBFC's credit that such risqué dialogue (by
the conventions of the time) was passed on to British
cinema audiences unscathed. However, Ecstasy
(Czechoslovakia, 1932, dir Gustac Machaty), a tale of
a country girl who takes a lover which is now mainly
noteworthy because Hedwig Keisler, better known as
Hedy Lamarr, appears completely nude, was not submitted to the BBFC, presumably because a ban would
have been automatic. However, it was shown at the
Film Society in March 1933.
    Due to off-screen American developments concern-
ing 'sex' films in the latter part of 1933, discussed
fully in the final chapter, I'm No Angel proved to be
the climax of the screen development of the sexually
liberated female star during the 1930s. Thereafter
until the Second World War the sexual content of film
melodramas was strongly watered down, either by the
BBFC or more often by the film industry itself, to
conform more closely to conventional standards of
morality. All the later Jean Harlow and Mae West
star vehicles lacked the sexual bite of the 1932-3

productions, while such topics as prostitution, free love, bigamy, adultery, seduction and divorce were all strongly discouraged at scenario stage in the BBFC throughout the remainder of the 1930s.[2] However, very late in the decade just after the outbreak of the Second World War the BBFC gave a certificate to In Name Only (RKO, 1939, dir John Cromwell) even though it took a sympathetic view of an extra-marital love affair between Cary Grant and Carole Lombard, prevented from blossoming into marriage by Grant's vindictive wife (Kay Francis) and her refusal to sue for a divorce.

Miscegenation

In January 1938 Mrs Crouzet wrote, 'I do not know if there is any special ban on the subject of mixed marriages'.[3] At that time she was considering a story involving an Englishman's marriage to a Chinese woman in the opening years of the 20th century, but her confusion is mystifying in that no BBFC ban on such marriages had ever existed. Indeed as recently before as April 1937 the BBFC had allowed in full The Wife of General Ling (1937, dir Ladislao Vadja) in which there is a marriage between a European woman and a Chinaman, although it eventually comes to grief, as such screen unions then invariably did. This decision had followed BBFC policy since 1913, for in the silent days of 1914 and 1918 Cecil B. De Mille had twice made The Squaw Man in which a British nobleman marries a Red Indian squaw who turns out to be a murderess and then commits suicide. The BBFC passed both versions as well as in 1921 what might have been the first film in which an English girl was married to a Chinaman, Li-Hang the Cruel (p. 26). In this case the wife had acted only under duress, and the union had emphasised the supposed lecherous impulses of Chinamen in general towards white women. In The Chinese Bungalow (1926, dir Sinclair Hill, remade in 1930 and again in 1939) a similar marriage is voluntarily entered into on both sides but turns out badly. Here the Chinaman (Matheson Lang) is driven less by promiscuity arising from his wife's infidelity than by the alleged Chinese conception of marital honour. In 1931 De Mille made his third version of The Squaw Man, but although the BBFC passed the film, times had changed sufficiently since 1918 for the title to be altered to The White Man. It is unclear whether this change was made by the BBFC or the distributors. Later came Java Head (Associated Talking Pictures,

1934, dir J. Walter Ruben), which the BBFC also
allowed. In this film an Englishman marries a Chinese woman (Anna May Wong) who commits suicide when
she learns her husband does not really love her once
they are living in Britain. Although the non-
European characters in these various screen mixed
marriages were sometimes portrayed in a favourable
light, the overall message came through loud and
clear - such marriages could never last.

      This message also applied to illicit liaisons
between easterners and westerners, as in White Cargo
(1929, dir J.B. Williams) where the Britons in one of
God's forsaken Malayan places are driven mad with
sexual desire for scheming native girl Tondelayo
(Gypsy Rhouma). Genuine love fared no better, as in
possibly the most interesting 1930s film touching
upon miscegenation, The Bitter Tea of General Yen
(Columbia, 1932, dir Frank Capra). In this an
American woman missionary in China (Barbara Stanwyck)
and her cultured Chinese warlord captor (Nils Asther)
fall for each other, which finally leads the warlord
to suicide. While because of its racial implications
this film was banned throughout the British empire by
the various colonial film authorities, the BBFC
passed it for showing in Britain in December 1932 and
upon its release it aroused no controversy. This
outcome is unsurprising in the light of the many
precedents already referred to in this section, despite which Hanna in particular with his long military
experience in India evidently continued to possess
qualms about miscegenation themes. When in December
1937 United Artists submitted a scenario based upon
Louis Bromfield's novel The Rains Came, Hanna opted
for its rejection whereas Mrs Crouzet was prepared to
accept it.4 However, when a modified version
scenario of the same story, which involves a doomed
love affair between a British-educated Indian doctor
and the wife of a British aristocrat, was resubmitted
in November 1938, he relented and was now willing to
give such a film the go ahead even though his reser-
vations had by no means disappeared.5 The BBFC
passed The Rains Came (TCF, 1939, dir Clarence Brown)
uncut in October 1939 with Tyrone Power and Myrna Loy
as the lovers.

      While it is plain that the BBFC did not bar
screen miscegenation in principle, there seems to
have been no such case of a film with a durable and
happy marriage involving children. Moreover, if
failed marriages between Europeans and Chinese or Red
Indians proved acceptable to the BBFC before 1939, no
film seems to have been produced depicting a marriage

between black and white. Indeed, as already mentioned (p. 60), the BBFC had specifically banned
marriages between black men and white women before
the end of the silent period. However, miscegenation
and resulting mulatto children as a central theme
have very seldom figured on the screen at any time
since 1939, so that any reluctance to bring this
subject out into the open on film was probably due
to film-makers themselves rather than to the BBFC.
There is apparently no recorded instance of the
BBFC's rejection of a film for containing, as the
main story line, a mixed marriage between black and
white partners or a successful mixed marriage between
other races which had produced children. If any BBFC
policy against such films existed unofficially, as
Mrs Crouzet's expressed uncertainty of January 1938
leads one to suspect, this was an attitude almost
certainly shared by the American and British film
industries in general and probably a majority of the
British people.

Images of the East

Before the talkies the overwhelming screen
image of Chinamen had been one of cruelty and evil as
personified by the notorious Fu Manchu and by
characters such as Li-Hang. In 1928 Dr Fu Manchu had
virtually reappeared as Dr Sin Fang (Harry Agar-
Lyons, the same actor who earlier had played Fu
Manchu), and no 'good' (i.e. western-educated and
sharing western values) Chinese had yet been placed
in a film as the dominating personality in the plot.
Through the experience with The Cheat (p. 26) between
1916 and 1923 the BBFC had already been made well
aware that English language films might exert an
influence on Anglo-Japanese relations. Moreover, the
BBFC's insistence in 1921 upon a foreword to Li-Hang
the Cruel pointing out that the villainous chief
character was not a typical Chinese (p. 26) had shown
a BBFC recognition of Chinese sensitivity to the
continued adverse film portrayals of Chinese. In
September 1927 the BBFC, at Foreign Office request,
had eliminated a scene from The Flight Commander
(Gaumont, 1927, dir Maurice Elvey) because it shows
a British bombardment of a Chinese town which might
have offended the Chinese government if the film had
been shown in China.
This episode makes it reasonably clear that the
BBFC knew of the Chinese government's concern at
China's poor image in American and British films.
The BBFC, too, could not have been unaware that the

Chinese government was making efforts in the opposite
direction through the occasional exhibition of
Chinese films in Britain. The first of these was
shown at the Shaftesbury Avenue Pavilion in 1929, a
romantic melodrama upon which The Times review of 23
September 1929 reported favourably and observed its
innocent character as compared to contemporary
western productions. In China the American and
British film companies had experienced official
difficulties over films consistently portraying
Chinamen in a bad light. Yet the BBFC had shown, and
continued to show, less sensitivity about Anglo-
Chinese relations than about Britain's relations with
European nations. No attempt was made to reject
films of the Fu Manchu and Sin Fang variety, which
emerged again persistently after 1929, whereas the
BBFC in 1931 invited a representative from the French
embassy in London to view with Shortt Dreyfus
(Wardour, 1931, dir F.W. Kraemer), a British version
of the celebrated French spy case of the 1890s which
had so greatly divided French society. As a result
of this viewing Dreyfus was cut in several places in
April 1931.
 The first sound version of Fu Manchu, the first
time he appeared in an American film, was The Mysterious Fu Manchu (Paramount, 1929, dir Holland Lee).
Here he is played by Warner Oland and dies by poisoning himself, but such a finale did not prevent the
production of three more films about him before the
end of 1932 with Oland (twice) and Boris Karloff
(once) personifying the Yellow Peril. The 1932
choice of Karloff, by then the illusion of unmiti-
gated evil and horror through his portrayal of Baron
Frankenstein's monster, rather than Oland, who had
begun the Charlie Chan B-feature detective series in
the previous year, was simply meant to stress to the
audiences of the time how great a world menace Fu
Manchu and China supposedly represented.
 Charlie Chan was the Honolulu detective of
Chinese origin created by Earl Derr Biggers. He had
occasionally been featured in films prior to 1931 but
never as the star character. The Charlie Chan films,
over 40 of them from 1931 to 1949 with Sidney Toler
taking over from Oland in 1938, signified Hollywood's
first serious attempt to placate China's hostility to
the apparently never-ending screen link of China and
Chinese with corruption, crime, sexual promiscuity,
untrustworthiness and vice. Later in the 1930s the
favourable image of Chinese generated by Charlie Chan
was built upon to a limited extent by the presentation of honourable and honest individual Chinese in

such films as The Bitter Tea of General Yen, Oil for the Lamps of China (Warner, 1935, dir Mervyn Leroy) and, most especially, The Good Earth (MGM, 1937, dir Sidney Franklin). The last was the only Hollywood pre-1939 film which endeavoured to look at everyday life in China from the standpoint of a humble peasant couple (Paul Muni and Luise Rainer) and to show that there were both good and bad Chinese people when western influences were absent. In this respect Chinese were at last shown as little different from the people of other nations. Furthermore, in 1938 the Charlie Chan image received reinforcement in the shape of another B-feature Chinese detective series focusing on Mr Wong (Boris Karloff) which, however, lasted only until 1941.

However, while these sporadic Hollywood attempts to improve the image of the Chinese people represented a break with film history, this should not distract attention from the fact that these attempts were only half-hearted, with the possible exception of The Good Earth. For the overwhelming screen treatment of China and Chinese remained unfavourable, China as a country being shown as rent by famine and pestilence, unstable, violent and always prone to revolution. This was even true of Oil for the Lamps of China and The Good Earth, not to mention for example Shanghai Express (Paramount, 1932, dir Josef Von Sternberg), The Painted Veil (MGM, 1934, dir Richard Boleslawski), Stowaway (TCF, 1936, dir William Seiter) and The Lost Horizon (Columbia, 1937, dir Frank Capra). In The Hatchet Man (Warner, 1932, dir William Wellman), the fundamentally anti-Chinese nature of which was meant to be concealed by a title change in Britain to The Honourable Mr Wong, a western-educated Chinese (Edward G. Robinson) resorts to tong warfare when called upon to do so and kills his best friend. The film's message is that the Chinese will never renounce their alleged ancient traditions, no matter how westernised they become. In addition Hollywood and the British studios poured out a constant stream of B-features, all now in a richly deserved oblivion which can easily lead one to overlook their sheer quantity. These fortified the presumed link of Chinese national characteristics, such as inscrutability, with crime and vice. Random instances over the 1930s were Chinatown After Dark and The Law of the Tong (1932), The Secrets of Wu Sin (1933), Chinatown Squad and Secrets of Chinatown (1935), Shadow of the Orient (1936), Dr Sin Fang (again!) and Shadows of Chinatown (1937), King of Chinatown and Shadows over Shanghai (1939). However, there appears to have been a decrease in this type of film after 1937 once the full-scale Japanese invasion of China got under way. The image of the Japanese was totally ignored in sound films until the 1937 emergence of the B-feature detective Mr Moto (Peter Lorre), but late in 1938 he disappeared from the screen as suddenly as he had arrived following widespread western revulsion at continued Japanese atrocities against the Chinese people during the hostilities in China.

From 1913 the BBFC had made only the most timorous of efforts to offset what can now be seen as sheer blatant anti-Chinese racialism. Other eastern peoples, like the Malays, also received similar screen treatment - for instance, in China Seas (MGM, 1935, dir Tay Garnett). Only the Japanese, probably due to their superior industrial development which in many western eyes equated Japan with western values of civilisation, were exempt until the real-life actions of the Japanese army in China could no longer be ignored. The evidence suggests that, in trying to respect foreign reactions to films in the west while simultaneously ignoring eastern reactions (except Japanese), the BBFC simply shared the sub-conscious anti-eastern prejudices of British society as a whole before the Second World War. All the anti-Chinese movies were allowed simply because they were not a source of political controversy within Britain.

Miscellaneous

The BBFC scenarios for the 1930s show repeatedly that bad language was frowned upon in films. Words like 'bloody' and 'bastard' were taboo, but in February 1938 a scenario appeared for Pygmalion, George Bernard Shaw's play in which Eliza Doolittle comes out with her immortal phrase 'not bloody likely'. Shaw himself, a persistent critic of the BBFC during the 1930s, was writing the script for the film and was determined to have the words included or mount a head-on challenge to Tyrrell and Brooke Wilkinson. On the scenario[6] both Hanna and Mrs Crouzet declared themselves in favour of deletion, but Shaw and the film's producer, Gabriel Pascal, decided to ignore BBFC objections. When the completed film was submitted in July 1938 (dirs Anthony Asquith and Leslie Howard), Dame Wendy Hiller as Eliza uttered the celebrated saying and Hanna as the sole censor, possibly bearing in mind the outcome of the Dawn incident, decided after all to let it through. This was the first time that a British

producer in the 1930s had openly and successfully
defied the BBFC guidelines. This was commented upon
in the press, and not long afterwards the government
attempts to influence newsreel content during the
Czech crisis came to light. The upshot was a Commons
censorship debate of 7 December 1938 which included
attacks on the political decision-making role of the
BBFC. This in turn led to a more determined assault
on BBFC values by the British film industry, for
which the Pygmalion affair more than any other single
event paved the way.

In investigating scenarios Hanna and Mrs Crouzet
were often keen to see that real institutions were
not named unless they had given their specific permission. In 1934 the murder mystery Death at Broadcasting House (ABFD-Phoenix, 1934, dir Reginald
Denham) required the approval of the British Broadcasting Corporation.[7] In 1933 a scenario entitled
Murder at Cambridge[8] had aroused Hanna's concern that
no shots of any real Cambridge college should be used
in the film, the story being set in the imaginary St
Mary's College, Cambridge. In 1936 and 1937 the
permission of the Bank of England and of Scotland
Yard was sought for certain scenarios.[9] A Yank at
Oxford (MGM Britain, 1938, dir Jack Conway) mentions
no specific college for its American student-hero
(Robert Taylor) and was passed uncut on 11 February
1938. On the other hand Commons debates were per-
mitted in The Masquerader (MGM, 1933, dir Richard
Wallace), Parnell (MGM, 1937, dir John Stahl),
Victoria the Great (British Lion-Imperator, 1937, dir
Herbert Wilcox) and The Four Just Men (Ealing, 1939,
dir Walter Forde) and a Lords debate in The Iron Duke
(Gaumont, 1934, dir Victor Saville).

The monarchy enjoyed special censorship protection. Portrayals of Queen Victoria and later monarchs
while any of her children remained alive were banned
in line with the Lord Chamberlain's theatre policy.
This probably reflected the wishes of the monarchy
itself until Edward VIII in 1936 granted Herbert
Wilcox permission to make Victoria's screen biography.[10] However, the production of Victoria the
Great had not commenced when in December 1936 Edward
abdicated to marry Mrs Simpson. On the day after the
abdication a Commons amendment was tabled to the
abdication bill to the effect that Britain should
become a republic. The ensuing debate saw the amendment overwhelmingly defeated by 403 votes to five,
but the fact that such an issue could be raised at
all was an indication that the principle of monarchy
might be at risk. As a result the coronation of

George VI was hurriedly arranged for 12 May 1937 -
Victoria, Edward VII and George V had all been
crowned more than a year after their accessions,
while Edward VIII was not crowned at all during his
ten-month reign and Elizabeth II had to wait all but
16 months. Victoria the Great was filmed soon afterwards as a pro-monarchical propaganda exercise when
the British ruling class rallied to the defence of
its key prop when this was threatened with mass un-
popularity. The film was produced with the permission of the Lord Chamberlain and presumably of the new
king. The BBFC allowed it in full as well as its
sequel, Sixty Glorious Years (Imperator, 1938, dir
Herbert Wilcox), during July 1937 and October 1938
respectively, all the previous pre-1936 bans being
conveniently forgotten. The participation of the
Permanent Under-Secretary at the Foreign Office, Sir
Robert Vansittart, in the script writing for both
films was concealed from the public at the time.
Victoria the Great and Sixty Glorious Years stand as
monuments to how far Tyrrell and the BBFC could perform a complete somersault on the usual avoidance of
current political controversy when establishment
expediency dictated. However, the undoubted popularity of both films, which owed much to the performances of Dame Anna Neagle as Victoria and Anton
Walbrook as Prince Albert, suggests that the Commons
vote of 11 December 1936 against republicanism reflected mass opinion. In this sense the abdication and
the continued existence of the monarchy were not
current political controversies at all.
　　Jeffrey Richards has drawn attention to the deep
BBFC concern to protect the professional image of, in
particular, doctors and the practitioners of law and
order.[11] Nevertheless BBFC guidelines on this were
sometimes infringed. For instance, Captain Blood
(Warner, 1935, dir Michael Curtiz), the first of the
Errol Flynn pirate swashbucklers, deals with the
wrongful conviction of a young British doctor (Flynn)
at the hands of Judge Jeffreys in 1685 during the
aftermath of the abortive Monmouth rebellion against
James II. This particular courtroom scene, which
might be interpreted as a criticism of British
justice, could not be deleted without making a non-
sense of the plot, so that the BBFC in January 1936
allowed it, evidently due to its historical setting.
The Will Hay comedy Ask a Policeman (Gainsborough,
1938, dir Marcel Varnel), passed in March 1939, is a
lampoon on the then current establishment wisdom that
the British police force was totally efficient and
morally beyond reproach. However, neither of these

films represented an earnest effort to look into the British system of law and order, and more noteworthy, because it was serious melodrama and near contemporary, was the scenario for The Citadel (MGM Britain, 1938, dir King Vidor) when it was delivered to the BBFC in July 1937. The film was based upon A.J. Cronin's novel which had been highly critical of the British medical profession, but for once Hanna was less perturbed than Mrs Crouzet, for he did not consider the scenario as a general attack upon doctors. He commented[12] that '...although it shows several undesirable types of doctor...I suggest that the faults of the undesirable types be not presented in such a manner as to shake the confidence of the nation in the medical profession'. Mrs Crouzet was much more scathing. She declared,

> There is so much that is disparaging to
> doctors in this book, that I consider it
> unsuitable for production as a film. I
> think it dangerous to shatter what faith
> the general public has in the medical
> profession, and in any case, if the story
> is considered at all the approval of the
> Medical Council should be obtained.
> Incidents showing doctor's (sic) petty
> jealousies, drunken doctor, incompetent
> doctors, a doctor refusing to answer the
> call of a poor boy...as well as scenes
> of operations, are in my opinion, prohibitive.

Significantly, neither of the censors asked themselves whether public confidence in doctors was either justified or a matter for them to decide, but despite the discouraging BBFC reaction MGM went ahead with the production along scenario lines. The story centres on the career of young Dr Andrew Manson (Robert Donat), an idealist who in 1924 becomes a doctor in a Welsh mining village. There with another doctor, the disillusioned, cynical, drunken visionary Philip Denny (Sir Ralph Richardson), he secretly blows up a sewer causing disease among the miners and thus compels the local council to build a new one. Under the later influence of a colleague motivated more by money than idealism, Freddie Hampson (Rex Harrison), Manson becomes a Harley Street specialist until one of his friends (Cecil Parker) blunders during a routine operation in which Manson's patient dies. It takes this incident and the loyalty of his wife, Christine (Rosalind Russell), to wake Manson up to how far he has wandered from his original ideals.

There was much more here to disturb the BBFC when the
full version was submitted in November 1938, but an
outright rejection was virtually out of the question
in the light of the Pygmalion affair earlier in the
year. Moreover, The Citadel was a prestige production of the newly established MGM studios in Britain
resulting from the new 1937 quota act of parliament.
However, if the basic theme could not be stifled, it
could be whittled down, and the BBFC went in for
mutilation on a grand scale. There were extensive
cuts and alterations, while the entire process of
censorship occupied all but three weeks when most
films were passed within a matter of days. Unfortunately it is not possible from the surviving BBFC
records to reconstruct the material left in and taken
out, for politics as well as medical ethics were
involved. Part of Denny's dialogue amounts to a plea
for a national health service, while the Welsh mining
village sequences are in places severely critical of
mining conditions owing to a visit to Wales beforehand by King Vidor,[13] whose wife wrote the screen-
play. The scope for BBFC modification was thus
great, but on the other hand it is hard to credit
that this cutting was performed so thoroughly that
the film's overall critique of medical practices was
totally erased. In fact it seems probable that the
BBFC concentrated more on politically sensitive
material than on the image of doctors, for in the
previous year South Riding (London Films, 1937, dir
Victor Saville) had also undergone extensive BBFC
revision. But in this case no general attack on
doctors had been entailed, whereas the minor character of a doctor (Sir John Clements) utters dialogue
advocating a national health service by implication
through criticism of private medical practice. In
addition the film vividly depicts the deprived social
conditions of the poor.

Religion

Religion had never proved a major problem for
the BBFC. From its creation in 1913 it had refused
to sanction the materialisation of Christ, and
although the 1928 annual report had announced that
this policy was under review following the success
of King of Kings, it was in fact to be retained until
well after the Second World War. In general the
BBFC's religious policy was the avoidance of anything
likely to offend any British religious denomination
or non-Christian religions within the British empire.
Accordingly in August 1929 the BBFC evidently made a

tentative decision to suppress a German film on the
life of Martin Luther because it might upset Roman
Catholics, as it had allegedly already done in Germany. However, on 26 August The Times published a
letter from the Protestant MP for West Belfast,
W.E.D. Allen, who attacked the ban on Martin Luther
and accused the BBFC of a pro-Catholic bias, presumably because O'Connor was a Catholic. In fact no
definite decision to refuse the film a BBFC certificate had yet been taken. Two days after the publication of Allen's letter an agreement was reached
between the BBFC and the British distributors for the
deletion of scenes showing Martin Tetzel's sale of
indulgences in Germany, the event which had sparked
off the Lutheran Reformation of the early 16th century. On this basis the BBFC allowed the cut version
of Martin Luther, to which there was no adverse
public reaction.
    After the Martin Luther episode religion posed
no special difficulties for the BBFC, either in
scenarios or films themselves, until 1936 when it was
confronted by the all-negro cast production of The
Green Pastures (Warner, 1936, dir William Keighley).
This depicts Old Testament stories as viewed by ill-
educated American blacks and contains a quite outst-
anding performance by Rex Ingram as De Lawd, the
preacher who leads his impoverished flock. The BBFC
on 13 November 1936 cut the film by 211 feet, but
this proved insufficient to prevent some press and
public criticism, mostly racially inspired. However,
this criticism was prolonged enough for Tyrrell to
refer to it in his published address to the CEA in
June 1937, but he continued to defend the BBFC's
decision in this instance on the ground that The
Green Pastures was reverential in approach and would
not prove to be the prelude to Hollywood religious
features of more dubious merit. Also the BBFC was
to raise no objection to the figure of the Roman
Catholic priest as social reformer in San Francisco
(MGM, 1936, dir W.S. Van Dyke), Boys' Town (MGM,
1938, dir Norman Taurog) and Angels with Dirty Faces
(Warner, 1938, dir Michael Curtiz) when played by
Spencer Tracy in the first two and Pat O'Brien in the
last. The BBFC was not subjected to any serious
public criticism as a result of these decisions, even
though Tyrrell was a Catholic.
    In January 1939 G.H.W. Productions submitted a
scenario, The First Easter, which covered events in
the life of Christ between the Crucifixion and the
Resurrection in a reverent fashion. The figure of
Christ would not be shown, only his shadow and hands,

although his voice was to be heard in one or two scenes. Both Hanna and Mrs Crouzet accepted the scenario but rejected the producer's request that the full figure of Christ should be seen but not his face.[14] The film was never made. When 20th Century-Fox (TCF) submitted a scenario for Brigham Young (1940, dir Henry Hathaway) in November 1939, Hanna and Mrs Crouzet feared that it might be converted into pro-Mormon propaganda.[15] However, since the film was passed in October 1940 with only minor cuts, the BBFC was evidently satisfied on this score.

The evidence from the scenarios and films between 1929 and 1939 suggests that, despite the Catholicism of its presidents, the BBFC pursued a policy of strict religious neutrality as between the various Christian denominations. However, its ban on the materialisation of Christ was probably over-cautious in the light of the success that King of Kings enjoyed during the late 1920s.

Crime, Gangsterism, Law and Order

From the outset the BBFC had been concerned about how crime was depicted on the screen, for its first annual report in 1913 had given 'excessively gruesome details in crime' and 'scenes calculated to act as an incentive to crime' as reasons for cuts to submitted films. The 1914 annual report had added the careers of notorious criminals as well as criminal methods of operation. By 1919 'subjects in which crime is the dominant feature' and 'the cumulative effect of crime' meant, if taken as literally as stated in that year's report, that crime films of any kind would be refused a certificate. But in practice that was not the case, and during the 1920s crime had continued to be mentioned regularly in the reports as a ground for banning or cutting films. 1923 had been the first time that crime was discussed in the text of the annual report when the BBFC had deprecated themes 'calculated to give an air of romance and heroism to criminal characters...whilst the constituted authorities and administrators of the law are held up to odium as being either unjust or harsh, incompetent or ridiculous'. In the 1926 BBFC codification crime had received a heading all to itself with no fewer than thirteen sub-divisions as grounds for rejection. As yet the BBFC had not been confronted with a film dealing with large-scale organised crime, but in the wake of prohibition in the United States during the 1920s real gangsters emerged like the infamous Al Capone. The first

screen attempt to depict a gang boss was in Underworld (Paramount, 1927, dir Josef Von Sternberg) in
which 'Bull' Weed (George Bancroft) is sprung from
prison by his moll, 'Feathers' McCoy (Evelyn Brent),
and his second lieutenant 'Rolls' Royce (Clive Brook)
but allows them to escape because they are in love
while he is captured as the law relentlessly closes
in. The film takes a sympathetic view of 'Bull', for
which reason it ran into considerable trouble at the
BBFC when submitted on 24 October 1927 under the
title of The Penalty. The BBFC insisted upon alterations, the film being resubmitted on 15 December
when however the BBFC remained unsatisfied. A third
submission was held over until April 1928 when the
BBFC, possibly with the intervening Dawn events in
mind, finally granted an 'A' certificate under the
title of Paying the Penalty in order to emphasise
fully that in the long run crime never paid. In the
process of the three submissions the film had been
reduced by 741 feet or twelve minutes running time.
    Nevertheless Underworld did not spawn more films
on American organised crime, as often claimed. Much
more influential was the famous St Valentine's Day
massacre of 1929 in Chicago, which led to a run of
gangster features. These have long since passed into
a mostly well merited obscurity, but important
examples, because they were soon to influence the
future development of the genre, were The Hole in the
Wall (Paramount, 1929, dir Robert Florey), Night Ride
(Universal, 1930, dir John Robertson) and Doorway to
Hell (Warner, 1929, dir Archie Mayo, released in
Britain as A Handful of Clouds). The first two
starred Edward G. Robinson and the last James Cagney,
although for the moment Cagney remained on the right
side of the law. Robinson's performance as gangland
boss Tony Garotta in Night Ride clearly foreshadows
his legendary role of Rico in Little Caesar (Warner,
1930, dir Mervyn Leroy). But even before Robinson's
performance as Rico had given the gangster image a
punch it had previously lacked, the trend towards
screen gangsterism had grown pronounced. The BBFC's
annual report for 1929 commented that,

> ...themes are often sordid, and the lives
> of the principal characters, if not actually
> immoral, are at all events unmoral in
> practice and principle. In many cases, there
> is in addition an admixture of the criminal
> or bootlegging element, with the introduction
> of an atmosphere of riotous luxury. One such
> film by itself may not be prohibitive, but

> the Board cannot help feeling that a
> continuous succession of them is sub-
> versive, tending to inculcate a lower
> outlook and to invest a life of irreg-
> ularity with a spurious glamour.

In 1930 one film, probably The Party Girl, was
rejected outright because the story was one 'in which
the criminal element is predominant', while the BBFC
annual report again complained about films with 'an
unrelieved atmosphere of sordidness'. None the less
there was no wholehearted BBFC effort to stifle
gangster films, and even Little Caesar, generally
regarded as the first of the classic gangster dramas,
ran into only minor difficulties and suffered merely
nominal cuts when allowed in February 1931. Indeed
in that same year the now relatively unknown The
Secret Six (MGM, 1931, dir George Hill), a bootlegg-
ing-cum-press melodrama, and Doorway to Hell
incurred much more BBFC displeasure. The Secret Six
was submitted on no fewer than five occasions between
20 April and 29 July and viewed by Shortt himself
before at length receiving an 'A' certificate. The
amount of reduced footage was not recorded. Presumably the film fared better than Doorway to Hell, for
this was submitted six times (and banned once) from
January 1930 to July 1932 before being cut by 342
feet, approximately 5 per cent of its full running
time. Almost simultaneously, on 22 June 1931, Shortt
was viewing The Public Enemy (Warner, 1931, dir
William Wellman), but it was almost two months later
before the BBFC declined to award it a certificate.
To the film buff of the 1980s there seems little to
distinguish The Public Enemy from the gangster dramas
previously let through, so that it is far from clear
why the BBFC took such drastic action against
Cagney's portrayal of hoodlum Tom Powers who eventually meets his death at the hands of other mobsters
rather than the law. No doubt, the scene in which
Cagney twists a grapefruit into Mae Clarke's face
did not go down well at the BBFC, but this hardly
explains a total rejection. The mystery is height-
ened by the fact that the 1931 report dwelt far more
on sex and scantily clad women than on crime and
gangsterism. This suggests that organised crime was
not the chief concern of the BBFC at this time, as
does the fact that in May 1932 the BBFC allowed a
modified version of Scarface (Howard Hughes, 1932,
dir Howard Hawks). The submitted print was almost
certainly heavily cut and reconstructed due to the
severe censorship problems the film had already

encountered in the United States. In the light of
this decision the ban on The Public Enemy was lifted
in the following month. Towards the end of the same
year I am a Fugitive from a Chain Gang (Warner, 1932,
dir Mervyn Leroy), in which Paul Muni's unjustified
sufferings in an American penal colony still assault
any audience's sensitivities far more than his devas-
tating portrayal of mob leader Carmonte in Scarface,
was viewed by Shortt after three submissions over a
six-week period during November and December.
Although technically not a gangster film, I am a
Fugitive from a Chain Gang touches upon the alleged
crime that brought Muni to the penal colony in the
first place and emphasises the difficulties that a
convicted man faces upon his release in trying to go
straight. This probably explains why the BBFC took
so long to pass it.

No crime or gangster film was rejected throughout 1932, and the whole topic was ignored in the last
of the regular published annual reports for that
year. The BBFC had thus bowed to commercial pressures and accepted organised crime in films provided
that the setting was the United States, whereas
scenarios covering organised crime in Britain were
strongly discouraged between 1932 and 1934.[16] Some
local authorities, most notably Beckenham and
Birmingham, thought the BBFC policy towards gangster
features too lax, the latter even going so far as to
ban Scarface outright. The early sound gangster
movies either made mobsters their central figures or
represented convicted criminals as the victims of
injustice. Invariably cloaked in a weakly emphasised
veneer of moral outrage, this was nevertheless sub-
ordinated to brutality and immorality even though
eventually society always caught up with the evil-
doers. By the end of 1932 this particular cycle had
run out of box office steam. The only major example
of the genre in 1933, The Mayor of Hell (Warner,
1933, dir Archie Mayo), in which Cagney plays an ex-
gangster who had seen the light and becomes the warden
of an American boys' reform school, began a change of
style in gangster personalities. This was to endure
for the remainder of the decade and reduced the
BBFC's problems over gangsterism to near zero. The
emphasis was shifted away from the unredeemable hoodlum to one who might be brought to see the error of
his ways and become a respectable and respected
member of society. Or, where that switch was too
incredible for an audience to swallow, he became a
criminal who possessed some redeeming features. He
was thus capable of considerate behaviour towards

others even if in the last resort his crimes had been
too serious for him to escape the ultimate sacrifice
which society demanded. The BBFC in 1933 did not
discern this coming change of emphasis, for when
Shortt viewed The Mayor of Hell on 22 July following
a resubmission, it was cut by 348 feet (four minutes)
and treated much as the earlier sound gangster
features. The BBFC's main concern was indicated by
the fact that a special foreword to The Mayor of Hell
was inserted to point out that the conditions in
British juvenile reform establishments were not so
bad as those depicted in the film.
     By 1935-6 Cagney and Edward G. Robinson had be-
come the protectors of the American public from
criminals - Cagney as the Federal Bureau of Investigation (FBI) recruit in G Men (Warner, 1935, dir
William Keighley) and Robinson as the crusading cop
infiltrating a gang led by Humphrey Bogart in Bullets
or Ballots (Warner, 1936, dir William Keighley). The
former film was in effect a propaganda vehicle for
the FBI, and as such it contained scenes favouring
the legal use of firearms by the FBI against armed
gangsters, which at the time involved Congressional
legislation and was opposed by some members of
Congress and of the American public. Possibly for
this reason G Men, despite its unequivocal pro-law
and order stance, encountered difficulties at the
BBFC, whereas Bullets or Ballots was allowed uncut.
The idea of arming the British police was then an
emotive public issue which the relevant scenes of G
Men might have stimulated. This probably accounted
for the modification of three reels and a cut of 134
feet before the film was allowed in May 1935.
     1937 saw the major cause of American screen
crime firmly linked with the world slump and unemployment. This cycle apparently began with You Only
Live Once (Walter Wanger, 1937, dir Fritz Lang) in
which, it is strongly hinted but never clarified
beyond doubt, a petty crook (Henry Fonda) is framed
and eventually killed by the police together with his
honest girl friend (Sylvia Sidney) as they try to
escape to Canada. Lang's preoccupation with the
possible innocence of the crook is played down. The
dominant impression on a first viewing is that the
crook is a victim of social circumstances outside
his control in that he could not obtain a job due to
the slump but nevertheless pays the inevitable
penalty for breaking the law, as does the girl for
eventually acting as his accomplice in trying to help
him to escape. The BBFC passed the film in February
1937 with only minor modifications. They Gave Him a

Gun (MGM, 1937, dir W.S. Van Dyke), passed in full in
May 1937, presses home much the same theme and ending, although in this case the inability of the
gangster (Spencer Tracy) to go straight is partly
blamed on his First World War battle experiences. On
the other hand Marked Woman (Warner, 1937, dir Lloyd
Bacon) was a minor hark back to the gangster melodramas of the early 1930s except that the central
figure is a prostitute, euphemistically described as
a night club hostess (Bette Davis), who despite a
severe beating up testifies in court against her
vicious gang boss (Eduardo Ciannelli). The film,
inspired by the recent trial of Lucky Luciano,
concentrates more than any other of this 1930s genre
upon the link between organised crime and prostitution, and Bette Davis's facial disfigurement after
her beating up is explicitly shown. The BBFC saw to
it that the film was first extensively modified and
then cut in April 1937, but nevertheless the fundamental theme remained easily recognisable when Marked
Woman appeared in British cinemas.
        Dead End (Samuel Goldwyn, 1937, dir William
Wyler) marked a swift return to slum conditions and
the slump as the genesis of crime, especially juvenile crime. The big-time gangster (Humphrey Bogart)
who returns to his run-down New York neighbourhood
before the law inevitably catches up with him is
contrasted with the unemployed college-educated
architect (Joel McCrea) who continues to go straight
and even aids the police to uphold law and order.
Even so the film at several points derides the use of
juvenile reform institutions as an antidote to crime,
while the dialogue once mentions police brutality
against women strikers. At scenario stage in June
1937 Hanna had been unenthusiastic about such a
production,[17] but even though the scenario failed to
mention that the gangster's ex-girl friend (Claire
Trevor) had turned prostitute, a fact fully brought
out in the film without the actual use of the word
'prostitute', Dead End was passed uncut in September
1937. This decision was a far cry from earlier
attitudes to the American gangster films and was
facilitated by contacts with American censors during
production. Although in principle the BBFC continued
to resist anything which smacked of organised crime
in Britain, the film which perhaps comes closest to
it in the 1930s, Edgar Wallace's story of The Squea-
ker (London Films, 1937, dir William Howard), was let
through uncut in August 1937.
        After the success of Dead End and the so-called
Dead End kids, the 1938 gangster genre moved into

deeper contact with juvenile delinquency in Crime
School (Warner, 1938, dir Lewis Seiler), Boys' Town
and Angels with Dirty Faces. In the latter two a
Roman Catholic priest (Spencer Tracy and Pat O'Brien
respectively) represents a potential reforming
influence on boys, while in the first two the success
of reform schools in handling juvenile delinquents is
the fundamental message. In Angels with Dirty Faces
the figure of the priest stands as the antithesis of
gangster Rocky Sullivan (James Cagney) from the same
poor district, a deprived social background thus
being projected as no excuse for a resort to crime.
The impact of such slick anti-crime propaganda is
slightly lessened by an ambiguous ending in which it
is unclear whether Cagney really turns coward before
his execution in the electric chair or merely feigns
cowardice at the priest's request in order to convince his juvenile admirers in his old district that
they would be well advised not to emulate him. Crime
School and Boys' Town passed the BBFC virtually unscathed, but despite its basic anti-crime posture
Angels with Dirty Faces suffered much alteration and
many minor cuts in November 1938.
     The remaining pre-September 1939 gangster movies
raised no particular difficulties for the BBFC, but
two related films - The Amazing Dr Clitterhouse
(Warner, 1938, dir Anatole Litvak) and the western
Jesse James (TCF, 1938, dir Henry King) - are noteworthy in a law and order context because both might
have been expected to meet more BBFC opposition than
they did. The first deals with a criminal psychia-
trist (Edward G. Robinson) who joins a gang to study
the criminal mentality. He eventually becomes the
leader and commits murder but evades the death penalty through an insanity plea. Shrouded in a comedy
format and based upon a well-known stage play, the
film comes close to suggesting that the middle class
is every bit as capable as the lower class of criminal activity, and that its superior education will
enable it to be more effective in carrying out crim-
inality. It was nothing less than astounding that in
July 1938 the BBFC passed the film uncut in the light
of the general BBFC reverence for law and order at
this time and insistence that criminals must never be
permitted to evade justice. By the time Jesse James
came before the BBFC in February 1939 the BBFC had
been expressly attacked during the Commons debate of
7 December 1938, and in consequence a relaxation of
previous policies had seemingly taken place. Even
so the film, based upon the life of the notorious
western bandit (Tyrone Power), is a near apologia

82

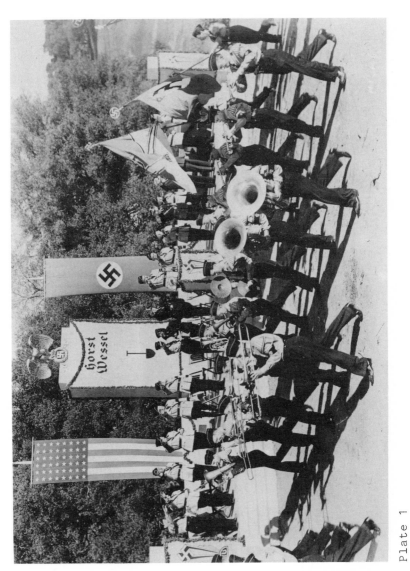

Plate 1

Plate 2

Plate 3

Plate 4

Plate 5

Plate 6

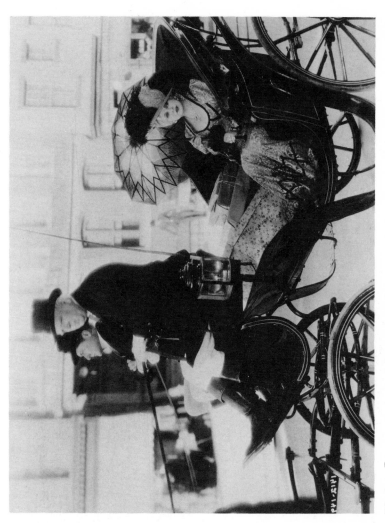

Plate 7

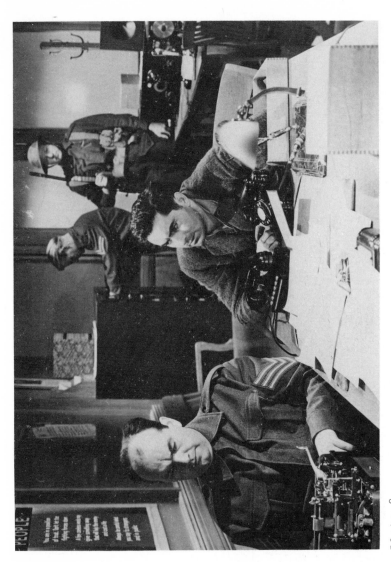

Plate 8

for law-breaking, as some British critics noted upon
its release. The BBFC cut Jesse James by 53 feet,
but this was probably due to a scene involving
cruelty to a horse rather than to the depiction of
crime, and the fundamentally favourable view of James
is consistent throughout the film. As it happened
the press concern over Jesse James was swiftly overtaken by the more pressing international events which
led to the outbreak of the Second World War.

Industrial Relations and the Labouring Classes

The BBFC objection to the coverage of industrial
relations, whether in Britain or elsewhere, on film
had dated back to 1915, but its attitude to the
depiction of working class living conditions had been
much less clear cut. For instance, the King Vidor
masterpiece The Crowd (MGM, 1927), the story of a
young New York couple's struggle to eke out a living
in typical overcrowded urban conditions, was granted
a certificate early in 1928. However, the rise of
Labour after 1919 had converted the condition of the
British working class into an ever-present political
issue which gained in intensity after 1929 under the
impact of the great slump and mass unemployment. On
the evidence of the scenarios and some mainly light
entertainment films, Jeffrey Richards has concluded
that the policy of the BBFC was to ban or discourage
films confronting British industrial relations head
on (i.e. entailing strikes, social unrest) and to
welcome films preaching class harmony and an uncom-
plaining acceptance of the social status quo. This
policy went so far as to embrace a scenario ban on
Love on the Dole.[18] Certainly it is no mere coincidence that so many films showing British working
class characters were comedies of the George Formby,
Dame Gracie Fields and Old Mother Riley (Arthur
Lucan) variety, unlikely to prompt serious political
thought even though they occasionally raised the
spectre of unemployment or the threat of it. However, a more serious depiction of British working
class everyday life also appeared now and again, as
in Song of Freedom (Hammer, 1936, dir J. Elder Wills)
where the early sequences dwell upon life in London's
dockland. Moreover, even if socialist doctrine
remained barred within a British context or in Soviet
films like Strike (USSR, 1925, dir Sergei Eisenstein)
and New Babylon (USSR, 1929, dir Yevgeni Enei), this
was not always the case with American films. By far
the most earnest pre-1937 American drama covering the
influence of the great slump was Our Daily Bread

(King Vidor, 1934, dir King Vidor, known in Britain
as The Miracle of Life), and amazingly this highly
committed left-wing film in an American setting
survived a three-month BBFC scrutiny from September
to December 1934 before the award of an 'A' certificate without cuts of any sort. A detailed examination of the plot and some of the dialogue reveals how
liberal the BBFC sometimes was over the poorer
classes and depression issues, even before the
Pygmalion episode of 1938.
 A young city couple, John and Mary Sims (Tom
Keene and Karen Morley), with the husband unemployed,
entertain the wife's rich uncle in the hope that he
will offer John a job. The couple's urban poverty is
emphasised by an inability to pay the rent, which
leads to eviction, and by the pawning of a cherished
banjo to pay for a scrawny chicken to serve the uncle
for dinner. The uncle does not offer John a job, but
he does offer a run-down farm in which neither he·nor
the bank holding the mortgage retain any interest.
The couple go to the farm and are soon joined by an
unemployed Swede, Chris Larsen (John Qualen), and his
wife. Advertisements for more men produce enough
labour for a collective farm. The enterprise is
threatened from outside in various ways, the most
serious of which is a shortage of food before the
planted crops have grown. One of the men, Louie
(Addison Richards), is a convict on the run with a
500 dollars reward on his head. He gives himself up
in such a way as to allow the farm to claim the
reward money, enabling the purchase of sufficient
food to tide the community over until the crops
ripen. Then drought menaces the crops, whereupon
John becomes despondent because his leadership is at
risk and turns to Sally, a Jean Harlow-type seduct-
ress (Barbara Pepper is even made to resemble Harlow
in appearance) who has come to the farm by accident
and whose heart is not in the collectivist spirit of
the farm's personnel. However, just as he is about
to desert the farm with Sally, John remembers Louie's
sacrifice and returns to get the power house to work.
He then induces the disheartened men to dig a long
ditch from the power house to the farm in five days
so that the fields can be irrigated. This they
succeed in doing during a final twelve-minute
Eisenstein-style sequence, and the farm survives as
the water is seen flowing into the fields.
 In itself this outline story conveys the message
that collectivism, ironically then on the wane in the
USSR, can ease or solve industrial unemployment, but
there is more subtlety to Vidor's film than this. He

hints that capitalism should be subverted by its own
unscrupulous methods. When the farm is threatened
with sale by auction, the farm's labour force turns
up in strength at the auction and physically intimi-
dates potential bidders not to bid, leaving the way
clear for the farm men to bid at a ludicrously low
figure which the sheriff-auctioneer is bound by law
to accept as the sole bid. Vidor also emphasises the
universal character of collectivism - Larsen is a
Swede rather than another American, while John
accepts men of economically unproductive occupations
for the farm, for example a violinist, an undertaker
and a cigar salesman. Furthermore Louie, the escaped
convict, becomes the farm's main upholder of law and
order. He protects one of the men when another tries
to push him off land which the former has just begun
to cultivate, saying, 'We are going to have law and
order here even if I have to clear up half the out-
fit'. This particular scene suggests that outside
the farm criminals may be simply the victims of
capitalism. Finally, politics openly intrudes into
a scene of a group discussion as to how the farm
should be run. One speaker states, 'We must have a
socialist form of government', to which another
replies that it was that kind of talk that had made
them unemployed and brought them to the farm in the
first place. Although Vidor's approach was basically
conservative in that it stressed rural values and
denigrated urban ones, it would have been most unlikely to have escaped a BBFC rejection if the setting had been in Britain, to judge from the fate of
the pre-war Love on the Dole projects. None the less
Our Daily Bread reveals how far the BBFC could bend
to permit a quasi-socialist viewpoint to be seen in
British cinemas.
     After the Commons debate of 7 December 1938,
with a general election due within two years if peace
was maintained and by-election results suggesting a
possible Labour victory, the BBFC seems to have
abandoned its resistance in principle to the subject
of British industrial relations. During 1939 two
films dealing with this were planned, The Proud
Valley (Ealing, 1939, dir Pen Tennyson) and The Stars
Look Down (Grafton Films, 1939, dir Sir Carol Reed).
The BBFC received no scenario for the former and it
was not completed until after war had broken out, so
that it is not now possible to know how the BBFC
would have treated the finished film in peacetime.
As it was the early emphasis in the film on racial
equality when Welsh miners accept black singer Paul
Robeson as one of themselves and on the poor living

85

and working conditions of the miners is balanced by
a late concentration on national unity as a result of
war. This was presumably the outcome of an amended
script, as the film was in the course of production
early in September 1939 and was not completed until
the end of the month.[19] At the close of June 1939
BBFC received the scenario for The Stars Look Down,
based upon A.J. Cronin's novel. Although it deals
with hostility between miners and mineowners and
contains a strike, rioting which leads to the looting
of a butcher's shop and a questionable prison
sentence for the leader of the men, Hanna raised no
objection to the fundamental theme. In fact he was
more concerned about over-long Biblical quotations
from Revelations and possible cruelty to pit
ponies![20] He appears to have judged the film suitable for production because in the plot the mineowner
works hard to save miners' lives when an unsafe mine
eventually floods. The Stars Look Down was completed
on the day Germany invaded Poland,[21] although it was
not released until January 1940. Its mild treatment
at the hands of the BBFC stands in stark contrast to
BBFC's pre-1939 application of its rules on British
industrial relations as shown by Jeffrey Richards.[22]
Times were certainly changing at the BBFC!

   However, although the BBFC was probably too
supine in its approach to British working class
characterisation, Labour ideology and industrial
relations prior to 1939, it was by no means as in-
transigent as a simple investigation of scenarios
and of British light entertainment films suggests.

Ireland

   Potentially the greatest source of friction
between the BBFC and American and British studios
from 1919 to 1939 was Ireland. When the cinema had
first taken root as a mass communication medium
during the early 20th century, the whole of Ireland
had formed a part of the United Kingdom. However,
following the Sinn Fein uprising of Easter 1916 and
the civil war against England in 1919-21, Ireland was
partitioned into Northern Ireland, which remained
within the United Kingdom, and the Irish Free State
(Eire after 1937), which in 1921 became a self-
governing Dominion within the British empire. A
minority of Sinn Feiners would not accept the separation of Northern Ireland with its Protestant majority from a Catholic united Ireland, with the result
that the Irish Republican Army (IRA) did not disband.
A civil war in the Irish Free State during 1923-4 led

to the defeat of the dissident Sinn Feiners, while
sporadic IRA activity in England was maintained until
1939 against a background of poor relations between
the Dublin and London governments throughout the entire inter-war period. In September 1939 Eire became
the only Dominion not to declare war upon Germany.
  With the possible exception of unemployment,
Ireland remained the most pressing British domestic
problem of the 1920s and 1930s. The BBFC was
directly involved in that Hanna had served in Ireland
from 1918 to 1922, when the 'troubles' were at their
height, and ended his military career there
immediately before joining the BBFC. Both the
American and British production companies probably
sensed instinctively that Ireland as a screen topic
would be a box office liability so close to the 1921
settlement, for films with even an earlier Irish 20th
century background seem to have been very rare indeed
in the silent and early talkie years. The most
important exception was a British silent 1928 version
of Liam O'Flaherty's novel The Informer (dir Arthur
Robison), while the BBFC also allowed Juno and the
Paycock (British International, 1929, dir Sir Alfred
Hitchcock), based on Sean O'Casey's play, even though
the 1916 uprising and the turbulence of the early
1920s formed the background. Thus references to
near contemporary Irish events were of themselves
not prohibitive at the BBFC, but when in February
1933 a scenario entitled The Man with the Gun
appeared with a story based mostly on 1921 Irish
events, Hanna dismissed it with the comment that it
was 'too recent history to be a suitable subject for
a film'. He continued, 'No matter how the subject is
treated, one side or the other will be angered and
much harm might result'.[23] The film appears not to
have been made. Universal in October 1934 sent a
scenario to BBFC under the title of Sir Roger
Casement. Casement was an Irish-born British
diplomat who had been executed in 1917 for trying to
persuade Irish prisoners of war in German hands to
fight for Germany against Britain and for his part
in successfully enlisting German aid for the 1916
revolt. The scenario concentrated mostly on
Casement's activities from 1914 to 1917, and he was
portrayed as an Irish patriot who had died for his
ideals. Hanna rejected the basic theme out of hand,
for to him Casement was 'an insignificant traitor to
his country who paid the ordinary penalty for his
offence',[24] a view which paid little heed to the fact
that most of Ireland had no longer been within the
United Kingdom for the past thirteen years. Again

the projected film seems to have been abandoned.

On the surface the prospects at the BBFC for any film dealing with Ireland from an anti-English stand-point were far from rosy, as RKO knew when it decided in the first half of 1935 to produce a remake of The Informer (dir John Ford). No scenario was submitted, although RKO undertook extensive indirect consult-ations with the BBFC prior to production. Ford's film, far and away the best on Ireland made in the 1930s, is set in a Dublin under British Black and Tan control in 1920 and deals with the retarded Gypo Nolan (Victor McLaglen), a member of a Republican resistance group who betrays his best friend to the British for 'a £20 reward' and an opportunity to emi-grate. An inescapable guilty conscience, combined with the relentless pursuit of the traitor by the other group members, ensures Gypo's discovery and downfall. Although seen in the film only here and there, the Black and Tans are the undoubted villains and by implication Gypo's colleagues are emphatically depicted as freedom fighters. The BBFC cut a modi-fied version of The Informer by 376 feet (over four minutes running time) on 6 June 1935, but its polit-ical commitment, if only rarely stated openly, re-mains nevertheless sharp and unimpaired.

The success of The Informer in the United States, where both Ford and McLaglen picked up Academy Awards for 1935, led RKO to make The Plough and the Stars (1936, dirs John Ford and George Nicholls Junior, the latter uncredited). A scenario for this had already been submitted to the BBFC be-fore the latter had considered The Informer, and on 8 May 1935 Shortt, Brooke Wilkinson and Hanna had agreed that this Sean O'Casey saga about the influ-ence of politics upon a Dublin family just before and during the 1916 Easter rising was basically accept-able.[25] O'Casey himself had drawn attention to Irish shortcomings in dealings with the English as well as Irish bravery, whereas the film centres upon the conflict between patriotism and love as this affects an Irish Republican officer (Preston Foster) and his wife (Barbara Stanwyck), who wishes him not to fight. After The Informer the BBFC was left with little alternative but to pass The Plough and the Stars despite Ford's continued anti-English approach, but the latter film lacks the charisma of the former, so that any lingering BBFC fears about the spread in Britain of anti-Irish Protestant opinion were soon to be laid to rest.

In April 1936 United Artists put forward a scenario for a story of the Irish 'troubles' which

bore some resemblance to the life of Irish revolutionary Michael Collins between 1920 and 1924.
Collins had been murdered in 1924 for signing the
1921 partition treaty, but the scenario suggested
that the film would play up love interest rather
than politics. The result was that Tyrrell personally approved the scenario.[26] Seldom during the
1930s was a BBFC President called upon for a decision
at scenario stage, so that Tyrrell's early involvement in the Michael Collins scenario, which does not
seem to have been converted into a film, indicates a
likely split over films on Ireland between the other
key BBFC staff. This is tentatively confirmed by
the comments of Hanna and Mrs Crouzet on the scenario
for Parnell in May 1936 when Hanna favoured rejection
but Mrs Crouzet recommended acceptance. In fact the
completed film on the life of the late 19th century
Irish Nationalist leader (Clark Gable) dwells largely
upon his affair with and subsequent marriage to Mrs
O'Shea (Myrna Loy). However, preponderant love
interest does not entirely submerge Parnell's politics, for it is made clear throughout that his fundamental political aim is Home Rule for Ireland.
Furthermore, in the film a Dublin mob orator uses
the phrase, 'English tyranny'. Nevertheless the
BBFC passed Parnell uncut in June 1937.
    However, BBFC opposition to Irish themes did not
wither altogether before September 1939. It is true
that Hanna was ready to accept a 1938 scenario called
The Rising, which covered Fenian revolution in
Ireland during 1866-7,[27] but his reaction to Irish
Story in May 1939 was very different. This Warner
Brothers scenario was set in Ireland immediately
following the 1921 treaty and concentrated upon the
Irish Free State civil war of 1923-4. Hanna observed
that Irish Story would be 'quite unpopular with the
Free State Government',[28] and advised against production. Mrs Crouzet on the other hand accepted the
theme, as did another BBFC staff member, who, however, with an extensive IRA bomb campaign in many
English towns and cities since the previous January
in mind, was moved to write, 'There is one point of
possible doubt, as to whether it would be advisable
to publish a film on this subject while the recent
outbreak of IRA outrages in Great Britain persist'.[29]
In the event, possibly because of the IRA terrorist
activities in England, neither The Rising nor Irish
Story was filmed and the BBFC was spared any possible
political difficulty.

Imperialism

In his masterly book Visions of Yesterday (1973)
and more recently in an excellent article for British
Cinema History (1983) Jeffrey Richards has shown how
the pro-imperialist ethos of the British Commonwealth
was projected onto the screen in such American and
British features as Rhodes of Africa (Gaumont, 1936,
dir Berthold Viertel), Sanders of the River (London
Films, 1935, dir Zoltan Korda), Lives of a Bengal
Lancer (Paramount, 1935, dir Henry Hathaway), The
Four Feathers (London Films, 1939, dir Zoltan Korda),
The Drum (London Films, 1938, dir Zoltan Korda) and
Gunga Din (RKO, 1939, dir George Stevens). From this
one might too swiftly conclude that the BBFC was
merely a vehicle for the transmission of pro-
imperialist propaganda, whereas in reality anti-
imperialist material was also let through. The
Tarzan films of Johnny Weissmuller, for instance,
invariably portrayed as the villains rapacious white
men bent on some form of greed or economic exploitation of the jungle, one justification for European
colonialism frequently advanced by its supporters in
Britain. The Hurricane (Sam Goldwyn, 1937, dirs John
Ford and Stuart Heisler), a disaster movie set on a
South Sea island, has early sequences which mount a
fierce assault on European justice as administered to
subject peoples in colonial territories. The BBFC
allowed this film almost uncut in December 1937.
Whether or not one interprets Old Bones of the River
(GFD-Gainsborough, 1938, dir Marcel Varnel) as a
spoof Sanders of the River, and there remains room
for debate on this score, Will Hay's comedy piece is
clearly less than admiring in its handling of British
imperial administration. One film, Song of Freedom,
even vaguely hints at the existence of African nationalism. In this production John Zinga (Paul
Robeson) plays a British-born black London docker who
becomes a famous opera singer before he discovers he
is the rightful king of a West African tribe. After
difficulties he manages to claim his throne and then
comes to Europe annually for a short concert tour to
raise money for his tribe to enjoy the benefits of
European civilisation. Here the message is that
Africans may progress towards civilised ways better
under the rule of British-educated Africans than
through direct British colonial administration. This
idea is given added force in that Song of Freedom
appears to have been the first British film with a
cast dominated by blacks. Also Zinga has the welfare
of his tribe at heart rather than personal power, the

usual motive attributed to those who wish to be rid
of British rule in the Sir Alexander Korda-style pro-
imperialist epics.

Germany and Nazism

The early talkies contained a number of First
World War films like All Quiet on the Western Front
(Universal, 1930, dir Lewis Milestone) which took up
where Dawn had left off in either emphasising an
anti-war theme or stripping war of false heroics.
Most of the remaining First World War films were
adventure espionage stories in which the Germans were
invariably the bad guys. This trend included The W
Plan (BIP-Wardour, 1930, dir Victor Saville) and Mata
Hari (MGM, 1932, dir George Fitzmaurice). Moreover,
the success of the silent Wings (Paramount, 1927, dir
William Wellman) had given rise to further First
World War air dramas like Hell's Angels (Howard
Hughes, 1930, dir Howard Hughes) and The Dawn Patrol
(Warner, 1930, dir Howard Hawks).
Such near contemporary history brought relatively new problems to the BBFC, of which Dawn proved to
be only an extreme instance. Wings suffered the loss
of an entire scene on 12 January 1928. The Dawn
Patrol was viewed by an Air Ministry representative
on 8 August 1930, after which the BBFC passed it with
minor cuts. Hell's Angels was passed on 23 October
1930 only after one Air Ministry viewing and two
viewings by Shortt. In the process the footage was
reduced from 11,800 to 9,045, a cut of approximately
35 minutes running time and massive by the standards
of any period in British cinema history. By the then
BBFC criteria it is hard to understand how so much
material came to be eliminated, even allowing for Air
Ministry reluctance to let anything through that
might have infringed official secrets; for Jean
Harlow's readiness to change into something more
comfortable before attempting to seduce Ben Lyon;
and for the many crude German character stereotypes
along First World War propaganda lines. However,
even this badly mutilated version of Hell's Angels
did not prevent a German protest to the Foreign
Office over the release of the film in Britain towards the end of 1930. However, the straight anti-
war or espionage films on the whole presented no real
difficulties to the BBFC at this time. It is true
that All Quiet on the Western Front was cut by 201
feet, but this was because some of the battle scenes
were considered too horrific. The W Plan was passed
uncut on 26 June 1930, but by contrast Mata Hari lost

408 feet, although this might well have been due to
the sexy appearance and acting of Greta Garbo in the
name part.

Anti-Germanism did not feature prominently in
any of these films except Hell's Angels. Indeed All
Quiet on the Western Front dealt with German experiences and sufferings. However, in 1930 the BBFC
accepted Westfront 1918 (Germany, 1930, dir Georg
Pabst) even though it mounted a strong attack on
aggressive German militarism and nationalism. On the
other hand in April 1933, when Hitler had already
been appointed German Chancellor, the BBFC also
passed with Admiralty agreement the fiercely nation-
alistic, pre-Nazi First World War U-boat drama
Morgenrot (Germany, 1933, dir Gustav Ucicky). As a
result of the trend towards a Nazi dictatorship in
Germany during the first half of 1933, the previously
established English language First World War genres
assumed a more germanophobic character than earlier.
A good example is I Was a Spy (Gaumont, 1933, dir
Victor Saville), allowed at the BBFC on 24 September
1933 after only superficial cuts. This film concerns
a Belgian nurse, Marthe Cnockaert (Madeleine
Carroll), who spies on the Germans in a German-
occupied Belgian town after 1914. The story bears a
surface resemblance to the career of Edith Cavell, no
doubt intentionally, except that the Belgian nurse,
although unmasked by the Germans, survives the war.
However, the background of the film is heavily anti-
German. There are many shots of German troops march-
ing through the town which add nothing to the plot,
Conrad Veidt turns in a stiff-necked German military
commandant performance reminiscent of later similar
roles, while German soldiers sing 'Deutschland Ueber
Alles' at an open air church service. There is also
an implied reference to German barbarism in the use
of poison gas, the choking effects of which on British prisoners of war are shown several times as they
arrive at a Belgian hospital, although no hint
appears in the film that the allies had also used
poison gas. Much of Victor Saville's work during the
1930s carries messages of this sort, constantly in-
veighing against the dangers of militant German
nationalism arising from strident Nazism, although
in this case there was also a general anti-war theme
characterised by British bombs on the open air church
service.

However, it was the outbreak of open anti-
Semitism initiated by the Nazi government-organised
boycott of Jewish goods and business premises on 1
April 1933 which most attracted the film studios

towards German affairs until well into 1934. The
BBFC strongly discouraged the making of two films, A
German Tragedy and City without Jews, when Gaumont
British submitted scenarios in May and June 1933[30]
because these dealt with contemporary anti-Semitism
in Germany and Austria respectively and the BBFC
regarded them as overt anti-Nazi propaganda. But in
May 1933 no exception was taken or major cuts made to
Loyalties (Associated Talking Pictures, 1933, dir
Basil Dean). This practically forgotten movie, still
the only one ever to concentrate upon anti-Semitism
within Britain, is based on a John Galsworthy play
and centres upon a wealthy Jew, Ferdinand de Levis
(Basil Rathbone), who has £1,000 stolen when a guest
at an upper class house gathering. On circumstantial
evidence he comes to believe in the guilt of a fellow
guest, Captain Dancy (Miles Mander). The host
(Algernon West), who is made to look exactly like
Hitler, wishes to suppress the evidence pointing to
Dancy's guilt to avoid a scandal, and he uses his
influence on the committee of de Levis's club to have
the latter blackballed when he openly accuses Dancy
of the theft. The committee persuades Dancy to bring
a slander action against de Levis, but during the
court case evidence comes to light which proves
Dancy's guilt. The case against de Levis is with-
drawn, but when the police come to arrest Dancy, he
commits suicide and de Levis is blamed even though he
had previously urged Dancy to flee the country to
avoid prosecution. In the dialogue de Levis's Jewishness is brought out on several occasions. The
club committee, forced to side with either Dancy or
de Levis, gang up against the latter who at one point
in the committee discussion is called a 'damned Jew'.
During the court case Dancy's counsel accuses de
Levis of racial motives in accusing Dancy owing to
Dancy's anti-Semitism. To his wife Dancy in private
justifies his theft because de Levis is a Jew. Even
when de Levis's accusation turns out to be correct,
he rather than Dancy has to shoulder the blame for
the resulting tragedy. The sheer timing of Loyalties
was sufficient for it to be linked with the contemporary anti-Semitism then sweeping through Germany,
and by contrast the BBFC had had deleted every expl-
icit reference to Disraeli's Jewishness from Disraeli
(Warner, 1929, dir Alfred Green). But, as the Nazis
tightened their grip on German society and anti-
Semitic practices became more blatant in the latter
part of 1933 and throughout 1934, both American and
British producers turned to films on European anti-
Semitism within a historical context. The remake of

The Wandering Jew (Gaumont-Twickenham, 1933, dir Maurice Elvey) covers the iniquities against Jews of the 16th century Spanish Inquisition and was allowed by the BBFC virtually uncut in October 1933. During 1934 the BBFC also passed Jew Süss (Gaumont, 1934, dir Lothar Mendes) and The House of Rothschild (20th Century, 1934, dir Alfred Werker), both of which deal specifically with historical anti-Semitism in Germany - Jew Süss in early 18th century Württemberg and The House of Rothschild in late 18th and early 19th century Prussia. The former for the most part keeps general anti-Semitism in the background and emphasises its influence upon the career of Süss (Conrad Veidt) as an individual, although the BBFC did let through one line of dialogue which runs, '1730-1830-1930. They will always persecute us (the Jews)'.[31]
   The House of Rothschild on the other hand dwells much more upon the effects of government-sponsored anti-Semitism for the Jewish population of Prussia as a whole. Nathan Rothschild and his banker father, both played by George Arliss, are portrayed throughout the film as freedom fighters for Jewish rights. The opening sequence shows a sign stating that all the Jews of Frankfurt in Prussia in 1780 must be inside the ghetto, symbolically styled Jew Street, by 6 p.m. This is at once followed by shots of demoralised, downtrodden Jews in Jew Street against a background of slow, sad Jewish music. Later it is made clear that Jewish taxation is extortionate compared to taxes on Gentiles, while two tax collectors address the Rothschild sons as 'Jew boys'. In family conversation it is revealed that Jews 'are forbidden to learn a trade'. When Nathan has grown up to become Europe's leading banker, he is resident in London where he once points out that there is no Jew Street. Late in the film government-organised Prussian pogroms against Jewish property in Frankfurt are expressly shown, while Nathan once states that Jews are being killed all over Prussia just for being Jewish. The contemporary analogy with events in Germany was too blatant to be overlooked, yet the BBFC on 16 April 1934 passed The House of Rothschild with only one small dialogue cut despite the heavy-handedness of its theme. However, contemporary settings for Nazi racial policies continued to be discouraged, as the adverse BBFC comments on a scenario entitled The Mad Dog of Europe in November 1934 make plain.[32]
   If anti-Semitism occupied pride of place in implicit film attempts to warn against Nazism before 1935, the international dangers from a revived

Germany under Hitler's thumb were by no means neglected. In this respect the film companies preferred to tackle the BBFC by stealth rather than head-on clashes. For example, as early as November 1934, when German rearmament above the levels allowed in the Versailles treaty was rapidly proceeding, the thriller The Man Who Knew Too Much (Gaumont-British, 1934, dir Sir Alfred Hitchcock) included among a gang of foreign spies operating in London the actor Peter Lorre who, although himself Hungarian, had acquired fame for his work in German films of the early 1930s, particularly as the Düsseldorf child murderer in the internationally acclaimed M (Germany, 1931, dir Fritz Lang). Hitchcock continued with the implication that Germany was a threat to Britain in The 39 Steps (Gaumont-British, 1935) with the choice of Austrian-born Lucie Mannheim as the mysterious victim with the guttural central European accent who is stabbed to death in the flat of Richard Hannay (Robert Donat) early in the film. By the time The 39 Steps was made Hitler had openly announced his intention of rearming above the limits imposed at Versailles, and the anti-German hints are more pronounced than in The Man Who Knew Too Much. In Sabotage (Gaumont-British, 1936, dir Sir Alfred Hitchcock), too, Austrian actor Oskar Homolka stars as a dangerous foreign agent in London, and again the guttural central European accent is much in evidence. However, Hitchcock's next film, Secret Agent (Gaumont-British, 1936), was the most overt anti-German feature he had yet directed because, since Sabotage was made, Germany on 7 March 1936 had sent troops into the demilitarised Rhineland zone in defiance of the Versailles and Locarno treaties. Secret Agent is ostensibly a First World War spy story in which the Germans are explicitly named as Britain's foe, but most of the action takes place in neutral Switzerland. Only the 1916 date given at the opening of the film and some late war action sequences give any real indication of the First World War. In between the manoeuvrings between the British and German secret services might easily be taken as contemporary. It was no accident that Gaumont-British produced all of these films as well as Jew Süss and submitted anti-Nazi racial policy scenarios, and that the anti-Nazi left-winger Ivor Montagu was associated with all four Hitchcock films. The BBFC passed each of them, subtle tactics proving a better way of circumventing the BBFC than direct challenges.

The BBFC was much more stringent with current international issues. This probably explains why the

earliest anti-Nazi documentary, Whither Germany?, was
not submitted to the BBFC but to the LCC which passed
it in December 1933. This remarkably prophetic
French film examines and explains the rise of Hitler
to advance the view that sooner or later Nazi Germany
would cause a European war in order to regain the
lost German territory of 1919. However, when in June
1934 a small British distribution company submitted
the pro-Nazi and anti-Russian Flüchtlinge (Germany,
1934, dir Gustav Ucicky), the BBFC rejected it. The
same fate befell an anti-Nazi documentary called
Hitler's Reign of Terror in September 1934 (by which
time the Nazis were virtually secure in power) and
Free Thälmann in February 1935. This was a short
documentary pleading for the release of Ernst
Thälmann, the German Communist leader and a defeated
presidential candidate in 1932 who was now languishing in a concentration camp where he was to die in
1936. The makers of this film were none other than
Adrian Brunel and Ivor Montagu! According to the
latter's testimony more than 40 years later in Before
Hindsight (Elizabeth Taylor-Mead, 1977, dir Jonathan
Lewis), he personally saw a BBFC representative
(probably either Brooke Wilkinson or Hanna) in 1935
but could not persuade him to pass Free Thälmann.
This outcome was hardly surprising in the light of
the BBFC's known antipathy to screen current affairs.

At about the same time as Montagu was once
again failing to win over the BBFC, the censors had
to consider Abdul the Damned (British International,
1934, dir Karl Grune). On the surface the film is a
straightforward historical account of the events in
the Turkish empire which led to the 1908 Young Turk
revolution and the consequent deposition of Sultan
Abdul Hamid II (Fritz Kortner). However, it was
produced by Max Schach who, like the director, was an
Austrian refugee from Nazi tyranny while working in
Berlin in 1933. The Sultan's despotic character in
the film represents a thinly veiled analogy with
Hitler which did not escape The Times's reviewer of 3
March 1935. Abdul the Damned slowly turns into a
study of paranoia as a mental basis for a political
dictatorship. The new constitution of 1908 in Turkey
forbids torture, but a prisoner who has tried to
assassinate the Sultan is nevertheless tortured to
death only to be described later by the Sultan's
government as having been shot while trying to
escape. To arouse popular feeling against the new
Young Turk liberal government, the Sultan plots with
his police chief (Nils Asther) for the latter to
disguise himself as a Young Turk and then murder the

loyal Old Turk leader (Walter Rilla). This was a
close parallel to the role of Hitler and his SS
chief, Heinrich Himmler, in the destruction of the
Nazi storm troop force, the SA, and its leader, Ernst
Röhm, during the Night of the Long Knives in Germany
on 30 June 1934 when at least 300 people perished.
When the round up of the Young Turks takes place in
the film, many of them are murdered in cold blood but
are referred to subsequently in the dialogue as having died while trying to escape, the usual Nazi
euphemism for liquidation. Shortt viewed Abdul the
Damned in the presence of Foreign Office staff, and
as a result it was cut by 625 feet, almost seven
minutes running time. Whether this was to avoid
possible difficulties in Anglo-German or Anglo-
Turkish relations remains unclear, especially as the
present National Film Archive print is 127 feet less
than the original version.
     Abdul the Damned was the last major 'message'
film concerning Nazi Germany until Secret Agent, more
than a year later. Although Nazi anti-Semitism
assumed legal shape through the Nuremberg laws of
September 1935, by then the focal point of international attention had switched from Germany to Italy as
Mussolini was preparing his invasion of backward
Ethiopia. In consequence Italy had been embroiled in
an open diplomatic crisis with Britain and the League
of Nations since the previous May. The Italian
invasion of Ethiopia began early in October 1935 and
occupied much British public attention until the
Italian conquest was completed in May 1936 and the
League economic sanctions against Italy were dropped
two months later. Scarcely had this crisis disappeared from British newspaper headlines and cinema
newsreels than the Spanish Civil War broke out in
July 1936. By the end of the year the Germans and
the Italians had intervened in support of the Franco-
led military revolt, while the Soviets were arming
the legal Republican government. Italian aid to
Franco was on a far larger scale than German, which
until 1938 made Mussolini appear a greater menace to
European peace than Hitler.
     Curiously, there seems to have been no anti-
Italian material in English language feature films
before the Second World War, but an anti-German
screen atmosphere concealed once more in First World
War stories emerged again from the start of 1937 as
passions in Britain were gradually aroused by the
atrocities committed in Spain by both sides. This
germanophobic trend apparently opened with the spy
drama Dark Journey (London Films, 1936, dir Victor

Saville), which was passed uncut on 27 January 1937,
and it received more or less simultaneous reinforcement with occasional more contemporary anti-German
material in lighter offerings - for example, Storm
in a Teacup (Sir Alexander Korda, 1937, dir Victor
Saville). This comedy, a satire on British local
politics, deals with an authoritarian local Scottish
provost with parliamentary ambitions (Cecil Parker).
He becomes politically embarrassed when a journalist
working for a local paper (Rex Harrison) on his own
initiative publishes, against the newspaper owner's
express orders, the fact that the provost has fined
an old lady (Sara Allgood) for not licensing her dog,
and that he intends to have the dog destroyed even
though she is too poor to pay. At one point the
provost acknowledges, and is acknowledged by, his
supporters outside a hall where he is about to
address a political meeting with a clan greeting
which is indistinguishable from the Nazi salute.
Moreover, during a scene in which the provost
attempts to browbeat the journalist into a retraction
of his offending press article, the latter retorts
that Britain is not Berlin or Moscow. None the less
the BBFC passed Storm in a Teacup uncut on 23 March
1937.
    For the remainder of 1937 and well into 1938 the
war in Spain distracted the attention of American and
British film-makers from Nazi Germany. The only film
which even indirectly touched upon Nazi policies was
the French The Golem (1936, dir Julien Duvivier), a
sound remake of the famous silent German classic on
anti-Semitism. This was submitted to the BBFC in
February 1937 but suffered extensive cuts before
being given a certificate under the title of The
Legend of Prague. Following the Nazi annexation of
Austria in March-April 1938, which brought a sharp
increase in the number of Jews under German rule,
anti-Semitic policies were intensified in the Third
Reich and stepped up again after the cession to
Germany in October 1938 of the German-speaking
Sudeten region of Czechoslovakia. As a result a
severely reduced version of The Golem was submitted
to the BBFC on 28 October 1938, and this time it was
passed uncut. The anti-Jewish pogroms in Germany of
the Kristallnacht of 9-10 November 1938 produced an
upsurge in anti-Nazi scenarios focusing upon Jewish
persecutions during 1939, but the BBFC rejected every
one.[33] Furthermore, the well-known but now unavail-
able Soviet anti-Nazi film attacking Jewish persecution, Professor Mamlock (USSR, 1938, dirs Adolf Minkin
and Herbert Rappaport), was refused a certificate on

26 May 1939 after a club showing at the London Film
Society in the New Gallery cinema two months
previously. However, on 27 July 1939 this film and
I Was a Captive of Nazi Germany (1939, production
company and dir Unknown) were allowed by the LCC.
The latter film is the true story of the 1934 arrest
and imprisonment in Germany of young American journalist Isobel Steele. The film also explores Nazi
injustice in general and the persecution of the Jews
in particular, which probably accounts for the BBFC
ban in May 1939 at a time when other anti-German
content was proving acceptable.
    The wish of some film studios to incorporate the
deteriorating European international situation into
feature films, at least by implication, grew stronger
after the Czechoslovak crisis and the Munich agreement of September 1938 when Britain, France and Italy
agreed to the German annexation of the Sudetenland.
Pinebrook Ltd. in January 1939 presented to the BBFC
a scenario called The Chinese Fish, a political
thriller set in the Balkans in which the Prime
Minister of Macedonia was on his way home from Slav-
onia with a peace settlement to be ratified by his
Cabinet. The contemporary analogy with British Prime
Minister Neville Chamberlain after Munich did not
escape Mrs Crouzet who commented that 'there should
be no mention of such real and recent events as the
Munich Pact',[34] although she went on to approve the
basic theme. Five days before the German occupation
of Prague on 15 March 1939 the BBFC allowed with only
minor cuts the First World War story of German
espionage in Britain, The Spy in Black (Harefield and
Sir Alexander Korda, 1939, dir Michael Powell). However, its release was held over until late July 1939,
presumably to give it the maximum amount of implied
topicality as German pressure on Poland intensified
and an Anglo-German war consequently loomed. Despite
the delicate international situation when The Spy in
Black first appeared in London, the BBFC apparently
made no effort to rescind its earlier decision.
    This was consistent with other simultaneous
decisions, particularly that relating to the April
1939 submission of a scenario for Nurse Edith Cavell
(RKO-Imperator, 1939, dir Herbert Wilcox). This
arrived with a covering letter from Wilcox to explain
that a foreword to his projected remake of Dawn would
emphasise the conflict between war and humanity, and
that the film would be basically accurate in fact
throughout. Tyrrell had been Foreign Office Permanent Under-Secretary at the time of the Dawn events in
1928, which probably did as much as anything to

ensure that the BBFC raised no objection to any
possible anti-German content in Nurse Edith Cavell.[35]
Another scenario carrying an even more glaring contemporary theme was yet another spy drama, Maginot
Line, a French production eventually released in an
English language version in Britain during June 1939
under the title of Double Crime in the Maginot Line.
In this story a divorced Frenchwoman falls in love in
Germany with an apparently ordinary German who is in
reality the head of the German secret service. She
discovers his true occupation only later when he
comes to France under an assumed name to gather information regarding the Maginot Line of defence
fortresses and meets her again by accident. She
eventually denounces him to the French authorities
when he refuses to promise her that he will not pass
back to Germany the secret information he has
acquired about French defences. The moral that
patriotism was more important than private happiness,
and the French rather than British setting, were
sufficient for the BBFC to pass the scenario in spite
of its current and overt germanophobic approach.[36]
The film itself was let through uncut on 25 May 1939.
    However, far and away the most astonishing BBFC
decision at this time in the light of its past
anxiety to avoid all controversy over Nazi Germany
was that to pass Confessions of a Nazi Spy (Warner,
1939, dir Anatole Litvak) with only one minor
dialogue cut. This spy drama, based upon a real case
in the United States of 1937-8, is centred on the
espionage activities of the German-American Bund as
directed from Germany herself, leading to their
collapse as brought about by persistent FBI investigator Ed Renard (Edward G. Robinson). The thriller
format scarcely conceals a very strong attack indeed
on the very nature of Nazism and its expansionist
aims. In the opening sequences a German Bund member
(Ward Bond, uncredited) who questions Nazi doctrines
and their compatibility with the American constitution at a meeting addressed by Bund leader Dr Kassell
(Paul Lukas) is beaten up by Nazi thugs. Later Dr
Kassell is shown delivering two fiery pieces of orat-
ory from Bund meeting platforms, a clear analogy with
Hitler. In the first of these a notice is displayed
stating, 'Morgen, die ganze Welt' (Tomorrow, the
whole world), which unambiguously implies that the
objective of Nazi foreign policy is world domination.
The actions of the Bund spies are linked with high-
level German policy when Kassell is called to Berlin
to recieve his instructions from Dr Josef Göbbels in
person. Göbbels is not mentioned by name, but the

actor concerned (Martin Kosleck, uncredited, a role
he was to repeat twice) bears a close physical resemblance to him and walks with a limp. This, incidentally, infringed the BBFC rule against the portrayal of contemporary political personalities. Moreover, information about an unmasked German spy in
Britain is passed on to the Americans by British
military intelligence, and the BBFC normally forbade
any overt mention of current British intelligence
activities. The spy narrative is also expressly
linked with the German annexation of Austria, the
subsequent German bullying of Czechoslovakia and the
Munich agreement. The film violated so many BBFC
rules that it was not surprising some time was taken
to arrive at a decision. It was submitted on 1 May
1939, when German pressure on both Britain and Poland
was being stepped up, but passed only on 6 June after
Tyrrell himself had viewed it. In the light of his
previous caution and the direct political character
of Confessions of a Nazi Spy at a time when the BBFC
was still opposing film attacks on Nazi anti-
Semitism, it is likely that Tyrell's go ahead had
received unofficial Foreign Office approval.
Certainly the decision represented a far cry from
that of 1938 to ban the March of Time documentary
Inside Nazi Germany, although the BBFC might have
allowed Confessions because it was based on fact
whereas Professor Mamlock, for example, was a work of
fiction. Not without justice did Graham Greene's
review in the Spectator of 23 June 1939 hail
Confessions of a Nazi Spy as the BBFC's abandonment
of appeasement towards Hitler! Finally, as German
pressure on Poland built up to a crescendo during the
summer of 1939 the French Le Monde en Action company
on 4 August submitted a scenario for an existing
French documentary on Danzig. This was the German
port which in 1919 had been placed under the theoretical supervision of the League of Nations but real
Polish control, and the ostensible German grievance
against the Poles in 1939 Nazi propaganda. Although
Hanna noted on the scenario that the Le Monde en
Action commentary put forward the Polish point of
view, he nevertheless did not object.37 Somewhat
belatedly but earlier than the British government,
the BBFC had in effect declared war upon Nazi
Germany.

Armaments and International Affairs

The Wall Street crash of October 1929 heralded
ten years of economic distress and international

instability, the worst manifestation of which was the rise of right-wing extremism in Germany. Prior to the appointment of Hitler as German Chancellor on 30 January 1933, international co-operation and disarmament as well as general anti-war sentiments had been uncontroversial British politics. Hence films on these topics had not aroused any special BBFC anxiety. For example, Kameradschaft (France-Germany, 1930, dir Georg Pabst), a plea for continued international collaboration through a coal mining disaster along the Franco-German frontier which brings both communities together in a sense of common tragedy, was passed in February 1931. Tell England (1931, dir Anthony Asquith), which does for the 1915 Gallipoli operation what All Quiet on the Western Front does for trench warfare, was passed uncut with an 'A' certificate in the same month, although later in 1931 the BBFC demanded minor cuts before agreeing to a 'U' certificate. As the world disarmament conference assembled in Geneva in February 1932 possibly the finest anti-war film of the inter-war era, the now comparatively unknown Niemandsland (No Man's Land, Germany, 1931, dir Victor Trivas), was submitted to the BBFC under the topical title of Disarmament. It was allowed uncut, although the BBFC changed the title to War is Hell.

By the end of 1932 the world disarmament conference had virtually collapsed due to Germany's withdrawal, and the Nazi seizure of power followed immediately afterwards. During 1933 Germany pulled out of the League, as did Japan when she refused to accept an adverse League judgement on her 1931-2 conquest of Manchuria. The post-1919 world order was in jeopardy, and against such an international background the subject of armaments became more controversial in British party politics. By 1934 MacDonald's Conservative-dominated National government was slowly edging its way towards a policy of unobtrusive rearmament against Germany, while Labour continued to advocate international disarmament and collective security against aggressors through the League. Little of this found its way onto the screen directly, but now and again general references to the evils of war appeared. For instance, in The Iron Duke, which covers episodes during the life of the Duke of Wellington (George Arliss) in 1815-16, when Wellington is congratulated by Prussia's Marshal Blücher on Britain's 'great victory', he answers that 'except for defeat, there is nothing more tragic than a great victory'. The BBFC allowed this dialogue on 28 November 1934 even though the government was then

under attack for its rearmament policy and the National Declaration Committee led by Viscount Cecil of
Chelwood was about to launch its anti-government
Peace Ballot. This was a private national referendum
of five questions regarding armaments, collective
security and British foreign policy which the Cabinet
had done its utmost to discredit before it began in
December 1934.

By the time the ballot was completed in June
1935 with some eleven million voters international
attention had become focused on the Ethiopian crisis.
In the following November the National government,
now headed by Stanley Baldwin, took the opportunity
to parade its support for the League against Italy
and hold a snap election with rearmament as a none
too prominent part of its programme. The government
romped home, but Labour more than trebled its Commons
representation, which gave it a firmer basis to
resist rearmament and drag it into the forefront of
British party strife. As Britain and the League
proved ineffective against Italian aggression in
Ethiopia during the early months of 1936, peace
politics in contemporary form at last found their way
onto film. The most striking example was Things to
Come (London Films, 1936, dir William Cameron
Menzies). Written by H.G. Wells and based upon his
own 1933 novel, this futuristic fantasy centres on
war in 1940, the ensuing devastation and survival
struggles of mankind. The dramatic opening scenes,
backed by superlative music from Sir Arthur Bliss,
are so realistic that they can easily be mistaken for
genuine Second World War footage. They also raise
the spectre of a law and order breakdown and of mass
panic, but nevertheless the BBFC allowed the whole
film on 20 February 1936. However, when in March
1936 a group of left-wing film-makers made a three-
minute propaganda short, The Peace of Britain, which
urged ordinary citizens to demand peace through
collective security as the Peace Ballot was approach-
ing its climax and the Italian army was deep into
Ethiopia, there were rumours that the BBFC had banned
the film. During a House of Lords debate on 8 April,
Lord Strabolgi criticised the BBFC for its 'obstruction' of the film and for allowing the War Office to
view it before a decision was taken. On the same day
MPs were given a private showing at Bush House, after
which George Lansbury, Labour leader from 1931 to
1935 and a prominent pacifist, expressed the view to
the press that it could not be banned when All Quiet
on the Western Front had been passed. However, the
rumours of a ban were without foundation, since the

BBFC records show that The Peace of Britain had
already been allowed uncut on the previous day after
a viewing by Tyrrell and a War Office member. When
Tyrrell addressed the CEA conference on 24 June 1936,
he defended the BBFC for its handling of The Peace of
Britain but simultaneously made it clear that he was
opposed to the introduction of films dealing with
contemporary political issues. However, this view
did not go unchallenged, The Times editorial of the
following day criticising Tyrrell and the BBFC for
over-caution.
    As Italy absorbed Ethiopia and the civil war
raged in Spain, the spirit of pacifism and opposition
to rearmament faded by degrees, but it nevertheless
remained alive to judge from certain anti-war feature
films of 1936-8. The Road to Glory (TCF, 1936, dir
Howard Hawks), the adventures of a French regiment
during the First World War, is a minor masterpiece
which deserves to be rescued from relative obscurity.
The Road Back (Universal, 1937, dir James Whale) was
an intended sequel to All Quiet on the Western Front
and was made in the same anti-war mood. The peace
movement in Britain no doubt also derived comfort
from the French anti-war productions La Grande
Illusion (1937, dir Jean Renoir) and I Accuse (1937),
Abel Gance's remake of his own 1918 masterpiece. The
BBFC passed all these films between August 1936 and
April 1938, although all suffered minor cuts and I
Accuse was even awarded a 'H' certificate.
    The Ethiopian crisis gave rise to two document-
aries which were implicitly pro-Ethiopian. The
first, Abyssinia, was submitted to the BBFC by
Wardour Films on 28 June 1935 before the Italian
invasion had been launched. This full-length film
was first modified at BBFC insistence and then cut
from 7,500 to 6,739 feet, but the most significant
thing was that the BBFC did not reject it outright
when Britain was exerting strong diplomatic pressure
on Mussolini to forego his planned conquest of
Ethiopia. On 7 October 1935, four days after the
Italian army had begun its advance, the BBFC passed
uncut the 40-minute International Productions film
The Real Abyssinia, but this decision was less politically risky because by then British government
policy, backed by Labour in principle, was anti-
Italian. The Ethiopian war proved to be too short to
register in the minds of film producers as a topic to
be brought out in features, however obliquely, whereas the Japanese penetration of China had been in
progress since September 1931 and was to continue unabated right up to the outbreak of the European war

THE TALKIES: SOME FILMS, GENRES AND THEMES, 1929-1939

in September 1939. The Spanish Civil War, too,
dragged on for almost three years, from July 1936 to
April 1939, and as a result these subjects eventually
confronted the BBFC.
    On the whole little film attention was paid to
Japanese actions and expansion before the Sino-
Japanese outbreak of mid-1937, but there was one
remarkable exception. This was East meets West
(Gaumont-British, 1936, dir Herbert Mason), which
first arrived at the BBFC in scenario form during
December 1935 as La Dame de Malacca. Its story is of
Audrey Greenwood, a lonely Irish girl who marries
Major Carter just before he takes up a posting in a
province of British-ruled Malaya. Upon arrival, she
finds her husband repugnant and is attracted to the
young Sultan of another Malayan province whom she has
met on the boat to Malaya. The Sultan wishes to
marry Audrey and blackmails the British governor of
the province to which Carter has been posted into
putting pressure on Carter to have his marriage
annulled. The Sultan's blackmail card is the threat
of a treaty with Japan to British detriment. Carter
agrees to the annulment and is accordingly promoted,
while the Sultan marries Audrey with the British
governor in attendance. The idea of fulfilled happy
miscegenation as well as mention of Japan as a
potential enemy of Britain met with unfavourable
BBFC comment38 and the project was evidently dropped.
However, early in February 1936 Gaumont-British submitted a scenario for The Scarlet Sultan which bore a
marked resemblance to the basic plot of La Dame de
Malacca. But this time the Japanese element is
introduced more directly in the shape of a Japanese
diplomat, Dr Shoshai. Furthermore, Carter is caught
in gin-smuggling by the Sultan's men, and now it is
the Sultan's Oxford-educated son with whom Carter's
wife has fallen in love. The Sultan uses these
events as pressure on the British governor to obtain
British subsidies, to gain a treaty with Britain and
to spare Carter from his death sentence. Meanwhile
Shoshai has incited the Sultan's son to arouse popular agitation for Carter's death, leaving the
Sultan's son free to marry Carter's wife. The Malay
province's relations with Britain would be shattered
beyond repair and the way would thus be open for a
treaty with Japan, but the Sultan foils this scheme,
Carter is reconciled with his wife and the province
concludes a treaty with Britain. These scenario
adjustments omitted the fulfilled miscegenation but
on the other hand emphasised Japanese involvement
more strongly than hitherto. It was therefore

scarcely surprising that the BBFC scenario scrutin-
eers still favoured rejection,39 but on 2 March 1936
Brooke Wilkinson spoke with the film's producer,
George Arliss, for whom the film was intended to be a
star vehicle. As a result Arliss promised that there
would be no references to Japan or Malaya, on which
basis Brooke Wilkinson and Hanna agreed that the
production could go ahead as originally written.
However, Arliss had the last word. Japan was not
named in the completed film itself, East meets West,
but the envoy possesses clear oriental features and
has his name changed to Dr Shagu. He is responsible
to the emperor of a great naval power, is described
at one point in the dialogue as a 'collector of china
(China?)' and is expected to commit suicide if he
fails to persuade the Sultan to sign a treaty with
his country rather than Britain. Finally, his henchman is named Takasato, which could hardly be ident-
ified with any Far Eastern nation but Japan. Carter
incidentally becomes an embassy official rather than
a serving British officer, which also cut across BBFC
rules. Despite Arliss's provocation, the BBFC
allowed East meets West uncut on 12 August 1936.
    By that time the Spanish Civil War had erupted.
The uncensored newsreels largely dwelt upon the evils
of war, as they had done during the Ethiopian crisis,
and adopted a neutral attitude as between Franco and
the Spanish Republican government. The same was true
of topical documentaries, the first of which was a
nine-minute offering from Exclusive Films entitled
Southern Spain, allowed uncut in September 1936. The
nine-minute Spain of Yesterday, submitted by Coronet
Pictures in April 1937, was also let through
unscathed. The first Hollywood feature to have the
Spanish conflict as background was The Last Train
from Madrid (Paramount, 1937, dir James Hogan), but
the political content was rendered so sparse and
innocuous that the BBFC passed it uncut on 17 June
1937. A film of quite a different kind was Spanish
Earth (Spain, 1937, dir Joris Ivens), a left-wing,
highly anti-Franco documentary and the first film
dealing with the Spanish Civil War to have been
filmed in Spain. Its commitment to the Spanish Republican cause was so strong at a time when the
National government was preaching non-intervention
and endeavouring to bring about a German, Italian and
Soviet withdrawal from Spain that it could not fail
to be embarrassing to the BBFC when submitted in
October 1937. The film was badly cut to approximately half of its 53 minutes running time, but it was
astounding that the BBFC awarded it a certificate at

all in the light of the clear Spanish Republican
leanings in Ernest Hemingway's commentary. However,
the decision might well have been influenced by the
fact that the Academy Cinema in Oxford Street had
made the submission, and that therefore the film was
unlikely to receive a general release, which indeed
it did not. A pro-Republican body called the National Conference on Spain produced three films during
1937-8. Nowadays the best known is Spanish ABC
(1937, dirs Sidney Cole and Thorold Dickinson), which
covers the efforts of the Spanish Republican government to maintain education in Spain during the civil
war and which the BBFC passed with only a minor dialogue cut in May 1938. However, at the time the BBFC
was more perturbed by Behind the Spanish Lines and
Non-Intervention. The first was eventually allowed
uncut on 2 June 1938, but only after Tyrrell himself
had viewed it, while the latter underwent a three-
month BBFC scrutiny before it was passed in July 1938
with an amended commentary and cuts which reduced the
footage from 1,412 to 879. Tyrrell's contacts within
the Foreign Office and consequent BBFC concern at the
manner in which the Spanish conflict was presented on
the screen probably explains why the political substance of the Spanish Civil War action drama Blockade
(Walter Wanger, 1938, dir William Dieterle) is diluted, mainly through pre-production censorship in
the United States, to the point where it is
impossible to know which side the hero is on! Under
such circumstances it was no surprise that the BBFC
allowed it uncut on 31 May 1938.
     The closing stages of the Spanish Civil War
gradually gave way in British public concern to the
German territorial expansion into Austria and
Czechoslovakia and to Japanese barbarism in China.
The rape of Nanking in December 1937, when for
several days on end Japanese troops murdered, plund-
ered and raped without restraint, proved to be the
prelude to much Japanese cruelty towards the Chinese
population, including the terror bombing of helpless
civilians. Western opinion in general was horrified,
and while none of this adverse reaction or pro-
Chinese sympathy found its way into feature films
directly, it did so in the occasional left-wing
produced short documentary like China Strikes Back
and Chinese War Songs. These were both filmed by
the Progressive Film Institute in 1938 and passed by
the BBFC, the former with a 73 feet cut during February 1938. However, it was certainly no accident
that the character of the genial, judo expert
Japanese detective Mr Moto (Peter Lorre), who had

first appeared on the screen just prior to the outbreak of the Sino-Japanese 'incident', vanished late
in 1938 when the series was brought to an abrupt
close after eight films whereas his Chinese B-feature
equivalent, Charlie Chan, continued to flourish.

Recent attention has been drawn to the deep BBFC
and Foreign Office involvement in attempts from
October 1937 to June 1939 either to suppress or to
alter several projected screen biographies of T.E.
Lawrence (Lawrence of Arabia).[40] The reason was fear
of offending Turkey at a time when Britain's
Mediterranean position was under threat from Italian
intervention in Spain and from an Arab revolt in
Palestine. But in July 1935, before either of these
threats had developed and only weeks after Lawrence's
death in a motor cycle accident in May, the BBFC
allowed in full a 36-minute Ace Films documentary
called Lawrence of Arabia without arousing Foreign
Office displeasure. When in the same month a feature
film on Lawrence was first mooted by Sir Alexander
Korda, the Foreign Office raised no objection in
principle. Then it was more worried about the exposure of First World War British broken promises for
independence to the Arab revolutionary leaders
against their Turkish overlords than about Turkish
susceptibilities.[41] It was the changing European
situation from October 1935 onwards which by 1937
brought about a change in the Foreign Office's
earlier readiness to accept a film on Lawrence and
his leadership of the desert revolt.

Chapter 5

THE SECOND WORLD WAR

The First World War had brought about an acute awareness among the British ruling classes that the masses
would play an important part in either the survival
or the destruction of the state during a war.[1]
Communist Russia stood as a monument as to what might
happen in the future to any state and its ruling
class when the people as a whole were pushed beyond
endurance by the strains of an unsuccessful modern
total war. This consideration had gained added force
through the slow emergence of the mass society in
Britain since 1918 and then the official expectation
during the 1930s that in the next war British cities
would immediately be heavily bombed. Within this
context the government had recognised the importance,
possibly the crucial role, of the cinema as a method
of influencing mass public opinion and sustaining
civilian morale in the face of the anticipated ensuing devastation from the air. Government preparations for the establishment of a Ministry of Information (MoI) had begun as early as October 1935 when
Italy had invaded Ethiopia and an Anglo-Italian war
had seemed possible. From the outset the proposed
functions of the MoI had included extensive media
censorship, but the specific topic of film censorship
had first been raised only on 3 January 1936 at a
planning sub-committee meeting by the Permanent
Under-Secretary at the Treasury, Sir Warren Fisher.
Then it had been agreed with Sir Russell Scott,
Fisher's counterpart at the Home Office, that the
latter department would look into the matter.[2] The
outcome had been a report a month later from a Home
Office permanent adviser, C.P.C. Robinson, which
deserves a lengthy summary because it was to become
the foundation stone of film censorship in Britain
throughout the Second World War.
    Robinson's report opened with a survey of film

THE SECOND WORLD WAR

censorship as this had developed since the 1909
Cinematograph Act. In origin the act had been
passed for safety reasons arising from the danger of
fire through the use of inflammable film, but since
1909 safer film had been introduced and therefore
current official control over film performances was
both precarious in law and incomplete by convention.
Robinson went on to recommend total government
control in wartime, to which end the government would
need a veto over any local authority decision to
allow a film considered undesirable on defence or
national security grounds. However, the responsibility for what Robinson termed 'moral' censorship
should remain with the BBFC. If any local authority
banned a film that the government wished to be widely
shown to promote the war effort, then it would not be
necessary for the government to possess the power to
reverse this decision. The publicity caused by such
a ban would equally well serve the government's
purpose, while those affected by the ban who wished
to see the film in question could travel to an
adjoining local authority area. Finally, Robinson
pointed out that Defence Regulations on film censorship had already been drafted. It would be an
offence to obtain, to attempt to obtain, to record or
to publish any information or material which might or
would be useful to an enemy, either directly or indirectly. The projected MoI would have the power to
suppress anything prejudicial to the conduct of the
war, including photographs and films, after submission to the MoI before publication or exhibition. In
this respect the Defence Regulations would provide
for the suppression of any film that had not received
MoI approval except those films the BBFC had already
passed and those shown in private houses to which the
general public was not admitted. In this way the
existing peacetime film censorship would be extended
to newsreels and other film not at present subject to
censorship.3
     When the planning sub-committee of the Committee
of Imperial Defence had discussed Robinson's memorandum only two days after he had written it, the sub-
committee had decided that film censorship lay outside its terms of reference. The subject was then
passed on to another sub-committee, the Standing
Committee on Censorship, which by the end of July
1936 was seeking in principle the co-operation of the
film production companies for a wartime censorship
system. At about the same time, as part of the
overall plan for the MoI, the Standing Committee had
recommended to the Committee of Imperial Defence that

the MoI should assume film censorship powers immediately upon an outbreak of war. The objectives would
be the suppression of propaganda films 'inimical to
the conduct of the war', of films showing movements
of service personnel and equipment, and of exported
films which might leak information to the enemy.
    The report of the Standing Committee had then
concerned itself with concrete details. It had
pointed out that the BBFC peacetime civilian censorship system was voluntary for the exhibitor and did
not cover all films intended for public showing and
export. The function of the peacetime system was
social, the Standing Committee deeming it undesirable
that the MoI should accept responsibility for both
social and security censorship in wartime. Thus the
existing system should be utilised as the agency for
wartime censorship as far as possible, but where the
BBFC was not equipped to perform this task, it should
have officials attached to it who would carry out
security censorship. A panel of representatives from
the three armed services should form a part of the
MoI, safeguard service interests in all film censorship matters, act as liaison officers between the
services, the BBFC and the MoI, and co-operate with
the film industry in the approval of scenarios and
film propaganda generally. In this way the BBFC
would retain its civilian character, independent
status and responsibility for social censorship. It
would also continue to issue its peacetime exhibition
certificate as shown on the screen at the beginning
of feature films, but the MoI should give some open
additional indication of suitability for wartime
public showing through the panel of service officers
attached to the BBFC. The existing peacetime system
did not cover newsreels, advertising films and
feature films intended for only private showing:
these were legal loopholes which the Standing
Committee wished to shut through a Defence Regulation
expanding the system to cover all film prior to
exhibition, whether for private or public showing.
The Standing Committee regarded it as impracticable
to recensor films already approved and shown in
public cinemas, so that the legal responsibility for
preventing the performance of suspect films in this
category once war broke out would have to rest with
both the exhibitor and the distributor who could
refer to the BBFC in doubtful cases. In the last
resort the MoI should have the power to ban all such
films outright. The last Standing Committee recommendation had been that all films for export would
have to be submitted to the BBFC, while a MoI

approval certificate would be necessary before the customs authorities accepted any film for export.[4]
　These far-reaching proposals, which had added substantial meat to the bones provided by Robinson's memorandum, had received Committee of Imperial Defence approval on a planning basis several months later.[5] It had taken approximately a year to finalise them in substance from an outline original. Those twelve months had witnessed the Italian invasion and eventual conquest of Ethiopia, the German military occupation of the demilitarised Rhineland and the outbreak of the Spanish Civil War. However, the Standing Committee's proposals had not been followed up with even preliminary implementation steps until 1938. The delay and relatively slight attention to film in overall planning for the MoI might have been due to the government's intention to close British cinemas indefinitely at an outbreak of war because, in urban areas at any rate, they were considered potential death traps in the event of sustained heavy bombing.[6] But it is equally plausible that once it had become clear that the Spanish conflict would not involve Britain in direct confrontation with Germany or Italy, the consequent danger of imminent war had receded and the urgency displayed from October 1935 to October 1936 over wartime film censorship had simply evaporated. None the less the appointed MoI Director-General designate from late 1936, Sir Stephen Tallents, had remained well aware of the likely importance of cinema in wartime. In his progress report of February 1938 for the Committee of Imperial Defence he drew attention to the need for government consultation with the film industry before a war broke out.[7] At this point he had sought authority for MoI officials to make the necessary overtures,[8] but he did not receive even a recommendation to this effect from the planning subcommittee until after German troops had occupied Austria in March 1938.[9] This recommendation to the Committee of Imperial Defence had also shown no great sense of urgency, for it had been made conditional upon advance dealings with the BBFC, although Tallents had been allowed discretion over the timing of any approaches. However, he had made no move in the direction of the BBFC until the Committee of Imperial Defence had at last ratified its sub-committee's recommendation on 12 May 1938.[10] Even then it was only as the Czechoslovak crisis was gathering momentum early in July 1938 that Tallents and Rear-Admiral H.E. Dannreuther DSO, the MoI chief censor designate, had conferred with Brooke

Wilkinson. It is difficult to know just how fully
Tallents and Dannreuther explained to Brooke
Wilkinson what was being planned, for the records of
their two meetings are very sparse and in theory all
planning for the MoI had yet to receive firm government approval. But it is clear Brooke Wilkinson was
informed that the BBFC peacetime system would be
extended to include newsreels, and that in principle
he accepted this arrangement without protest, presumably on account of his First World War censorship
experiences. It was not until 16 September 1938,
when an Anglo-German war over Czechoslovakia had
seemed more a probability than a possibility, that
MoI officials appear to have given Brooke Wilkinson
fuller details when he met them at the Home Office.
    At this meeting the government representatives
had specifically stated that Defence Regulations
would provide for the censorship of all films, and
they had proposed that the wartime censors should be
accountable to the MoI rather than to the film
industry. Brooke Wilkinson had demurred and held out
for a repetition of the First World War system in
which the BBFC censors had acted for the Admiralty
and the War Office and referred to them when in
doubt. However, the government officials had been
insistent on this point and on the attachment to the
BBFC of advisers representing the three services.
Consequently Brooke Wilkinson had felt obliged to
give ground, but he had obtained a concession in that
the service advisers at the BBFC were to be either
civil servants or service officers rather than members of the film industry. It was further agreed that
there would be no consultation with either the industry or local authorities before the announcement of
the Defence Regulation bringing the MoI into official
existence. The Home Office would inform the local
authorities of exhibitors' responsibilities under the
new censorship requirements, while the BBFC would do
the same for the film industry including the newsreel
companies. If film producers inserted censorable
material into film after it had been censored and
passed, prosecution under the Defence Regulations
would follow. To prevent such insertions, the BBFC
would seal films for export after approval. These
agreements were later submitted to Tallents and
Tyrrell for final approval, with any detailed matters
subsequently arising to be settled between Brooke
Wilkinson and the designated MoI staff.[11]
    Up to this stage the draft Defence Regulations
had presupposed compulsory film censorship, but once
the Munich agreement had been signed two weeks later

and the immediate danger of war had once again
receded, doubts on this score had soon arisen.
According to Tallents's report of November 1938 for
the Committee of Imperial Defence, he had already
experienced qualms about compulsory film censorship
while the MoI contacts with Brooke Wilkinson had been
in progress. In drawing attention to an anomaly
whereby there would be voluntary censorship for press
photographs but compulsory censorship for films,
Tallents had also pointed out that the draft Defence
Regulations had envisaged permits for cameras in
public places during a war, and that presumably
cinema apparatus would fall into the category of a
camera.[12] In the light of such considerations and
possible pre-war consultation with the film industry
if censorship was to apply to films already shown to
the public, he had deferred a decision over compulsory or voluntary film censorship. Accordingly a MoI
censorship sub-committee on 14 December 1938 had
discussed whether or not film censorship should be
mandatory when voluntary censorship was intended for
the press along First World War lines.[13] A subsequent meeting of representatives from the MoI, the
Home Office and the War Office a week later came down
in favour of a voluntary system (unless local authorities allowed films which had been refused a security
clearance) and of direct discussions with the film
industry over possible pre-script 'advice'. However,
when a member of the Home Office staff present at the
meeting of 21 December 1938 had informed Brooke
Wilkinson early in January 1939 of the decisions
reached, the latter took strong exception to prior
censorship discussions with the film industry rather
than with the BBFC. He argued that his long experience as BBFC Secretary since 1913 had led him to the
conclusion that the industry would accept accomp-
lished facts after a war had broken out, whereas if
it was consulted beforehand, it would raise many
difficulties. Brooke Wilkinson declined to recognise
the validity of Home Office analogies with the
position of the press, for he maintained that the
British press held a stronger sense of public responsibility than the film industry because the latter
was largely in the hands of American film
companies.[14] No doubt his marked hostility to prior
censorship consultation with the film production
companies was influenced by their growing unwillingness at this time to accept BBFC policies in the
aftermath of the Pygmalion affair in February 1938
(pp.70-1) against the background of the increasingly
unstable European political situation. This new-

found opposition had been evidenced in the dwindling
number of scenarios submitted to the BBFC - 95 in
1938 compared to over 160 in 1936, over 130 in 1937
and well over 100 in every other year since 1932.

Brooke Wilkinson's view had prevailed with
Tyrrell and within the government. As the Polish
crisis had gained in force during the summer of 1939
the BBFC had finalised the censorship arrangements
with the MoI officials designate along the lines of
the various discussions which had taken place since
July 1938. When Britain declared war on Germany in
September 1939, these agreements were at once put
into effect via the Defence Regulations, although as
all cinemas were closed down until mid-September
only the export provisions were immediately applicable. Even so problems soon emerged. The MoI
included a Censorship Division under Admiral C.V.
Usborne and a Films Division under Sir Joseph Ball.
When a German submarine torpedoed the British liner
Athenia on 3 September, the very day that Britain
declared war on Germany, Ball specially asked the
newsreel companies to take shots of the survivors
landing in Britain for speedy showing in the United
States. This was evidently to try to evoke memories
there of the First World War when the sinking in 1915
of the Lusitania had resulted in a large number of
American deaths. The newsreel companies complied
with Ball's request and arranged for the resulting
footage to be sent to the United States by the air
clipper leaving Britain on the afternoon of 5 September, only to find that the MoI censorship procedures would cause a delay. In the event the footage
missed the clipper for other reasons, but the representations of the newsreel companies made to Ball
on the morning of 5 September prompted him to raise
the matter with Usborne. Ball emphasised that the
transport of footage from the newsreel studios at
Acton, Denham, Dorking, Elstree and Shepherd's Bush
to either the BBFC offices or to the special censorship facilities then being set up at Langley Park,
near Slough in Berkshire, and possibly back again to
the studios for modification and final submission
would consume much time to little effect. He therefore proposed that the five British newsreel companies be given some general indication of what material
should not be filmed and then left to use their own
discretion, but Ball's arguments left little impression on Usborne. Although it is not clear from the
MoI files how this disagreement was resolved, it
seems probable that Ball had his way when the government allowed the cinemas to reopen. The newsreel

companies expressed their satisfaction at new
arrangements during a meeting at the MoI in mid-
September, as noted in handwriting at the foot of
Ball's typed memorandum on the <u>Athenia</u> episode.[15]
Almost simultaneously another problem arose, for
Brooke Wilkinson in person had rejected a GPO Film
Unit production made on behalf of the Home Office
because it contained shots of anti-aircraft guns and
barrage balloons. This delicate situation was
corrected by the diplomatic intervention of Admiral
G. Thomson, Dannreuther's assistant acting for
Usborne, as a result of which the BBFC received the
latter's express sanction to relax the Defence
Regulations at its own discretion.[16]

   In September 1939 the BBFC censors were Hanna,
Major R.H.W. Baker, Lieutenant-Colonel A. Fleetwood-
Wilson, and Miss Madge Kitchener, the niece of Lord
Kitchener. Mrs Crouzet appears to have been concerned solely with scenarios. After war broke out they
were joined by Major-General Bruce Hay, both the MoI
and the War Office having approved his appointment in
advance. A certain Lieutenant Kite acted as MoI
censor for the services, viewing all the newsreels
and some feature films where these touched upon service matters, whereas the BBFC censors remained
primarily concerned with feature films. The new
system initially irritated the local authorities, who
had been represented on the pre-war Film Censorship
Consultative Committee and the Cinema Advisory
Council, for they now found themselves excluded from
the censorship structure. During October 1939 both
Kent County Council and the LCC made efforts to
remedy this situation, but Tyrrell, Usborne and
Brooke Wilkinson on 27 October agreed that local
authority participation in the revised censorship
machinery was undesirable. Accordingly the Kent and
London demands were rejected, and the local authorities were reduced to a less important censorship
position for the entire war. Ball was soon to
discover that the BBFC had added to its peacetime
approval certificate shown on the screen at the beginning of features the words 'and complies with the
requirements of the Ministry of Information'. He
complained to Usborne on the ground that MoI censorship was better conducted in secret, the offending
phrase being dropped from the certificate in October
1939.

   The war brought about a steep increase in work
for the BBFC censors. During September 1939 alone
they examined and sealed 1,236 items for export to
neutral countries and the empire.[17] Moreover,

administrative censorship problems persisted within
the government. In practice Kite was the War Office
censor while the Admiralty and the Air Ministry each
delegated censorship duties to one of its own serving
officers, with results that were not always satisfactory at the MoI. Sir John Reith, the former head of
the British Broadcasting Corporation, succeeded Lord
Macmillan as Minister of Information in January 1940.
Reith at once set about reorganising the MoI, one
outcome being the absorption of Usborne's Film Censorship division into the Press and Censorship Bureau
under Walter Monckton. In March he was called upon
to deal with an incident whereby the photographic
section of the bureau banned from the press a still
photograph of a German aircraft which had crashed in
Berwick while two newsreel companies had had film of
the same crashed German bomber passed for showing by,
presumably, the Air Ministry censor. To avoid future
occurrences of this sort, Monckton sought the second-
ment to his bureau of all the service censors, so
that security film censorship and that for still
photographs could be co-ordinated. However, neither
the Admiralty nor the Air Ministry was responsive.
Indeed the Admiralty went to some pains to point out
to Monckton that its censor from its Press Division
spent only a small part of his time on censorship.
His main duties were to advise on, assist in and
arrange facilities for the filming of newsreel naval
material and any other naval film.[18] Nevertheless
Monckton's pressure was not without effect, for the
Admiralty agreed that as a matter of routine its
film censor would report to the photographic section
of the MoI Press and Censorship Bureau any footage
censored out of a particular film as well as a list
of items passed and banned in entirety. But even
this reform did not eradicate error. In May 1940,
after Germany had broken the 'phony war' stalemate
of the early months by invading first Denmark and
Norway on 9 April and then Belgium and the Nether-
lands on 10 May, the MoI photographic section at the
request of the Norwegian legation in London banned a
still photograph showing Norwegian merchant sailors
being trained in Britain to use rifles. After consultation with the Admiralty's Norwegian section the
Admiralty censor had passed a film of the same event,
although as it turned out the film was suppressed in
time. After this MoI Press and Censorship Bureau
censors were always present whenever Admiralty and
Air Ministry censors viewed film.
   By this time Winston Churchill had replaced
Neville Chamberlain as Prime Minister. In the next

month France fell, Italy declared war on Britain and
Hitler became the master of western Europe. Britain
thus had her back to the wall against Germany and
Italy without a major ally until the Germans attacked
the·Soviet Union on 22 June 1941. Japan attacked
Pearl Harbor on 7 December 1941, whereupon a German
declaration of war on the United States four days
later provided Britain with another powerful ally.
However, both the Soviet Union and the United States
required time to recover from initial setbacks and
mobilise their full resources for war. Under such
circumstances Britain, despite her success against
the Luftwaffe after the evacuation of the British
army from the Dunkirk beaches, continued to face
imminent defeat until well into 1941 and possible
eventual defeat until late into 1942. In such a dire
crisis it was not surprising that film censorship
squabbles within the MoI disappeared, to judge from
the absence of documentation on the subject during
this period in the MoI files. With the entry of the
Soviet Union and the United States into the war the
censorship of newsreels and documentary films became
much more extensive and complex. From mid-1941 the
work of the censors included the viewing of German
and Soviet footage for possible incorporation into
British newsreels, the translation of German and
Soviet commentaries and the arrangement of special
screenings for the armed forces.[19]
    As the prospects for an ultimate victory became
rosier, tensions within the film censorship system
asserted themselves once again during the second half
of 1942. In particular co-ordination between the
various branches of the MoI as well as between the
MoI and the BBFC showed itself to be less than per-
fect. For instance, in August 1942 MGM submitted a
scenario to the BBFC for, and simultaneously asked
the MoI Film Censorship section to advise on, a
projected film called Sabotage Agent which eventually
saw the light of day as The Adventures of Tartu (MGM,
1942-3, dir Harold Bucquet). This deals with a
British spy (Robert Donat) dropped by parachute into
German-occupied Europe to blow up a poison gas
factory. The BBFC objected only to some bad language
but sought careful treatment of a torture scene and
of one in which a plane ran over a German pilot.[20]
However, the MoI Film Censorship section wished to
delete a bomb disposal sequence early in the film
because of a total MoI ban on any material relating
to bomb disposal, only to find that several months
earlier MGM had consulted the MoI Films Division
which, without notifying the Film Censorship staff,

had approved the plot. On the strength of this
approval the bomb disposal scene had already been
filmed. The Film Censorship section was disposed to
ignore the incident, since the scene in question contained no technical information liable to be of use
to the enemy, but the matter had come to the attention of the Chief Military Advisor to the MoI Press
Censorship Division, who wanted the scene cut from
the film.[21] The outcome is unclear, but the release
of the film was delayed until October 1943. By then
Italo-German resistance had ceased in North Africa,
the allies had taken Sicily and landed in Italy, the
German army had suffered defeats at Stalingrad and
Kursk and the Japanese were on the defensive in the
Pacific. The tide of war was turning strongly in the
allies' favour, and censorship bungles could now be
more easily let through.

By October 1942 work had begun on Squadron
Leader X (RKO, 1942, dir Lance Comfort), an implausible propaganda piece in which a Nazi hero (Eric
Portman) poses as a British pilot in order to escape
from Britain to Germany. The film now has little to
commend it except Portman's repeat performance of a
stereotype ardent Nazi, a role he had already played
so convincingly as the U-boat officer stranded in
Canada attempting to reach the then neutral United
States in 49th Parallel (GFD-Ortus, 1941, dir Michael
Powell). However, Squadron Leader X included a brief
scene, essential to the plot, of RAF personnel
escaping from German-occupied Europe. This particular scene had been shot in collaboration with the
Air Ministry and with the approval of the Films
Division of the MoI, but the film as a whole had not
undergone censorship before production and the topic
of escape from enemy-held territory was in theory
prohibited by the MoI altogether.[22] As so often, the
precise outcome of bureaucratic muddle is obscure
from the MoI documentation, although the BBFC records
show that the film was passed uncut in October 1942.
Presumably as a result of the mishaps concerning The
Adventures of Tartu and Squadron Leader X the MoI
Films Division in January 1943 wrote to the British
Film Makers' Association giving a list of banned
subjects and drawing attention to the fact that MoI
Films Division approval of a film or a basic theme
did not of itself signify that no further censorship
was necessary. The letter recommended producers to
consult the MoI Film Censorship Division in advance
if they intended to make a film touching upon any of
the prohibited topics.[23] These were spies; counter-
espionage; delayed action bombs; escapes of serving

personnel from enemy-occupied territory; treatment
of prisoners of war; use of gas; parachutists,
commando raids (except as approved by the MoI Film
Censorship Division); and secret equipment. After
this letter episodes of The Adventures of Tartu and
Squadron Leader X variety seemingly ceased. Exactly
when this MoI list of banned topics came into force
is unclear, for One of Our Aircraft is Missing (British National, 1941-2, dirs Michael Powell and Emeric
Pressburger), one of the most noteworthy British wartime propaganda productions both at the time and in
retrospect, had dealt entirely with the exploits of a
British bomber crew who after crashing escape with
the help of the Dutch resistance from enemy-held
territory. This film had been released uncut in
March 1942 and does not seem to have incurred any MoI
displeasure.

     Collaboration with the Soviet Union and the
United States over films after June 1941 presented
difficulties of a politically sensitive nature for
the MoI censors and for other government departments
with which they had not previously had to contend.
Soon after the German attack on Russia the Churchill
government agreed to allow the performance of Soviet
films in Britain, although these were to be subject
to the normal censorship process. The films were
distributed by the Soviet War News Film Agency, later
the Soviet Film Agency, and even before Pearl Harbor
short Soviet newsreels, propaganda films and war
documentaries were released to the British public.
Titles included Raid on Moscow, Hitler's Dream,
Russian Salad and Strong Point 42. There were also
five ten-minute art newsreels dealing with various
aspects of Soviet cultural and social life before the
German invasion. All were allowed through uncut even
though the newsreel themes at times came perilously
close to ideological pro-Communist propaganda. In
November 1941 the first full length (one hour) Soviet
production, Soviet Frontiers on the Danube, arrived
in Britain and was also released in full despite the
fact that it implicitly raised the question of the
Soviet boundary with Rumania after the war, the
disputed area being Bessarabia. From then until the
end of the war a regular stream of Soviet full length
features, full length and short documentaries, newsreels and short interest films was seen by British
audiences. The vast majority were shown in entirety,
although a few suffered slight mutilation at the BBFC
during 1944 and 1945 on account of their uncompromising depiction of German atrocities in Russia. Some,
like State Poultry Farms (1943), praised alleged

pre-war achievements and by implication lauded the
Communist way of life. Material of this sort,
coupled with American and British pro-Soviet films
and the successes of the Red Army as it drove the
Germans out of Russia and swept into Poland early in
1944, helped to produce an upsurge of pro-Soviet
feeling in Britain. This alarmed the Polish govern-
ment-in-exile in London which in February 1944 asked
Britain to suppress a film the Soviet Union was
supposedly making called Fighting Poland. This was
reported to be in Polish dialogue and devoted to the
subject of Polish troops in the Red Army fighting
against Germany. The Poles apparently feared a
Soviet effort to influence British public opinion
against automatic Polish independence at the end of
the war. Both the Foreign Office and the MoI were
sympathetic towards the Polish request, but it was
felt within the British government that the Soviets
would inevitably find out about any suppression of
Fighting Poland on whatever pretext, for which reason
the MoI declined to take action against it. As it
happened the film never reached Britain, but a more
serious problem involving Anglo-American relations
emerged late in May 1944. Then the Admiralty sought
two cuts from a British documentary entitled Eve of
Battle before its release in the United States. This
dealt with the preparations for the Normandy invasion
which took place on 6 June 1944, and the shots the
Admiralty objected to were of rocket gun ships towards the end of the film. On 1 June the MoI Films
Division urgently cabled the Americans to make the
cuts before issue, but for reasons which are unknown
this request was not met in time. For a while relations between the British service censors and the
Americans were less than cordial, but there seems to
have been no repetition of the incident.

From May 1940 onwards the MoI film censorship
files are scrappy regarding newsreels, documentaries
and the security aspects of feature films. However,
the evidence from this source suggests that, with
only isolated exceptions, the system evolved before
the war and improved during its early stages through
Sir John Reith's reorganisation at the MoI proved
effective right through to August 1945 despite a
great increase in the amount of film censorship work
after June 1941.

Regarding the non-security political and social
content of feature films, the BBFC was by and large
left to its own devices. The Defence Regulations
empowered the MoI to suppress any film in the last
resort, but the power appears never to have been

exercised. From this one can reasonably assume that
the ideas in the content of the feature films shown
in Britain either had positive MoI approval or did
not arouse sufficient official disapproval for any
action to be taken in the direction of suppression.
Politics presented little problem to the BBFC, for
routine party political strife was suspended for the
duration of the war in September 1939. Labour
remained in official opposition until it joined
Churchill's administration in May 1940, but because
war exigencies were slowly causing unemployment to
dwindle Labour leaders did not seek to stir up domestic disunity during the 'phony war' period. Nor did
they do so after the publication of the Beveridge
report in December 1942, advocating a welfare state
in Britain, evidently captured the public imagination
and raised the question of post-war social policy in
the context of Britain's war aims. Churchill himself
discouraged all public discussion of this subject,
but inevitably it came more and more into the political forefront as final victory loomed. Once Germany
had surrendered in May 1945 and the war in Europe was
over, Labour left the Churchill coalition to precip-
itate a general election in which post-war reconstruction figured prominently as a campaign issue.
Within such a tranquil internal political framework
the BBFC censors enjoyed a comparatively easy time
over domestic politics compared to the 1930s, and
much the same was true over international affairs.
Although a certain regard had to be paid to opinion
in the neutral states prior to Pearl Harbor, by the
end of 1941 the position of Britain's friends and
foes, as likely to appear in allied feature films,
had been thoroughly clarified. However, as the war
progressed the BBFC played an increasingly subord-
inate role to the MoI in feature film censorship.
Both the American and British film production
companies as well as individual British producers
and directors such as Anthony Asquith, Sir Noel
Coward, Leslie Howard and Michael Powell preferred to
deal direct with the MoI and the services when making
war films rather than submit scenarios to the BBFC.
In the United States the American film companies were
in direct contact with the American Office of War
Information in the production of war films. Under
such circumstances the BBFC had little option but to
refrain almost always from even minor cuts to either
American or British propaganda productions, even
when these sometimes transgressed the BBFC's pre-1939
rules. This was also the case for the Soviet feature
propaganda offerings shown in Britain, relatively few

in number compared to the Anglo-American output.
Where propaganda features were actually set in the
Second World War, the BBFC was all but impotent. But
when propaganda was merged into popular pre-war
genres made without the co-operation of either
American or British government departments, the BBFC
was more prepared to attempt to enforce its pre-1939
policies. With features which had no connection with
the war the BBFC concentrated on keeping them clear
of bad language, extreme brutality and overt sexuality.

Horror films, gangster films and thrillers were
tame stuff when set against the actual wartime
experiences of many Britons, especially after the
'phony war' had ended. Conscription into the armed
forces, where the use of bad language in the ranks
was so commonplace as to constitute the normal state
of affairs, brought many men into daily contact with
those from different social backgrounds on a far
greater scale than before 1939. Even when servicemen
were not sent abroad, the disruption to pre-war
family life caused by the prolonged absence of
husbands, fathers, sons and brothers was acute. Unmarried adult daughters and wives without children
were either conscripted into the services or worked
on the land. If they escaped these fates, they, like
men unfit for service in the armed forces, were
liable for compulsory direction into work at armaments factories. Second World War features helped to
make those at home more aware of the dangers faced
by their loved ones in theatres of operations. Sim-
ilarly service personnel abroad were given some idea
of what civilians in Britain might undergo through
the activities of German bombers, the rationing of
food and clothes, and fire watching, for example.
Violence of one kind or another, not to mention death
or at least the possibility of it, had entered the
lives of many British men and women, even if rural
areas often remained comparatively unaffected.
Mothers with children of school age sometimes took up
war work, even though this might mean that the children could not be looked after as well as before the
war. Children continued to find their way to cinemas, sympathetic adult cinemagoers seldom failing to
respond to the children's requests to take them in to
circumvent the 'A' certificate regulations.

Normal family routine, except for the very
elderly, was decimated and pre-war sexual conventions
came under great strain. The long absence of a
marital partner inevitably led to a proliferation of
extra-marital affairs. With many more women either

at work or in the services they had more social
contact with men than before the war, which produced
a goodly share of casual sexual liaisons. This situation was exacerbated after 1942 by the presence in
Britain of well paid American service personnel and
of growing numbers of German and Italian prisoners of
war. In urban areas unattended children had opport-
unities for mischief, sometimes involving difficulties with the police. All this evidence of social upheaval caused the BBFC some concern. Nevertheless
outright bans of films were extremely rare between
September 1939 and August 1945. Only four films
suffered permanently in this way (See Appendix 3).
None had any connection with the war, but the BBFC
banned a fifth, No Greater Sin, on 30 March 1942 and
was not persuaded by the MoI to give way and allow
the film until 13 February 1943. It was then released under the title of Social Enemy Number One with
an 'A' certificate. The cause of BBFC resistance in
this case was the subject matter of venereal disease,
the incidence of which had risen dramatically since
the outbreak of war. The film warned against prom-
iscuous sex but at the same time diluted its message
by specifying in detail what precautions should be
taken against the spread of the disease if one
contracted it.

     In September 1939 the MoI gave the BBFC no guid-
ance as to how pre-war censorship rules should be
modified to suit wartime conditions. As late as
November 1939 Mrs Crouzet complained, 'I would be
grateful to know any new wartime rulings.'[24]
However, Tyrrell's express approval of Confessions of
a Nazi Spy in June 1939 had paved the way for a
complete reversal of policy over anti-Nazi films. As
soon as the cinemas reopened in mid-September the
BBFC pre-war bans on I was a Captive of Nazi Germany
and Professor Mamlock were lifted. During October
and November 1939 anti-Nazi scenarios were approved
for Liberty Radio, which was eventually released in
February 1941 as Freedom Radio (Columbia-Two Cities,
1941, dir Anthony Asquith); Report on a Fugitive,
released in May 1940 as Night Train to Munich (TCF,
1940, dir Sir Carol Reed), a wartime version of
Hitchcock's The Lady Vanishes (Gaumont-British, 1938)
reflecting some naive British 'phony war' attitudes
to Nazi Germany; and The Mad Dog of Europe.[25] This
had first been submitted to the BBFC in November 1934
as a story of the sufferings in Germany of an Aryan
and a Jewish family linked by marriage occasioned by
the Nazi seizure of power. The BBFC had then rejected it, and the project had been abandoned until the

outbreak of war. Columbia then revived it with only
a slight modification to the outline story. Despite
BBFC approval Columbia did not proceed with the film,
although MGM was to produce the similar The Mortal
Storm (1940, dir Frank Borzage), based on Phyllis
Bottome's novel of 1938. The initial BBFC confusion
over wartime censorship is perhaps most hilariously
evidenced in The Mad Dog of Europe scenario where one
recommended cut was a scene in which Nazis replaced
a picture of Jesus Christ with one of Hitler![26]
   Films with an anti-German or anti-Nazi bias by
implication which had been made before the war were
passed at the BBFC without serious qualms during the
latter months of 1939. Nurse Edith Cavell, already
approved at scenario stage in April, was passed on 14
September after having been regarded as anti-German
propaganda in some quarters in the United States when
shown there on the very day that Germany moved into
Poland two weeks previously.[27] On 27 December the
BBFC allowed Alexander Nevsky (USSR, 1938, dir Sergei
Eisenstein), the story of Prince Alexander Nevsky's
13th century defeat in Russia of the invading Teuton-
ic knights. Although placed in a remote historical
setting, the implicit anti-Nazi approach of the film
can scarcely be overlooked. The brutality and heart-
lessness of the knights is emphasised in their treatment of the citizens of captured Novgorod, and at one
point in the film a swastika is explicitly shown as
a symbol of church approval for the knights' aggression and religious support for their victory in a
coming battle. Ironically the BBFC welcomed
Alexander Nevsky in Britain for the very reason that
it had been banned in the Soviet Union at this time
following the conclusion of the Nazi-Soviet non-
aggression pact in August 1939. The subsequent
Soviet benevolent neutrality towards Germany in the
face of German aggression against Poland, as well as
hostile Soviet actions against Finland culminating in
a Finnish-Soviet war from November 1939 to March
1940, possibly explains the BBFC tolerance of anti-
Soviet feature film material in the early months of
the war.
   Early in the 1930s the BBFC had been concerned
over British Agent (Warner, 1934, dir Michael
Curtiz). This had originally been based upon the
secret anti-Bolshevik activities in Russia of Sir
Robert Bruce-Lockhart from 1912 to 1918, particularly
during the revolutionary upheavals of 1917. At
scenario stage in March 1933 the BBFC had considered
it unsuitable for production but had nevertheless
submitted it to the War Office for further

consideration. Evidently the War Office had given
the go ahead in principle, but the plot had then
undergone many amendments leading to a relatively
sparse coverage of 1917 and the Bolshevik revolution.
A heavier emphasis was also placed on the British
agent's (Leslie Howard) romantic attachments. The
completed film thus bore only a superficial resemblance to the March 1933 scenario, but when submitted
to the BBFC in August 1934, it received ponderous
consideration all the same. Shortt and representatives from the Foreign and Home Offices did not view
it until 26 October. Even then they had viewed it a
second time on 8 November, but it was not passed
until 7 December, by which time the BBFC had deleted
266 feet or three minutes running time and drained it
of any possible political significance.

By contrast to some extent the BBFC had raised
no objection to Tovarich (Warner, 1937, dir Anatole
Litvak) even though it had contained a highly unsym-
pathetic portrayal of Soviet commissar Gorotchenko.
The choice of Basil Rathbone for this part when he
had within the previous few years played such harsh
roles as Murdstone in David Copperfield (MGM, 1935,
dir George Cukor), Karenin in Anna Karenina (MGM,
1935, dir Clarence Brown) and the Marquis St
Evremonde In A Tale of Two Cities (MGM, 1935, dir
Jack Conway) is a sufficient indication of Tovarich's
antipathetic approach to the Soviet Union against the
real background of the Stalinist purges. However,
this prejudice had been partially tempered in the
script with a recognition that Gorotchenko was a
Russian patriot even if he was depicted as villainous
by comparison with the Tsarist aristocrats-in-exile
in Paris (Charles Boyer and Claudette Colbert). But
Ninotchka (MGM, 1939, dir Ernst Lubitsch) was an
anti-Soviet satire pure and simple. It centres on
Ninotchka (Greta Garbo), a young female Communist
envoy sent on official business to Paris where she
falls in love with a western playboy (Melvyn
Douglas). The resulting conflict between basic
human emotion and Communist beliefs is well brought
out in a lively script supported by high quality
acting. The BBFC passed the film uncut on 13 November 1939, but on the other hand to have attempted to
suppress or mutilate on anti-Soviet grounds a Garbo
star vehicle when she was at the height of her fame
and popularity might easily have brought the BBFC
problems of a different kind with the film companies
in the United States when they were establishing
studios in Britain to meet the quota requirement of
British films laid down by law in 1927 and amended in

THE SECOND WORLD WAR

1937. The Soviet defeat of Finland in March 1940
perpetuated anti-Soviet feeling in Britain until June
1941, and another satire similar to Ninotchka, Com-
rade X (MGM, 1940, dir King Vidor), was allowed by
the BBFC in February 1941. This tale of an American
reporter in the Soviet Union (Clark Gable) who is
blackmailed into smuggling a devout young girl Communist (Hedy Lamarr) to the west by her anti-Communist
father (Felix Bressart) lacks the cinematic sparkle
of Ninotchka, but its anti-Soviet message is sharper
and easily picked up by even unsophisticated audiences.
     Not even the German attack on Russia brought an
end to anti-Soviet sympathies in Britain. This became evident when Mission to Moscow (Warner, 1943,
dir Michael Curtiz) was shown in Britain in 1943. An
account of the work of American Ambassador Joseph E.
Davies in Russia from 1936 to 1938, it adopts a
favourable view of pre-war Soviet foreign policy.
Before its arrival in Britain the Conservative
Central Office vainly tried to induce the Minister of
Information, Brendan Bracken, to impose a ban.[28] The
cause of annoyance was dialogue attributed to Stalin
which was critical of pre-1939 Anglo-French policy
towards the European dictators. Stalin's actual
words in the film to Davies as the latter was giving
up his post in Moscow were,

     The reactionary elements in England have
     determined upon a deliberate policy of
     making Germany strong. At the same time
     they shout lies in the press about the
     weakness of the Russian army and disorder
     in the Soviet Union...there is no doubt
     that their plan is to force Hitler into a
     war with this country. Then when the com-
     batants have exhausted themselves, they
     will step in and make peace. Yes, the kind
     of peace that will serve their own interests.
     In my opinion the present governments of
     England and France do not represent the
     people. Finally the Fascist dictators will
     drive too hard a bargain, and the people
     will bring their governments to account.
     But then it may be too late.

However, Bracken's refusal to intervene did not
settle the matter. When Mission to Moscow was submitted to the BBFC on 1 July 1943, it was referred
to Tyrrell who viewed it six days later. On 12 July
members of the Foreign Office also viewed it, after

which it was cut by almost two minutes running time, 162 feet. Since there is nothing else in the film's substance which offended the BBFC and MoI rules, it is highly probable that at least a part of Stalin's dialogue to Davies was omitted from the version seen in Britain. This speculation is reinforced by the relative lack of criticism for the film in the Conservative press upon its release.

Between I was a Captive of Nazi Germany in September 1939 and Tomorrow The World (United Artists, 1944, dir Leslie Fenton) in February 1945 cinema audiences in Britain were subjected to an incessant spate of what were in the main crude anti-German or anti-Nazi screen diatribes from both American and British studios. In both American and British wartime features the Italians were usually lampooned rather than regarded as enemies worthy of respect. Perhaps the best examples are Filippo Del Giudice's comic portrayal of an Italian Fascist leader in The First of the Few (Melbourne-British Aviation, 1942, dir Leslie Howard) and the character of Captain Tonelli in Casablanca (Warner, 1942, dir Michael Curtiz), of whom the French prefect of police, Captain Louis Renault (Claude Rains), disparagingly says that if he gets a word in edgeways with the Germans, it would be a major Italian victory. Japan was treated more seriously, most of the anti-Japanese material emanating from the United States. In all three cases national stereotypes were the overriding image conveyed on the screen. Although these attitudes to Germany were double-edged, the anti-Fascist Italian and the anti-militarist Japanese were all but non-existent in English language cinema while the war was actually in progress. In the anti-Japanese wartime features the basic themes were brutality, torture, rape and general barbarism allied with duplicity and treachery both before and during the war. So far as the author has been able to discover only one film, Behind the Rising Sun (RKO, 1943, dir Edward Dmytryk), attempted any sort of distinction between good and bad Japanese before and after Pearl Harbor in a Japanese setting.

Although Pearl Harbor had made China an ally of Britain and the United States, the adverse pre-1939 cinematic image of China and the Chinese by no means vanished even if it was no longer the dominating one. Charlie Chan had at least placed a Chinese on the side of law and order through, it was implied, an American upbringing, while The Good Earth had portrayed the Chinese peasantry sympathetically. However, the general impression of China as a country

had remained one of political instability, poverty,
vice and violence. This image was perpetuated in The
Keys of the Kingdom (TCF, 1944, dir John Stahl), the
story of a Catholic priest (Gregory Peck) in 19th
century China based upon A.J. Cronin's novel. The
Purple Heart (TCF, 1944, dir Lewis Milestone) deals
with American flyers who had bombed Japanese cities
when put on public trial in Japan for war crimes.
Tortured and finally executed, the airmen are first
turned over to the Japanese by a treacherous Chinaman
eager for money when they had bailed out over China.
On the other hand the Chinese are depicted as indust-
rious, persevering, happy, loyal and courageous
allies in Night Plane from Chungking (Paramount,
1942, dir Ralph Murphy), Dragon Seed (MGM, 1944, dir
Jack Conway), Thirty Seconds over Tokyo (MGM, 1944,
dir Mervyn Leroy) and God is My Co-Pilot (Warner,
1945, dir Robert Florey).29 To reinforce this
favourable image of the Chinese, the Charlie Chan
series continued throughout the war.

The MoI and the BBFC made no effort to interfere
with propaganda which was ambivalent in terms of
allies and foes and their national stereotypes.
Neither the American nor the British production
companies ever entirely lost sight of the 'decent'
(i.e. anti-Nazi) German, a trend of which both the
MoI and the BBFC were exceptionally tolerant under
wartime circumstances. The idea of anti-Nazis in
Germany seems first to have appeared in Let George Do
It (Ealing, 1940, dir Marcel Varnel), a George Formby
comedy released in March 1940 in which he plays a
ukelele player who goes to Norway by mistake and is
taken for a German spy in Bergen. This contains an
extraordinary dream sequence in which Formby descends
from a balloon into a Nazi rally to knock Hitler
unconscious as he is speaking from the rostrum.
Thereupon the Nazi audience becomes joyous and shakes
hands with one another in delight. This clear mis-
understanding of the Nazi stranglehold over Germany
and consequent over-optimism in Britain that the war
would produce an anti-Nazi coup in Germany was not
entirely dispelled until the fall of France. This
same erroneous belief lay behind the first serious
wartime anti-Nazi British film, Pastor Hall (Charter,
1940, dir Roy Boulting), based upon a play by Ernst
Toller. This was reportedly the case of Pastor
Martin Niemoeller, a clergyman (Wilfrid Lawson) who
was persecuted and then executed (in the film but not
in reality - he survived the war) before the war for
his anti-Nazi beliefs and actions. This film was
produced in the 'phony war' period and passed uncut

by the BBFC on 24 April 1940, but by the time it
reached the cinemas on general release the 'phony
war' was well and truly over and France was veering
towards collapse. As a result Pastor Hall was not
well received and has since fallen into an unmerited
obscurity. It is well made, movingly acted and the
only serious wartime British screen endeavour to
examine what Nazism meant for dissenting Germans before September 1939. A chilling performance from
Marius Goring as an ardent Nazi makes a telling contribution to the overall impact. If this was blunted
at the time by force of circumstances, its image of
the 'good' German was not as a consequence sunk without trace. Before the end of 1940 it had appeared
again in American films like The Mortal Storm (in the
persons of Margaret Sullavan, James Stewart and eventually Robert Young) and Escape (MGM, 1940, dir
Mervyn Leroy). In this a famous German actress,
Emmy Ritter (Nazimova), languishing in a concentration camp for her anti-Nazi ideals, is rescued by her
American-born son (Robert Taylor) aided by other
Germans. As the war grew in intensity, the idea of
the 'good' German understandably faded into the
background on the screen, but it never disappeared
altogether and neither the BBFC nor the MoI took
steps to discourage it, no matter how dire the war
situation.

In 49th Parallel a member of the U-boat crew
(Niall MacGinnis) wishes to live in peace with a
German religious community in Canada rather than
reach the neutral United States to continue to participate in the war. In 1942 the 'good' German image
was given a new twist in The Pied Piper (TCF, 1942,
dir Irving Pichel), an American production which
tells of an old Englishman (Monty Woolley) who while
on holiday in the France of mid-1940 finds himself
fleeing from the German advance and in the process
assuming responsibility for several refugee children.
At length he falls into Gestapo hands but is nevertheless allowed to proceed to Britain by a Gestapo
chief (Otto Preminger) who does not believe in an
ultimate German victory. In April 1943, almost simultaneously, there came before the BBFC the American
The Moon is Down (TCF, 1943, dir Irving Pichel) and
the British The Life and Death of Colonel Blimp (GFD-
Archers, 1943, dirs Michael Powell and Emeric Pressburger). The former concerns the resistance of a
Norwegian village to German occupation. Based on a
John Steinbeck novel, the film reaches a standard of
realism and intelligence far above the average wartime resistance drama. In the German garrison a

THE SECOND WORLD WAR

young homesick officer (Peter Van Eyck) heartily
dislikes the deeds of the occupation force carried
out in the village in the name of his country as
retaliation for resistance activity. A unique feature of British wartime cinema was the thinly disguised discourse on 20th century Anglo-German relations
in Colonel Blimp. This is personified by a friendship struck up in 1902 between a young British army
officer, Clive Candy (Roger Livesey), and a young
Prussian officer, Theo Kretschmar-Schuldorff (Anton
Walbrook). They have to fight a duel in Berlin over
an alleged insult Candy has delivered to the German
imperial army and, both wounded, end up in the same
hospital. Eventually the German comes to Britain as
an anti-Nazi refugee and convinces Candy that Nazi
Germany will have to be defeated by Nazi methods
rather than by pre-1914 British standards of honour
and fair play. The BBFC passed both films uncut,
even though Churchill had personally tried to prevent
the production of Colonel Blimp altogether and was
later to succeed in having it decimated for export.30
As the war neared its closing stages the BBFC also
passed uncut The Seventh Cross (MGM, 1944, dir Fred
Zinnemann), a concentration camp story set in Germany
in 1936. The seven anti-Nazi escapees are recaptured
save one, George Heisler (Spencer Tracy), who manages
to leave the country. He is greatly assisted by an
apolitical friend, Paul Roeder (Hume Cronyn), who
places personal friendship above obedience to his
government. In the varied reactions of the German
personalities whom Tracy contacts in his bid to
secure permanent freedom Fred Zinnemann strongly
emphasises human nature more than political belief.
The Seventh Cross was the American equivalent of
Pastor Hall and a particularly courageous film in the
light of an impending German defeat and the prospect
of allied retribution. It provoked no public hostility in Britain on its release in September 1944,
although it might well have done so had the full
horror of the Nazi death camps been public knowledge
at the time. It took the revelations of the holo-
caust against the Jews and other Nazi atrocities in
1945 to convert the English language cinema to a more
anti-German, as opposed to anti-Nazi, stance in the
post-war era than had characterised its propaganda
during the European war itself.
        The plight of the Jews in Germany or German-
occupied territory was touched upon, with varying
degrees of emphasis and intensity, in The Mortal
Storm, The Great Dictator (Sir Charles Chaplin, 1940,
dir Sir Charles Chaplin), Once Upon a Honeymoon (RKO,

1942, dir Leo McCarey) and Mr Skeffington (Warner, 1944, dir Vincent Sherman). Nazi anti-Semitism never entirely deserted the American film industry throughout the war, but it was left to the British to produce what seems to have been the solitary English language wartime fiction film dwelling upon Nazi anti-Semitism as a central theme. This was Mr Emmanuel (Two Cities, 1944, dir Harold French), a full print of which unfortunately no longer survives. But even this film contained a key role for a 'good' German in the shapely form of a cabaret singer (Greta Gynt) who uses her emotional hold over a Nazi leader (Walter Rilla) to save from death the elderly Jew of the title (Felix Aylmer, his only starring part). However, Emmanuel survives Nazi persecution, unlike some of the Jewish personalities in the American films previously cited in this paragraph. Jewish deaths arising from Nazi anti-Semitism in wartime films took place on an individual basis, systematic wholesale extermination never being even remotely hinted at, so that neither the BBFC nor the MoI had any reason to contemplate suppression on horror grounds.

Political problem films were few and far between during the war. With unemployment gradually vanishing any sting the pro-working class The Stars Look Down and The Proud Valley might have generated upon their release in 1940 during the 'phony war' was soon overtaken by the course of the war itself. Consequently the BBFC did not even cut, let alone attempt to suppress, Love on the Dole (British National, 1941, dir John Baxter) when it was submitted in April 1941 - by contrast with BBFC policy before the war - despite the fact that it contravened BBFC pre-war rules on several counts. Nor did the BBFC and the MoI interfere with feature films possessing pacifist inclinations. The first of these during the war was We are not Alone (Warner, 1939, dir Edmund Goulding), based upon James Hilton's novel of an English small town doctor (Paul Muni) who is falsely accused of murdering his wife (Dame Flora Robson), found guilty and executed in 1914. This film must have been troublesome to the BBFC on several scores - it covered a near contemporary miscarriage of British justice which, unlike Captain Blood, is not eventually corrected, it strongly hints at hysterical and unwarranted anti-German prejudices in Britain on the eve of the First World War and it provides the doctor in the condemned cell with anti-war dialogue. We are not Alone had begun production before the war, but it was not submitted to the BBFC until 17 January 1940.

However, it was passed with minor cuts on 2 February
but not released in Britain for a further three
months, by which time the 'phony war' was at an end.
Although the screen version of George Bernard Shaw's
Major Barbara (Gabriel Pascal, 1941, dirs Gabriel
Pascal, Harold French and David Lean) not only to
some extent held up the Salvation Army to ridicule
but also called into question the morality of war and
armaments production, the BBFC passed it uncut on 9
January 1941. Probably the most dangerous problem
film of the war from the viewpoint of the BBFC and
the MoI was This Above All (TCF, 1942, dir Anatole
Litvak). This was based on a novel by Eric Knight
and was the only English language wartime film which
was actually set in the Second World War itself yet
questions the purpose of the conflict. A British
conscientious objector (Tyrone Power) is drafted into
the services but deserts because he believes the aim
of the war is to preserve the British social system
and the privileges of the ruling class. He falls in
love with a surgeon's daughter (Joan Fontaine) and ·
redeems himself through his bravery in an air raid.
This feature was one of the very few during the war
that Tyrrell was called upon for a decision, but
eventually it was passed uncut on 1 July 1942. One
wonders whether this would have been the case if the
hero had not seen the error of his ways!
    In contrast to the First World War the BBFC took
no exception to films portraying cowardice under
fire, although it seems probable that this tolerance
was extended only to a cowardice which ultimately
redeemed itself. In Ships with Wings (Ealing, 1941,
dir Sergei Nolbandov) Sir John Clements, echoing to
a certain extent his Harry Faversham role in The Four
Feathers, is dismissed from the Fleet Air Arm before
the war due to doubts about his bravery but loses his
life in a suicide mission to Greece. In Which We
Serve (Rank-Two Cities, 1942, dirs Sir Noel Coward
and David Lean) saw Sir Richard Attenborough's debut
as a young stoker in HMS Torrin who deserts his post
in action but, after his commander (Sir Noel Coward)
had only admonished him, shows next time he had
learned his lesson by his display of endurance and
valour in an open dinghy when HMS Torrin is sunk.
    Changes also emerged in BBFC attitudes on social
questions which had seemed important before the war
but had been swept into the background by events
after September 1939. Cancer, for instance, was a
near taboo subject in both American and British
cinema before the war. This was perhaps best evidenced in Dark Victory (Warner, 1939, dir Edmund

Goulding), a tale of a frivolous society girl (Bette
Davis) who discovers she is dying and turns over a
new leaf before her death. Now chiefly remembered as
a Bette Davis star vehicle, the film in its early
sequences delivers a strong plea for more open discussion of terminal illness. Although this message
is eventually lost in the later tear-jerking scenes
as Bette Davis nears her demise, and the exact nature
of her complaint is glossed over through the use of
official medical terms, the BBFC had none the less
imposed a one-minute cut on 29 March 1939. However,
during the war the word 'cancer' occurred in the
dialogue of Rebecca (Selznick, 1940, dir Sir Alfred
Hitchcock), King's Row (Warner, 1941, dir Sam Wood)
and None But the Lonely Heart (RKO, 1944, dir
Constantin Bakaleinikoff), all of which appeared
uncut in British cinemas. More significantly, King's
Row also strongly suggests that Dr Henry Gordon
(Charles Coburn) has amputated both the legs of Drake
McHugh (Ronald Reagan) for personal reasons rather
than medical necessity, although the point is not
clarified beyond doubt.

If the horror genre paled into insignificance
compared with wartime reality in many adult lives,
the BBFC appears never to have lost sight of the
possibility that due to wartime conditions parental
control over children was more lax than before 1939.
As a result children might gain admission to horror
films more easily. The only four films which
remained banned throughout the war all seem to have
been horror films of one sort or another - Buried
Alive (1940), The Corpse Vanishes (Warner, 1942, dir
D. Ross Lederman - ultimately passed on 26 June 1946
as The Body Disappears), The Mad Monster (1944 -
passed on 10 January 1952 with an 'X' certificate)
and The Mystic Circle Murder (1944). 'H' certificate
films were reduced to a trickle of two until 1945.
These were The Monster and the Girl (Paramount, 1940,
dir Stuart Heisler), a story of a wrongfully executed
man whose brain is transplanted into a gorilla, and
The Ghost of Frankenstein (Universal, 1942, dir Erle
C. Kenton), another brain transplant theme wrapped in
a 1930s genre setting with Boris Karloff, Bela Lugosi
and Lionel Atwill to lend substance to the horror
atmosphere. In 1945 four films were awarded 'H'
certificates (see Appendix 2), but one of these was a
United Nations war crimes documentary. Not until
1946 did the horror genre once again flourish, the
BBFC giving no fewer than nine 'H' certificates in
that year. Howevever, during the war the BBFC
allowed many horror films to have an 'A' certificate

134

which, even with cuts, would probably have been given
a 'H' certificate before the war. Random examples
are Dr Cyclops (Paramount, 1940, dir Ernest
Schoedsack), The Mummy's Hand (Universal, 1940, dir
Christy Cabanne) and I Walked with a Zombie (RKO,
1943, dir Jacques Tourneur).

The BBFC's opposition to bad language on the
screen had not broken down before September 1939 as
much as one might have expected following the 'not
bloody likely' breakthrough in Pygmalion of 1938, but
the war brought further challenges to this aspect of
the BBFC rules. Far and away the most dramatic
further inroad came with In Which We Serve, in which
one of the characters (James Donald) clinging to a
dinghy in open water as German aircraft sweep in to
machine gun them says, 'Here come the bastards
again.' Later in the film Bernard Miles also uses
the word 'bastards' to describe German bombers in
action. To judge from the BBFC register of films
passed, which records that one word was cut from the
dialogue, the BBFC must have been defied on this
occasion, for in the author's memory the word
appeared in the film shown to British audiences at
the time. Furthermore, with Sir Noel Coward's
express agreement, it was cut from the version shown
in the United States by the Hays Office.[31] Although
In Which We Serve did not lead to the use of down-
to-earth language in British films on a large scale,
there were other, less blatant instances. In a scene
from The Bells Go Down (Ealing, 1943, dir Basil
Dearden), a solidly made homage to the work of the
London Fire Brigade during the blitz, a semi-
inebriated soldier (Charles Victor, uncredited) tells
the film's hero (Tommy Trinder) in a public house
that as a fireman in 1940 he was drawing a wage 'for
sweet Fanny Adams', i.e. doing absolutely nothing. In
fact 'sweet Fanny Adams' was a polite version of
service jargon in widespread use, the phrase usually
being either 'sweet fuck all' or 'sweet F.A.'.
Nevertheless the BBFC passed The Bells Go Down uncut
on 6 April 1943.

Before the war the BBFC had not permitted mention of individual drugs, but once more the rules were
relaxed in wartime. For instance, in Next of Kin
(Ealing, 1942, dir Thorold Dickinson - he had been
active in the pre-war London Film Society), a
propaganda piece warning against careless talk in
public disguised as a thriller, Mrs Webster (Mary
Clare), a German agent, blackmails a stage dancer
(Phyllis Stanley) into remaining a Nazi spy by
threatening to withhold cocaine. This is described

in Mary Clare's dialogue both as 'coke' and 'cocaine' - a far cry from Herbert Wilcox's difficulties with the BBFC in 1922! (pp. 29-30). Next of Kin was allowed without cuts on 11 May 1942, while in The Woman in Green (Universal, 1944, dir Roy William Neill), passed uncut on 21 June 1945, a woman hypnotist (Hillary Brooke) attempts to drug Sherlock Holmes (Basil Rathbone) with what she names as 'cannabis japonica'.

The real violence of even the 'phony war' reduced the pre-war fantasy violence of the screen to unimportance, and it was not long before this fact was reflected in wartime films and BBFC policy. As early as September 1939 a little known British production, an espionage thriller called Traitor Spy (Pathé, 1939, dir Walter Summers), was submitted to the BBFC and extensively cut on account of a brutal beating up sequence and scenes in a seedy night club hinting at illicit sex and drugs. It took almost a month before the film was restructured to the BBFC's satisfaction and even then it was subjected to further minor cuts. However, at the same time there was sufficient left of the offending material in the version which the BBFC finally let through on 23 October 1939 to represent an initial significant relaxation of the BBFC's pre-war attitude to screen violence. The famous western Destry Rides Again (Universal, 1939, dir George Marshall) suffered great modification and cuts at the BBFC in January 1940, but a long scene was retained in which the bar room girl Frenchie (Marlene Dietrich) rolls around the floor when fighting another woman (Una Merkel) before the laconic Destry (James Stewart) ends the brawl by pouring water over both of them. Fighting between women was prohibited material before the war. On the other hand The Hunchback of Notre Dame (RKO, 1939, dir William Diertle), the remake of the 1923 Lon Chaney Senior classic with Charles Laughton superb as Quasimodo, was cut, the scene objected to almost certainly being that in which the gipsy girl Esmeralda (Maureen O'Hara) is tortured with the brodequin, a steel boot which is fitted to the foot and tightened. None the less enough of this sequence remains to leave the audience in no doubt about the nature of the torture and its effectiveness in extracting a confession from the unfortunate girl. Of Mice and Men (Hal Roach, 1939, dir Lewis Milestone), based on John Steinbeck's book and passed uncut on 13 March 1940, contains a fist fight scene in which the mentally retarded Lon Chaney Junior systematically crushes all the bones in one hand of

his adversary (Bob Steele). Pastor Hall includes a
concentration camp whipping scene which, although not
shown explicitly, depicts the severity of the old
anti-Nazi clergyman's flogging through a prolonged
lingering on his suffering as manifested by his hand
struggles in thick straps.

1941 continued in the same vein. Love on the
Dole saw British policemen using truncheons on demonstrators protesting against unemployment, on which
the BBFC had laid down an absolute ban in the 1930s
and before. However, strangely enough, the tendency
towards more brutal screen violence was more evident
at this time in the offerings of the neutral United
States than of belligerent Britain. The most glaring
example in 1941 was Man Hunt (TCF, 1941, dir Fritz
Lang), the story of a British big game hunter (Walter
Pidgeon) who had tried to assassinate Hitler. He is
caught and tortured by the Gestapo but manages to
escape to Britain, only to realise that his chief
Gestapo tormentor (George Sanders) has followed him
there. The torture is not shown, but its physical
results are, yet the BBFC allowed it in full on 30
August 1941. In the film there is also a brutal fist
fight scene when Pidgeon is discovered by a SS guard
outside Berchtesgaden just as he is lining Hitler up
in the telescopic sights of his rifle and is about to
pull the trigger. The Maltese Falcon (Warner, 1941,
dir John Huston) was allowed in entirety at the BBFC
on 20 November 1941 even though it contains a scene
in which a drugged and prostrate Sam Spade (Humphrey
Bogart) is kicked in the head by gunman Wilmer Cook
(Elisha Cook Junior).

After Pearl Harbor screen violence in various
American genres became much more pronounced, the Hays
Office evidently encountering much the same problems
as the BBFC in trying to enforce pre-war censorship
policies. As with earlier film developments, Cecil
B. De Mille soon sensed a new public mood over violence in both Britain and the United States and
pointed the way to the future with Reap the Wild
Wind (Paramount, 1942, dir Cecil B. De Mille). This
now rarely screened period adventure set in Georgia
is most remembered for its spectacular underwater
fight involving a giant squid, but it also has a
scene where John Wayne rams a large lighted lantern
straight into the face of another man. Although the
film suffered a minor cut when passed on 1 April
1942, the lantern scene was untouched. Later in the
same month the BBFC had to deal with This Gun for
Hire (Paramount, 1941-2, dir Frank Tuttle), which
appears to have been responsible for introducing to

137

the screen the professional 'hit man' in the form of
the psycopathic killer Raven (Alan Ladd, his first
starring role and arguably his best). In the opening
sequence Raven slaps a room maid full across the face
- men striking women had been banned at the BBFC
before the war - and later shoves a man (Marc
Lawrence) down the full length of a cellar staircase,
but nevertheless the BBFC passed the film uncut on
29 April 1942. Next of Kin centres on the activities
of a German spy ring in Britain prior to a British
commando raid in Europe. At one point Mervyn Johns,
a German spy, knocks out Nova Pilbeam with a fist
landing flush on her jaw just after she has stabbed
Stephen Murray, another member of the spy ring posing
as a bookseller, in the back with a letter opener.
In the commando raid itself, following a bout of
hand-to-hand combat, a British soldier is seen
bashing in the head of a German with two blows from a
rifle butt. Next of Kin went through the BBFC in
full on 11 May 1942. In The Spoilers (Universal,
1942, dir Ray Enright), a Yukon adventure along
traditional western lines, John Wayne and Randolph
Scott engage in a fist fight which was so bloody and
protracted by contemporary standards that it prompted
one press reviewer to write that, 'for mobility,
length, ferocity, noise, damage, and general uproar
(it) rivals anything yet seen in all the violent
history of the cinema'.[32] What this anonymous reviewer would have thought of the scene, which the BBFC
passed uncut on 2 June 1942, if he or she could have
peered into the future of the cinema can be only
speculation, but within a few months The Glass Key
(Paramount, 1942, dir Stuart Heisler) was to break
new ground. A political thriller, the film opens
with ruthless politician Paul Madvig (Brian Donlevy)
hurling a man through French windows into a swimming
pool and treating it as a joke. Later Jeff (William
Bendix), a hired thug, persistently and brutally
beats up Madvig's henchman, Ed Beaumont (Alan Ladd),
who eventually escapes Jeff's attentions by plunging
straight through a glass skylight into the room below. The BBFC allowed The Glass Key without cuts on
3 September 1942. In Sherlock Holmes and the Secret
Weapon (Universal, 1942, dir Roy William Neill)
Holmes (Basil Rathbone), in a dive bar disguised as
an Indian seaman, breaks a bottle on the bar counter
and threatens another seaman with it. Here the
violence among seamen is implied rather than shown,
although the use of bottles in brawls was frowned
upon at the BBFC before 1939. More important, there
are shots of the inventor of a secret bomb sight, Dr

Tobel (William Post Junior), being tortured by Nazis
under the supervision of Professor Moriarty (Lionel
Atwill) to induce him to reveal its whereabouts.
From the existing print it is unclear precisely what
form of physical torture is employed, but it is
accompanied by several piercing screams to bring home
to the audience its horrible nature. On 25 September
1942 the BBFC cut the film by 34 feet - about a third
of a minute - and since the torture scene on the
extant British print is disjointed, it is all but
certain that this is where the BBFC imposed the cut.
    For the rest of the war the personal violence
which the BBFC was called upon to view was chiefly
connected with wartime Axis brutality, concerning
which there were limits to the censors' tolerance.
Hanna and his colleagues sometimes toned this down,
as in Hitler's Children (RKO, 1943, dir Edward
Dmytryk), in which Bonita Granville is tied to a post
and whipped by a Gestapo man. However, the BBFC was
never able to erase violence of this sort altogether
during the war, for as personal violence tended to
die away in traditional Hollywood genres after the
upsurge of 1942 - for instance, the brutality of This
Gun for Hire and The Glass Key was rarely repeated in
later wartime thrillers - it emerged in British
melodramas. In The Man in Grey (GFD-Gainsborough,
1943, dir Leslie Arliss), the first of a successful
series of period costume melodramas which continued
after the war, the loathsome and sadistic Lord Rowan
(James Mason) whips Margaret Lockwood to death. The
deed is not shown, the scene ending as the whipping
is about to begin, but even implied violence along
these lines against women had not been allowed before
the war. The film also contains a vicious fist fight
between James Mason and Stewart Granger, which
probably owed much to The Spoilers, but the BBFC
passed the entire version on 21 June 1943 despite a
certain amount of press criticism of the John Wayne-
Randolph Scott fisticuffs in The Spoilers. The
Seventh Veil (Theatrecraft-Sydney Box-Ortus, 1945,
dir Compton Bennett) sees James Mason crash a walking
stick down on the hand of Ann Todd as she is playing
the piano. This was depicted explicitly, yet the
BBFC allowed the film in full on 24 July 1945,
although it was not released until after the war.
    The forward sexual antics and snappy dialogue of
Mae West and Jean Harlow in the early 1930s had been
stamped out by American censorship by 1934. As a
result the image of the forward, wisecracking,
sexually aware and rough diamond female had virtually
disappeared from the English language cinema by 1939.

Nor, in spite of the real sexual laxity that was a
product of the war itself, was this image revived for
some time into the war years. This was likewise true
of socially sensitive matters closely related to sex.
It was not until 1940 that the sex element intruded
into feature films, even then on only a small scale
and implicitly rather than explicitly. Unmarried
miscegenation figured in The Letter (Warner, 1940,
dir William Wyler), a remake of an early talkie
version of the Somerset Maugham novel (Paramount,
1929, dir Jean de Limur), which the BBFC passed uncut
on 20 December 1940 even though Hanna and Mrs Crouzet
had expressed misgivings about the scenario when it
was submitted in June 1939.[33] Rape or marital rape
was obliquely hinted at in Of Mice and Men and Gone
With the Wind (MGM, 1939, dirs Victor Fleming,
George Cukor and Sam Wood, the last two uncredited)
without incurring major censorial displeasure in
March 1940. Dr Ehrlich's Magic Bullet (Warner, 1940,
dir William Diertle), possibly the best of the Hollywood screen biographies, approached the subject of
venereal disease somewhat tentatively but suffered
merely a minor cut to the dialogue when the BBFC
passed it on 29 March 1940.
    However, as the 'phony war' gave way to more
serious hostilities and wartime pressures on conventional sexual morals increased, both American and
British features delivered a more direct challenge to
the pre-war values of the Hays Office and the BBFC.
In Love on the Dole Sally Hardcastle (Deborah Kerr,
her first major part) becomes the mistress of well-
to-do local bookmaker Sam Grundy (Frank Cellier) in
order to obtain jobs for her unemployed father and
brother. In Hatter's Castle (Paramount British,
1941, dir Lance Comfort), an A.J. Cronin novel which
the BBFC had strongly discouraged at scenario stage
in November 1938[34] but allowed at the same stage in
April 1941,[35] references were made to the birth of
an illegitimate child to the daughter (Deborah Kerr)
of tyrannical Scottish hatter James Brodie (Robert
Newton). These scenes had been the main basis of
the BBFC's pre-war objections to the film, but it
was allowed in full on 29 October 1941. That Hamilton Woman (London Films, 1941, dir Sir Alexander
Korda), filmed in the United States and released in
Britain as Lady Hamilton, in effect defends the
extra-marital liaison of Emma Hamilton (Vivien Leigh)
and Lord Nelson (Sir Laurence Olivier) despite the
fact that it had destroyed both their marriages.
The BBFC passed it on 19 May 1941 even though it
also presents none too flattering a picture of Lady

Hamilton's sexual morals before she meets Nelson.

In 1942 Next of Kin shows a prolonged, sexually provocative dance by Phyllis Stanley in which the outline of her nude body is clearly seen behind near transparent clothing. In the same production Mervyn Johns, while waiting to see Stephen Murray in the latter's bookshop, picks up and thumbs through a book entitled L'Art de Catalon. He stops at a page which has a picture of a woman nude to the waist with both breasts prominently displayed. During 1943 British companies were more prepared than hitherto to depart from accepted sexual stereotypes and poke fun at conventional sexual morality. When We are Married (British National, 1943, dir Herbert Mason), a J.B. Priestley play set in the 1890s, deals with the re-actions of three Yorkshire couples who on their silver wedding day discover that they had never been legally married. This thinly veiled challenge to the sanctity of marriage was allowed uncut on 9 March 1943. The Man in Grey introduced to the British screen the deep-eyed villainess without a redeeming feature in its 18th century story of decadence, duplicity and ruthlessness among the British upper class. In the process Margaret Lockwood was converted into a British equivalent of Bette Davis as the latter appeared in The Little Foxes (Samuel Goldwyn, 1941, dir William Wyler), which may have reflected the changing, more positive position of women in British society brought about by wartime necessity.

By 1943 the sexual implications of the war were being brought home more forcibly to the United States, with consequent repercussions in American features. A notable example was the euphemistically named Lady of Burlesque (United Artists, 1943, dir William Wellman). This concerns the then famous American striptease dancer, Gypsy Rose Lee (Barbara Stanwyck), and her part in unravelling a series of baffling show business murders. The subject of striptease offended American puritanical tastes, and this film was probably the first time a striptease dancer had been the central character, although the plot was heavily wrapped in comedy and mystery ingredients. Perhaps for this reason the BBFC took not the slightest exception to the film, not even to the more titillating British title of Striptease Lady at a time when striptease as a public phenomenon was almost unknown in Britain outside a few night clubs in the major cities. However, far and away the strongest American challenge of the war to the sexual outlook of the Hays Office and the BBFC was The

Miracle of Morgan's Creek (Paramount, 1943, dir
Preston Sturges). An American girl (Betty Hutton)
becomes pregnant after a dance by a soldier she has
only just met. When drunk, she marries him but then
cannot remember who he is. The contemporary setting
of the film gave great impact to its biting and witty
script. Moreover, its basic plot could have happened
in any of the allied countries and certainly in
Britain. For all its comedy veneer, when her chival-
rous but timid and bumbling boy friend (Eddie Bracken)
tries to protect her from the consequences of her
actions, the issue of casual sexual intercourse and
resulting pregnancy in a Second World War context was
raised head on for the first time. The BBFC let it
through uncut on 1 September 1943.

Despite a more broadminded approach to sex than
before the war, itself possibly dictated by wartime
conditions and amicable Anglo-American relations, the
BBFC did not altogether relax as the course of the
war veered in the allies' favour. In particular it
remained sensitive to rape or sexual assault except
when this was committed by enemy forces. Early in
1944 the BBFC had to deal with The Lodger (TCF, 1943-
4, dir John Brahm). This was a remake of the 1926
Hitchcock film, but with the crucial difference in
the plot that the sinister lodger (Laird Cregar)
turns out to be the real Jack the Ripper instead of
an innocent suspect. The print submitted to the
BBFC, the full version, was cut on 7 February 1944 by
325 feet, a very large cut indeed for the Second
World War years. For all their retreats from their
pre-war positions on a variety of topics, neither the
Hays Office nor the BBFC would permit any overt reference to prostitution during the war. This can be
clearly seen in The Woman in the Window (International, 1944, dir Fritz Lang), passed uncut in Britain on
22 December 1944. This is the tale of an unwordly
criminology professor (Edward G. Robinson) who stays
behind at home while his wife and son go on holiday
and who becomes innocently involved with a girl (Joan
Bennett) and kills her rich boy friend in self-
defence. The girl's occupation is never referred to,
but her style of dress and the luxury of her flat
indicate wealth. The dead man turns out to be a rich
tycoon who has conducted his liaison with the girl
under an assumed name. There appears to be no
personal affection between them, the implication
that he has been visiting her as a high class call
girl being very strong.

In the war's closing stages the BBFC was confronted with a scenario for The Wicked Lady

(Gainsborough, 1945, dir Leslie Arliss). A 17th
century noblewoman, Lady Skelton (Margaret Lockwood),
befriends a highwayman (James Mason) and becomes his
mistress and accomplice. In attempting to avert
discovery of her secret life she suffocates an
elderly faithful family servant (Felix Aylmer) with
a pillow. The film in essence was a star vehicle for
Margaret Lockwood, enabling her to exploit further
the image of the merciless upper class villainess she
had already created in The Man in Grey. However, in
the relationship between the aristocrat and the highwayman there was a strong suggestion of illicit sin,
to which the female sexual urge was making at least
an equal contribution. In the scenario the theme of
the sexually disloyal, ruthless femme fatale concerned Mrs Crouzet far less than a projected scene involving a scene of sexual double entendre between three
groomsmen. She decided to consult Brooke
Wilkinson,36 whereas before the war she would almost
certainly have rejected such a theme and scene out of
hand. Although in the event this dubious scene was
not included in the final version submitted to the
BBFC, The Wicked Lady was allowed without cuts on 7
November 1945.
The BBFC scenarios for 1940 were lost when
bombing destroyed Carlisle House in May 1941, while
those for January to May 1941 may be incomplete.
Just fewer than 140 scenarios remain for 1941 to 1945
inclusive compared to over 100 for each year after
1932 except 1938 (95) and 1939 (69). Indeed for 1936
there were more than 150. The 140 scenarios of 1941-
5 include some American and unmade features. Many of
the most acclaimed British Second World War films do
not appear among the 140 which represent a minority
of the British films produced and only a tiny fract-
ion of the total number of feature films shown in
Britain from September 1939 to August 1945. No
precise record of MoI cuts to feature films has yet
emerged or now seems likely to emerge. The surviving
BBFC registers give an indication of which features
were cut, while an examination of the films themselves in combination with the BBFC registers tentatively suggests that the war greatly accelerated the
pre-war erosion of BBFC values in feature film content. However, those values were never completely
abandoned, no matter how drastically times had
changed at the BBFC through new political and social
developments in both Britain and the United States.
The wartime adaptability and apparent growing lib-
eralism at the BBFC has also to be considered in the
context of the diminishing amount of footage viewed

per annum due to reduced film output. In 1938, the
last full year of peace, the BBFC had viewed just
over six million feet of film. This figure had
dropped by approximately one million during 1939. It
dropped further to between four and four and a half
million in 1940, 1941 and 1942. Less than four
million feet were viewed in 1943, 1944 and 1945. Between 1948 and the mid-1950s the figure was to rise
again to more than five million. Under the economic
circumstances of a progressively shrinking footage
and the loss of spacious premises after May 1941 the
BBFC, which used viewing facilities provided by the
film production companies located in Soho for the
rest of the war, was unlikely to have applied its
pre-war standards as strictly as it might have
wished.
     Of course the BBFC was hamstrung to a large
extent by the impact of the war on film production in
Britain and the United States, by the political need
for Anglo-American and Anglo-Soviet collaboration and
by the influence of the war on public film tastes in
Britain. The MoI censorship files demonstrate beyond
doubt that many American and British film companies
dealt direct with the MoI both prior to and during
production rather than with the BBFC. It even seems
possible that some British features might have received unofficial MoI financial backing or that
official interest proved a prelude to financial investment in prestige propaganda productions from
influential film personalities like J. Arthur Rank.
At the same time it is plain that MoI records do not
reveal the whole censorship picture, for The Life and
Death of Colonel Blimp affair (see p. 131) does not
appear anywhere in the MoI film censorship files.
However, on the whole BBFC and MoI documentation
indicates that serious wartime wrangles over feature
film censorship either between the BBFC and the MoI
or between either of them and film companies or other
outside bodies, including the local authorities, were
few and far between. Whatever Brendan Bracken as
Minister of Information after mid-1941 might have
achieved overall, so far as film censorship was
concerned he simply inherited a system evolved in
substance before the war. After initial teething
troubles once the war began it was already function-
ing smoothly through Sir John Reith's MoI reorganisation before Bracken arrived at the MoI.

Chapter 6

THE AMERICAN CONNECTION AND A BRITISH PERSPECTIVE,
1907-1950

From the years immediately prior to 1914 British
cinema screens have been dominated by American productions, American censorship thus being bound to
have a crucial influence on British censorship. As
the cinema emerged as a major communication medium
in American cities, the same concern with the content
of movies appeared as in Britain. In November 1907
the Chicago City Council passed the United States's
first film censorship law, the constitutionality of
which was upheld in the Illinois Supreme Court. As
the result of official hostility in New York City,
the New York Association of Motion Picture Exhibitors
in March 1909 created a citizens committee to view
all films due to be shown in New York State in
advance of public exhibition. This body of worthies
developed into the National Board of Censorship of
Motion Pictures, renamed the National Board of Review
of Motion Pictures in 1915. It possessed no legal
standing, neither distributors, exhibitors nor producers being under any legal obligation to submit
films for censorship. The board did not have the
power to decide whether or not any film should be
shown but instead compiled a weekly bulletin which
classified films as 'passed', 'passed with changes as
specified' or 'condemned'. This was sent to 450
'collaborators' in more than 300 American towns and
cities. In theory the National Board banned eight
subjects - obscenity; vulgarity verging towards
indecency; representation of crime in detail which
could be copied except where this was given as a
warning to the public; morbid scenes of crime; unnecessary elaboration or prolongation of scenes of
suffering, brutality, vulgarity, violence or crime;
blasphemy; libel and questions of fact in criminal
cases yet to come before the courts; scenes which,
because of subtle elements, have a deteriorating

tendency on the basic moralities or necessary social
standards.[1]
     However, the establishment of the National Board
in New York City failed in its prime objective, to
avert official state censorships. In 1911 Pennsylvania passed the first state film censorship law,
Kansas and Ohio following suit in 1913, measures
which in themselves showed that National Board
rulings did not command universal confidence, but on
the other hand state censorship was very much the
exception rather than the rule. To a large extent
the American film industry had staved off the threat
of official censorship, which was probably the overriding influence on the British film industry's
overtures in 1912 to the Home Office for the creation
of the BBFC. Events in Britain possibly had some
influence on censorship in the United States, for in
August 1913 New York City appointed a licence commissioner for cinemas ostensibly to enforce building
and fire safety regulations. But in practice he was
soon using his powers to control film content,[2] much
as some British local authorities had latched on to
the 1909 Cinematograph Act for the same purpose.
     From its inception in 1913 the BBFC was called
upon to perform an onerous if not impossible task.
On the one hand it sought to protect the film industry from an official censorship, while on the other
it wished to allow the industry as much latitude and
artistic licence as possible to promote cinematic
growth. On occasions, due to the activities of
vociferous pressure groups or local authorities or
both, these two fundamental functions were to prove
irreconcilable, the BBFC being compelled to show
undue favour to one function or the other. In the
years before the First World War it is hard to
estimate how well-founded was the British film
industry's fear of a central government censorship,
but the danger was unquestionably real. However, it
was not until 1915 that the first unsuccessful
attempt took place in the American Congress to create
a federal film censorship. There were several
further efforts made in this direction before 1921,
while Maryland joined Kansas, Ohio and Pennsylvania
in forming a legal state censorship body. No doubt
American events played an intangible part in the
formation of the abortive 1916 Samuel proposals for
an official British government censorship. From
these only the fortuitous fall of the Asquith coalition government in December rescued the BBFC. By
July 1916 the National Board of Review had fallen so
far into American disfavour for its liberal rulings

that American directors and producers decided to
form the National Association of the Motion Picture
Industry (NAMPI) with a self-censorship programme of
eleven basic points[3] which were not far removed in
substance from O'Connor's 43 rules of 1917 in
Britain. Under his guidance from 1917 to 1929, ably
supported by Brooke Wilkinson's liaison with government departments during and after the First World
War, the BBFC gradually won over the Home Office
bureaucracy and Home Secretaries as varied in political outlook as the reactionary Conservative
Joynson-Hicks and Labour's Clynes. However, this
development came about only by degrees, for during
the war, against a background of rising cinema attendances in both Britain and the United States, there
had been a flood of American features with crime,
drugs and erotic content which the NAMPI code of July
1916 had failed to dam up.
    This trend continued after the war. The result
was a renewed pressure for stricter censorship in
both Britain and the United States. The crucial
years were 1920 and 1921 when a series of Hollywood
'scandals', played up by the sensationalist press,
included the Arbuckle case, the unsolved murder of
British director William Dean Taylor and the marriage
of Douglas Fairbanks Senior to Mary Pickford. A
marriage might seem an unexceptionable event by any
social standards, but this one involved Mary
Pickford's divorce from her first husband, which the
Attorney General of Nevada had unsuccessfully tried
to invalidate, thus ensuring much press coverage.
Such off-screen occurrences generated almost 100
censorship bills covering 37 states during 1921 alone
when even previously liberal New York State set up an
official state censorship. Against this American
background O'Connor and Brooke Wilkinson trod warily
during the early 1920s until the American censorship
position was clarified. The first major step in this
direction came in December 1921 when film industry
representatives approached Will H. Hays, President
Warren Harding's Postmaster-General then about to
resign, to ask him to become the head of a new organisation to replace NAMPI. Hays accepted the offer,
NAMPI being superseded by the Motion Picture Producers and Distributors Association (MPPDA) of America
in March 1922. Hays assumed the mantle of film
industry protector from censorship at a time when
cinema attendances in the United States were in
decline. As he saw matters the industry was faced
with self-censorship or external suppression. He
probably assessed the situation correctly, for by

1922 the number of states with censorship laws had
risen to seven and there was the prospect of one more
in Massachusetts if a referendum during that year
voted in favour of a censorship law already passed
by the state legislature. In the referendum campaign
the MPPDA came out against censorship, which was
rejected by the Massachusetts voters. After this
result censorship bills failed in three other states
during 1922 and in 24 more states by 1925. However,
movement was not all in one direction, for in 1923
and again in 1924 the Governor of New York State
failed to gain the repeal of the state censorship
law. From 1922 to 1927, the golden years of the so-
called Jazz Age when many in both Britain and the
United States blamed films for supposed moral
decline, no fewer than 45 film censorship bills were
introduced into various state legislatures, although
all were defeated.[4] Furthermore, one pressure group
lobbied sufficiently energetically to have a federal
censorship bill introduced into the House of Representatives in 1926, but the indirect intervention of
President Calvin Coolidge killed it at committee
stage.[5] Nevertheless Hays's work at the MPPDA was
impressive enough to ensure that the pro-censorship
pressures in the United States gained no further
ground before the coming of sound.

In September 1923 Hays visited Britain and met
O'Connor as well as leading figures in the British
film industry who evidently made no secret of their
dislike of American domination in the British film
market. Hays concluded from these contacts that his
efforts in the United States were of equal importance
for Britain,[6] and it was no mere coincidence when
shortly afterwards, in February 1924, the MPPDA endeavoured to tighten up its censorship procedures.
It was proposed that each studio should submit to the
MPPDA a synopsis of every book, play and story it was
considering for a film, whereupon MPPDA would advise
non-acceptance where appropriate. The MPPDA members
in June 1924 undertook not to produce films which
included excessive drinking, vulgar speech in the
sub-titles and illicit sex, but observance was
optional and no MPPDA machinery existed for enforce-
ment. None the less criticisms of films died down in
the United States during the mid-1920s, but pressures
for a stricter American censorship never completely
disappeared any more than they did in Britain at the
same period.

By 1927 the MPPDA rules of 1924 had been
complied with sufficiently well to ease the work of
the BBFC and permit more liberal decisions, although

148

even in the early 1920s the BBFC had taken risks in
this respect and by so doing incurred a certain
amount of local authority odium. In fact the BBFC
pursued a more liberal policy throughout the entire
inter-war period than a reading of its published
annual reports might lead one to suppose. At times
the gap between what was shown on the screen to
British audiences and the general tone of the reports
was very wide. Indeed it is conceivable that the
reports were to a certain extent a public relations
exercise designed to foster the impression that the
BBFC was more conservative than in reality in order
to ward off critical local authorities and a variety
of right-wing pressure groups. Between 1924 and 1927
Hays and the BBFC in combination had shaped a censorship structure for Britain which was settling down as
an acceptable compromise between conflicting views
when declining cinema attendances in the United
States threatened to undo their work. The MPPDA
members became steadily less co-operative. Even
before the great slump of October 1929 less than half
of them were observing the 1924 rules based on
'don'ts and be carefuls' and only about one fifth of
the film scripts were submitted to the MPPDA in
advance.[7] Competition between the Hollywood studios
grew very cut-throat, which largely explains the by-
passing of the BBFC over King of Kings in the latter
part of 1927 because of the BBFC's long established
practice of banning the materialisation of Christ and
excluding religious ceremonies from all films.
Recently fortified by the quota system, the British
companies too became caught up in the film rat race,
as demonstrated by Wilcox's exceptional persistence
in defying the BBFC over Dawn during early 1928.
This affair, when O'Connor's political judgment for
once deserted him, might well have undone all of his
and Brooke Wilkinson's previous efforts if it had not
taken place so close to the sound revolution. As it
was a combination of the two events, coupled with the
advent of the great slump and O'Connor's near simultaneous death in November 1929, provided the occasion
for a revival of strong pressure in the direction of
a government-controlled film censorship for Britain.
     The renewed growth of the American film industry
from 1927 to 1930 generated by the talkies produced
new script writers who were unfamiliar with the MPPDA
guidelines of 1924. Studios also scrambled among
themselves to acquire Broadway stage successes which
before sound would have been considered as unsuitable
for the screen. Finally the slump intensified the
competition among the large production companies

during the early 1930s as unemployment rose and
cinema attendances again declined. The outcome was
the virtual destruction of the MPPDA 1924 rules within the United States and in consequence much greater
difficulties for the BBFC, posed by a stream of films
which particularly emphasised gangsterism, sex and
violence. The British production companies were of
course also by no means immune from the effects of
economic hardship, but the slump hit Britain with
less force than the United States and cinema attendances continued to rise during the early sound
period. However, the BBFC at the outset of Shortt's
presidency in 1929 found itself once more at the
centre of domestic film politics, just as the Hays
Office was in the United States. There early in 1930
Martin Quigley, a major film trade paper publisher,
and the Reverend Daniel A. Lord, who had acted as a
technical adviser to Cecil B. De Mille on King of
Kings, drew up a new code of practice for the MPPDA.
They were both Roman Catholics who first submitted
their ideas to Hays before further transmission to
the studios. This new code, to be known as the
Production Code, was agreed to in April 1930 and came
into operation in January 1931 when its Catholic
origins were hidden from the American public. MPPDA
members were now supposed to submit all film scripts
in advance of production. After the Hays Office had
passed a script, with or without suggested modifications, it viewed the completed print, but no penalty
for non-compliance by members was laid down. It was
no accident that the first pre-production scenario
submitted to the BBFC arrived in November 1930, so
soon after the new American experiment had been
mooted.
    The new code considerably extended that of 1924
in detail along the lines of the 1926 BBFC codification,[8] but as box office receipts in the United
States continued to drop as a result of the ever
deepening slump - attendances plunged from 100
millions a week in 1930 to 60 millions in 1932 and by
early 1933 approximately one third of all American
cinemas open in 1930 had closed[9] - producers turned a
blind eye to or evaded the 1930 code more and more.
Despite the box office success of horror and gangster
films, many studios faced bankruptcy late in 1932.
Until then official American censorship bodies had
been more concerned about crime and brutality than
sex, but in the early days of the slump women in
screen life increasingly resorted to prostitution
and the 'fallen woman' image became more commonplace.
Even Greta Garbo portrayed such a figure in Anna

Christie (MGM, 1930, dir Clarence Brown), but what
transformed the female character on celluloid were
the Jean Harlow and Mae West star vehicles of 1932-3.
Red Dust, _She Done Him Wrong_, _I'm No Angel_, _Red-
Headed Woman_ and _Bombshell_ were all produced within a
year between late 1932 and late 1933 when the American film industry's financial crisis was at its most
acute. Never before had the woman who enjoyed her
sexuality without guilt been portrayed so boldly, a
sexual image that soon aroused the wrath of religious
groups in general and the American Roman Catholic
hierarchy in particular. Shortly after the New York
City release of _She Done Him Wrong_, the sauciest of
the five films, Catholic periodicals attacked the
film industry. In October 1933, by which time _Red-
Headed Woman_ had also been released, the presidential
address to the National Council of Catholic Women
declared that films 'are a menace to the physical,
mental and moral welfare of the nation...'.10 This
grave charge was soon taken up in public by the
Catholic higher clergy, and in November 1933 a conference of the American Catholic bishops in Washington
DC demanded the complete overhaul of the 1930 code
and appointed a film committee to study the situation.
      These events formed the prelude to the formation
by the Catholic bishops' committee of the Legion of
Decency in April 1934. The Legion's members were
invited to sign a pledge 'to rid the country of its
greatest menace - the salacious moving picture'.11
In practice Legion policy was to persuade Catholics
and non-Catholics to boycott both films which the
bishops' committee labelled offensive and the cinemas
where such films were shown. This was a shrewd
effort to strike at the American film industry where
it hurt most, the box office. Ten million American
Catholics signed the Legion's pledge. Catholics
represented some 20 per cent of the American population, and most lived in the heavy industrial urban
areas where there were many cinemas. Moreover,
Catholics in important foreign markets like Italy and
Spain comprised a much higher percentage of the population, while in any case the Legion's campaign was
supported by both American Jewish and Protestant
groups. Similar support abroad might have far-reaching repercussions. The very existence of the American film industry was at stake, the Legion relenting
in June 1934 only when the MPPDA promised to put
teeth into its 1930 code and make it fully effective.
The result was provision for a 25,000 dollars fine on
MPPDA members who released any film without a MPPDA

certificate and seal of approval. No cinema controlled by a MPPDA member was allowed to book a film
which lacked the seal of approval. These two main
provisions came into immediate effect, while a
Catholic, Joseph Breen, took over the MPPDA's Production Code Administration (PCA), which gave him much
the same position as Brooke Wilkinson enjoyed at the
BBFC. Under this new régime the Hays Office swiftly
brought recalcitrant studios into line, although the
Legion remained in existence to ensure the continuing
effectiveness of the 1934 code. These American developments had considerably facilitated the BBFC's task
over the talkies by the time Hays himself came to
Britain in December 1936 at the end of a European
tour. Then he met Tyrrell to confer about PCA religious policy in the aftermath of the BBFC's controversial decision to allow The Green Pastures.[12]
     Breen's strong control over the PCA was most
welcome at the BBFC, for even before the emergence of
sound Hollywood films had been arousing the concern
of British pressure groups. From the end of 1927
the London Public Morality Council, a body with a
strong ecclesiastical element, had been in contact
with Hays to have film prints changed for British
audiences before the films arrived in Britain.[13]
Whether for this reason or because of PCA contacts
with the BBFC, the American studios had altered many
of their productions when these were sent to Britain
by 1931.[14] In the early sound era public pressures
had mounted from both right and left for a committee
of enquiry into the structure of British film censorship. The LPMC complaints about some films passed by
the BBFC were supported by the Birmingham branch of
the National Council of Women which after July 1930
allied itself with the Birmingham Cinema Enquiry
Committee in bringing pressure to bear on Clynes and
the Home Office. At the same time a number of MPs,
mostly Labour and Liberal, had formed themselves into
the Parliamentary Films Committee, with Labour MP
Ellen Wilkinson as its Secretary, which sent a deputation to Clynes on 15 July 1930 when the BBFC's list
of banned subjects was described to Clynes as a serious infraction of political liberty.[15] The deputation's basic objective was to press upon Clynes the
need for an enquiry into film censorship because the
existing system was felt to be unduly restrictive.
Already the Parliamentary Films Committee had made
direct representations to the LCC on 19 March 1930 to
plead for private film societies to be allowed to
screen uncensored films.[16]
     The Home Office was fundamentally opposed to any

change in film censorship, but as Clynes had come under increasing pressure from both sides during the first half of 1931 he had felt obliged to give ground in the shape of the Film Censorship Consultative Committee. By the time he left the Home Office in August 1931 he had paved the way for this new body, although it was left to his successor, Sir Herbert Samuel, to establish the committee formally in November 1931. Since 1916 Samuel had become more liberal in his attitude to films, and he was a regular attender of Film Society shows in London as well as a member of the Parliamentary Films Committee. Indeed he was a part of the deputation to Clynes of 15 July when he had insisted that there should be no political censorship of films.[17] However, the Film Censorship Consultative Committee turned out to be a concession of shadow rather than substance despite its domination by the local authorities. The committee held seven meetings from November 1931 to October 1932 but recommended no reforms to the Home Office during that time and did not meet again before its replacement by the Cinematograph Advisory Council in 1938. Its solitary tangible achievement was the introduction of the advisory 'H' certificate for horror films early in 1933 following LCC and Surrey County Council complaints about the BBFC decision to pass Frankenstein.[18]

After the installation of sound apparatus at the BBFC in January 1930 all four censors could no longer view each film. The sheer number of films, and often as important the time consumed in viewing again - frequently necessary and sometimes more than once - due to the technical aspects involved, meant that a consistent application of and full central control over BBFC policy within the BBFC itself was virtually impossible. It was only when the BBFC moved from Wardour Street to Carlisle House late in 1936 that it became possible for the censors to view different films simultaneously.[19] Thus during the first half of the 1930s, a dangerous time for the BBFC, much had to be left to the discretion of the individual censors of necessity. Moreover, the Film Censorship Consultative Committee was not empowered to view films before release but could only react to BBFC decisions or to complaints concerning those decisions laid before it by local authorities or private citizens. Shortt, Tyrrell and Brooke Wilkinson were then obliged to defend BBFC decisions against criticism or confess ineptitude. Even the authoritarian instincts of Brooke Wilkinson and Hanna could not entirely overlook the influence on the censors' morale of having their rulings too often overthrown by external influences. How far the very existence of the Film Censorship Consultative Committee, which could always have been reactivated from 1933 to 1938, shaped BBFC policy in practice must remain a matter for conjecture on present evidence. The very large number of banned films during Shortt's brief presidency might indicate equally the contemporary ineffectiveness of American censorship from 1930 to 1934, his own personal prejudice against sound films, his fear of Consultative Committee reaction if there were too many protests against the BBFC or the overcaution of the censors in the face of unfamiliar technical developments and the consequent conversion of the cinema in Britain into indisputably the most important mass medium of communication. Tyrrell was singularly fortunate during the early years of his presidency in that the emergence of the Legion of Decency in the United States during 1934 had brought about a more effectual American censorship and greatly simplified the BBFC's function.

However, Tyrrell was unlucky in the same period that the expansionist policies of Germany, Italy and Japan broke down the British internal consensus on foreign policy that had prevailed between the Locarno treaties of 1925 and the rise of Hitler. He was doubly unlucky in that his appointment as BBFC President coincided with the general election of November 1935 when Labour, after near obliteration in the election of October 1931, resurrected itself as a credible alternative to the National government. As the international climate deteriorated thereafter and the likelihood of war in Europe increased, so the temperature of British domestic politics rose correspondingly. As a result the BBFC in the late 1930s became the subject of Opposition attacks and was regarded in such quarters virtually as an unofficial branch of government. Although understandable in the light of the BBFC published annual reports, this attitude was in fact erroneous, but under growing pressure after 1938 from both the British studios, which sought to capitalise on a renewed quota system, and from the Opposition Labour and Liberal parties the BBFC decided to allow topics previously deemed prohibitive. This even extended in some degree to foreign affairs, the most glaring instance being the decision in the summer of 1939 to pass the highly committed anti-Nazi Confessions of a Nazi Spy. How far this new peacetime approach would have penetrated the BBFC in the long run cannot be judged because the Second World War intervened at too early a stage of

its evolution and created fresh social conditions
which militated against the pre-1938 censorship
principles.

During the war the BBFC was relatively impotent,
great dents being inflicted upon the pre-1938 rules.
It is arguable that this simply reflected the new
BBFC policy of the late 1930s or that more radical
changes were inevitable due to the war itself and the
ensuing new political and social situation. When the
war ended in August 1945, the top brass of the BBFC
had been in harness for some time, all were on the
wrong side of 70 and comparatively rapid personnel
changes were inevitable during the immediate post-war
years. The extant scenarios of 1945-7 and the first
half of 1949 suggest that the BBFC staff was divided
over the wartime developments, and that initially
some BBFC members sought to recover a part of the
lost ground or at least not to surrender any more.
On the other hand some allowed films themselves point
in an opposite direction and also indicate that the
British studios were not going to abandon their wartime reputation for new found realism without a
fight. The advent of the first majority Labour gov-
erment under Clement Attlee in July 1945 introduced
an atmosphere of radical reform into British society,
which in itself partly accounted for the bolder British challenge to the BBFC which occurred from 1945 to
the early 1950s. The British film industry was also
anxious to expand during the post-war boom period in
entertainments generally, while the Attlee government
was concerned about the adverse influence on Britain's balance of payments of American film imports.
A large British customs duty on American films in
August 1947 during an acute balance of payments
crisis led the American studios into a boycott of the
British market which lasted until May 1948. This un-
expected development opened up the British market to
dubious French films (by pre-1938 standards) and simultaneously encouraged British producers to greater
efforts now more noteworthy for quantity than
quality.

The Attlee administration was pledged to the establishment of the welfare state along the broad lines
of the 1942 Beveridge report and to the wholesale
nationalisation of key industries. Privilege was to
come under attack via the philosophy of equality or
equality of opportunity for the British lower classes. Unemployment was reduced to miniscule proport-
ions by pre-war standards on a wave of new large-
scale government expenditure, but British economic
decline and dependence upon American capital was

highlighted by the 1949 devaluation of the pound
sterling. The post-war entertainments boom reached
its climax in 1946 until its virtual disappearance by
1950. It was kindled by the phased-out demobilisat-
ion of the armed forces and the readiness of almost
everyone to seek personal enjoyment as a pent up
escape route from wartime rigours and discipline.
Crime flourished in the shape of the so-called 'black
market', when scarce or rationed commodities changed
hands at inflated prices. The figure of the 'spiv',
obtainer and seller of such goods while wartime rationing remained in force until 1954, became the tar-
get of official and press hostility, not to mention
public contempt. Petty crime and violence also increased. These often involved juvenile offenders,
although this feature was exaggerated in the public
mind through sensationalist press coverage of a
number of particularly ghastly murder cases by the
standards of the time. The double sex murderer Heath
was executed in October 1946, the Soho shooting of
Alec de Antiquis led to the execution of three men
under 23 in September 1947 and acid bath murderer
Haigh was executed in August 1949 after a prolonged
trial. However, when the Commons in April 1948 on a
free vote suspended capital punishment for five years
as an experiment, the Lords and some vociferous public disquiet soon compelled the abandonment of the
measure. Moreover, marriage as an institution came
under strain as wartime marriages entered into in
haste under extraordinary conditions collapsed under
peacetime routine and pre-war marriages resumed after
a long period of separation. Many women were no
longer willing merely to be housebound wives and
mothers when women had frequently worked hard in outside employment and earned money during the war. The
pre-war, essentially middle class sexual conventions
with their strong emphasis upon stable marriage did
not simply slot back into place after a temporary
disruption. For all these reasons the divorce rate
in the late 1940s rose to then unprecedented heights.
To a large extent the immediate post-war British
social scene was still in evidence when the Conservatives regained office in October 1951. Television
as a challenge to the cinema as the chief medium of
communication to the masses was then only in its
infancy, for in 1950 British television licences
numbered less than 500,000, whereas by 1955 the
figure had risen to some four and a half millions.
        Overseas Britain's main concerns were the four-
power (Britain, France, the Soviet Union and the
United States) occupation of Germany pending a final

peace treaty with Germany, as agreed at the Potsdam
conference of July 1945, and the future of the British Commonwealth. In August 1947 Britain commenced
what grew into a full-scale withdrawal from imperial
commitments over the next two decades when she
granted independence to India and Pakistan. This
relatively spontaneous decision entailed the complete
removal of British troops and, together with a deteriorating economy, probably influenced the Labour
government later in the same year to hand over the
British League of Nations mandate in Palestine to the
United Nations by 15 May 1948. In Palestine after
1945 there had emerged a Jewish terrorist campaign
against British troops, spearheaded by fanatical
Zionists, while Britain strove to prevent further
Jewish immigration from Europe in order not to exac-
erbate deteriorating relations with the Arab population. However, the Zionists' most potent weapon was
the full revelation of the Nazi extermination policy
against the Jews and other concentration camp atrocities. These were to produce in Britain in the years
immediately after 1945 a deeper anti-German revulsion
than had existed during the Second World War itself,
a sentiment kept alive until well into 1947 by numer-
ous war crimes trials, especially those of the Nazi
leaders at Nuremberg. Such a development virtually
guaranteed continued widespread British sympathy for
that portion of European Jewry which had escaped the
Hitlerian genocide and which was trying to enter
Palestine illegally in defiance of British policy.
British efforts to defuse Arab-Jewish tension within
Palestine, which included the execution of a few
condemned Jewish terrorists, were widely misunder-
stood, especially in the United States. There
President Harry Truman, coming up for re-election
within a year, brought pressure on Britain to abandon
her opposition to the creation of a Jewish national
home within Palestine.
    However, by the end of 1947 American-Soviet and
Anglo-Soviet relations came increasingly under
strain. From 1945 the western allies had been in
control of western Germany and the Soviets of eastern
Germany, while Berlin had been divided on the same
basis. This was meant to be a temporary arrangement
pending ultimate German reunification, but after the
war the victorious allies could not agree about
Germany's future. What was to crystallise into the
'cold war' broke out into the open in 1948 when the
Soviets attempted to isolate the American, British
and French occupation zones in West Berlin. Air
relief saved West Berlin from a possible Soviet

occupation, but the crisis had hardened attitudes on both sides. The outcome was the division of not only Germany but also much of Europe into two armed camps. The reunification of Germany and a definitive peace treaty were indefinitely postponed, although the western allies went on to form their occupation zones into the German Federal Republic while the Soviets reacted by establishing the German Democratic Republic in eastern Germany. Anglo-American concern at the Soviet 'threat' intensified with first the explosion of a Soviet atomic device to counter the nuclear weaponry of the United States and then the almost instantaneous emergence of Communist China in October 1949. In both Britain and the United States the latter event was often regarded, quite incorrectly, as the work of the Soviet Union. Against this background the immediate post-war allied hostility to all Germans in Britain gradually gave way to wider political considerations. By October 1951, when Churchill returned to Downing Street, the 'cold war' was an established fact of international life.

At the end of the war the MoI was disbanded, the BBFC and the local authorities resuming their pre-war dominant censorship position. Tyrrell was now close to 80, while both Brooke Wilkinson and Hanna were well past 70. Mrs Crouzet remained as a scrutineer of scenarios, and of the September 1939 censors Baker, Fleetwood-Wilson and Madge Kitchener were still serving. Since the BBFC practice of publishing annual reports was never to be resumed after 1945, the BBFC code was no longer open to parliamentary and public criticism as it had been before the war. Hence the extant scenarios for 1945-9 (with 1948 missing), in combination with the films themselves of course, assume a key importance in assessing immediate post-war BBFC policies.

The evidence from the scenarios for late 1945 sometimes points in opposite directions and suggests a certain ambivalence at the BBFC derived from the war. For instance, Hanna in October 1945 came down decisively against Green for Danger (Rank-Individual Films, 1946, dir Sidney Gilliatt), the story of patients who die mysteriously on the operating table in a military hospital during 1944 when the murderess turns out to be a nurse (Rosamund John), whereas Mrs Crouzet took no exception to the main theme. However, she recommended that operating theatre scenes did not infringe established BBFC standards, and that the nurse should not deny morphia to patients.[20] As ever, religion proved a touchy subject which, however, had caused the BBFC no real problems during the

war. To judge from the box office success of The
Song of Bernadette (TCF, 1943, dir Henry King), Going
My Way (Paramount, 1944, dir Leo McCarey) and The
Keys of the Kingdom, the war had engendered a religious revival in Britain despite the fact that in each
of these films the central figure was a Roman
Catholic. None of these features had been placed in
a Second World War setting, but religion had been
utilised as justification for the allied cause in
such misleading titles as God is My Co-Pilot, a
routine war drama allowed in full without a title
change at the BBFC on 29 May 1945. By contrast the
near-sacrilegious approach of Major Barbara had made
no tangible adverse impact on public opinion. This
Shavian work concerns the daughter (Dame Wendy
Hiller) of a millionaire armaments manufacturer
(Robert Morley). She joins the Salvation Army out of
idealism but resigns when it accepts a donation from
her father, whereupon he taunts her with the famous
line, 'What price salvation now?' In this wartime
context the BBFC in December 1945 had to consider a
MGM scenario for Risen Soldier. Hanna was in
hospital at the time, so that Mrs Crouzet was free to
comment on the scenario alone. She believed the subject to be prohibitive on the ground that there were
New Testament incidents, and that to parallel Mary's
maternal sufferings after the crucifixion of Jesus
with the similar sufferings of a dead American air-
man's mother after a bombing raid on Rumania would
cause offence. She consulted Tyrrell and Brooke
Wilkinson, who agreed that the film could be produced
if Jesus did not appear and the theme was reverently
handled. MGM was notified in this sense on 12
December 1945, when the BBFC recommended cuts, all
but one of which dealt with the religious content.[21]
It seems as though the film was never made, but the
reaction to the scenario indicates that on this subject at least the BBFC assumed that the war had not
changed public attitudes.
    The films passed late in 1945 also suggest BBFC
inconsistency. One of the year's largest cuts was
imposed on The Fallen Angel (TCF, 1945, dir Otto
Preminger), the tale of a husband who intends to
murder his wife in order to marry another woman.
Instead the latter herself is murdered. This potentially humdrum crime melodrama is saved from cinematic
obscurity by strong direction and the sleazy American
small town atmosphere, but BBFC cuts on 21 November
1945 amounted to 276 feet or three minutes running
time. On the other hand the BBFC on 23 August 1945
allowed The Lost Week End (Paramount, 1945, dir Billy

Wilder) which narrates two drunken days in the life
of an alcoholic author (Ray Milland). This was the
first time that dipsomania as a central theme had
been allowed in British cinemas. Equally daring
against the background of real post-war marital
instability was Brief Encounter (Cineguild, 1945, dir
David Lean), the British film approved at scenario
stage while the war was still in progress and passed
uncut on 28 September 1945. This was the first film
which dealt with middle-aged love outside the con-
fines of marriage in its story of a middle class
housewife (Dame Celia Johnson) who meets a married
local doctor (Trevor Howard) on one of her weekly
shopping expeditions to the local town. They fall in
love, but the affair is physically unconsummated before he goes to Africa permanently in order to
preserve his marriage. Duties and responsibilities
to others ultimately triumph over sexual desire and
emotion, but had the ending been otherwise, the BBFC
might not have been so tolerant of Sir Noel Coward's
current, socially explosive topic.

The election of the Attlee government had rendered pre-war radical politics on film less controversial. As a result Soviet features, newsreels and
documentaries continued to be shown in Britain until
well into 1946, although in the main these were
either culturally and politically innocuous or
strongly anti-Nazi. Examples in late 1945 or 1946
were Zoya (USSR, 1944, dir Lev Arnshtam), Girl No.
217 (USSR, 1944, dir Mikhail Romm), Soviet Sport,
The End of an Aggressor and Hello Moscow. Such
films, coupled with the four-match soccer tour of
Britain by Moscow Dynamo towards the end of 1945 and
the mere existence of a Labour government, conspired
to perpetuate the illusion that a new era in Anglo-
Soviet relations had dawned. Attacks on social privilege along semi-Communist lines were now in accordance with the will of the Commons. The BBFC
adjusted accordingly, most evidently in its decision
of 11 October 1945 to allow in full The Rake's
Progress (GFD-Individual, 1945, dir Sidney Gilliatt).
This British film charts the reckless career of an
upper class playboy (Rex Harrison) during the 1930s.
He is eventually responsible for the death of his
father (Sir Godfrey Tearle), after which his remorse
leads to his own death from personal heroism in the
war's closing stages. Cloaked in a veneer of comedy
and personal melodrama, the film is in effect an
obituary notice for the pre-1939 upper class. As
such it would have experienced the utmost difficulty
in getting through the BBFC before 1938.

THE AMERICAN CONNECTION AND A BRITISH PERSPECTIVE

Early in 1946 Mrs Crouzet became an ordinary
censor and Madge Kitchener took over her duties on
scenarios. As the year progressed the BBFC settled
down into something like its pre-war routine until
Hanna left the BBFC in the closing months, although
a lack of permanent premises until the move into the
present offices at 3 Soho Square in 1950 proved to be
a handicap. None the less even Hanna realised that
changes would be inevitable due to the war and post-
war conditions, which for example is clear from a
scenario entitled Rope. Submitted on 2 January 1946,
it was based on a successful play by Patrick Hamilton
and eventually converted into a film more than two
years later (Transatlantic, 1948, dir Sir Alfred
Hitchcock). The story concerns two homosexuals who
murder a friend and conceal the corpse in a trunk,
but Hanna in 1946 raised no objection to the fundamental theme whereas when a similar scenario had been
submitted in March 1943 he had declared, 'I can find
no reason for saying that this play is unfit for rep-
roduction, but I cannot see what good purpose it can
serve.'[22] At that time Mrs Crouzet had condemned
Rope out of hand.[23] Other January 1946 scenarios
reveal that by then Hanna was ready to accept organised crime in Britain and child illegitimacy as
suitable screen subjects.[24]
    Caravan (Gainsborough, 1946, dir Arthur
Crabtree) demonstrates as vividly as any feature the
challenging mood of the post-war British film
industry to the pre-1938 BBFC code. This now justi-
fiably little remembered period melodrama, based on a
novel by the authoress of The Man in Grey, Lady
Eleanor Smith, covers the mission in Spain of a young
man (Stewart Granger) who is attacked by the agents
of his rival (Dennis Price) for the hand of a young
lady (Anne Crawford). Left for dead, the young man
is saved by a gipsy girl (Jean Kent) who falls in
love with him before he returns to good health and
gains subsequent revenge for his maltreatment. Realistic brutality is impressed on the audience from
the very beginning when Granger fights robbers in a
London back street and in the process bangs one
robber's head against a wall several times, while the
climax sees Granger whip Price full across the face
to produce a deep scar. In between viewers are
treated to Jean Kent's sexy cabaret dancing and the
outline of her nude body swimming only just below the
surface of the water. The film suffered only very
minor cuts on 4 April 1946, so that most of this
material was undoubtedly left in the censored print.
However, this liberal decision is not easily

reconciled in retrospect with the anxiety of Hanna
and Madge Kitchener that a prostitute should not be
referred to as such in the dialogue or be seen tout-
ing for her trade, as in the scenario for For Them
That Trespass (Associated British Pictures, 1948, dir
Alberto Cavalcanti).[25] Both censors seem to have
been unaware that a scene very close to that of a
prostitute (Joan Bennett) picking up a man (Edward G.
Robinson) in the street had recently been passed on
16 January 1946 in Scarlet Street (Universal-Diana,
1945, dir Fritz Lang). Even more surprising was that
the same film had, for the first time that the author
has been able to uncover, depicted unpunished murder
and the execution of an innocent man (Dan Duryea),
albeit in the United States. The same team's earlier
The Woman in the Window might have been the first but
for a dream ending, supposedly added by the studio
without Lang's knowledge, possibly to circumvent
censorship problems.
     In April 1946 the BBFC was called upon to
consider a scenario for The Snake Pit (TCF, 1948, dir
Anatole Litvak). The story of a woman (Olivia De
Havilland) in a New York mental hospital and her
reactions to violent treatment there, the film represents a plea for a more understanding attitude
towards mental illness and breakdown. Such an intent
was evidently lost upon both Hanna and Madge
Kitchener when they commented on the scenario, for
both wished to ban it outright even though the woman
was cured and discharged from the mental hospital.
On the woman's treatment Hanna remarked,[26]

          The drastic and alarming 'shock therapy'
          and the 'tubes and wet pack' cure, plus
          the strait jacket and forcible feeding,
          read more like Nazi tortures than curative
          methods. It is a repellent picture that
          emerges from the fogged descriptions given
          by the muddled mind of this insane woman...
          a film should not be made of this book
          because there is so little story...As the
          therapeutic treatment is described from
          only the patient's point of view it
          appears almost horrific. I fail to see how
          a certificate could be given to any version
          of this unpleasant book.

Shortly afterwards on another scenario[27] Hanna observed that if BBFC passed a film on mental derange-
ment, this might set a dangerous precedent. Madge
Kitchener also took exception in The Snake Pit

scenario to the treatment scenes as well as a scene
of women fighting and expletives like 'bitch',
'bastard', 'Christ' and 'Holy Mother of Jesus'.
Despite BBFC discouragement 20th Century-Fox went
ahead but not until 1948, when the cinema was just
beginning to lose ground to television in the United
States but not yet in Britain. The completed film
was submitted to the BBFC in February 1949, by which
time Tyrrell, Brooke Wilkinson and Hanna were all
dead. Sir Sidney Harris, knighted upon his retire-
ment from the Home Office in 1946, had succeeded
Tyrrell in March 1947, Arthur Watkins (also a former
Home Office member) had become the Secretary in July
1948 and Fleetwood-Wilson had taken Hanna's place towards the end of 1946. Nevertheless the BBFC adopted
a cautious approach to The Snake Pit. According to
Watkins's letter to a critic after the film had been
released in Britain,[28] a BBFC ban would have been
consistent with previous policy, but the film was
sincere, well made, well acted and had been shown in
other countries without public opposition. The BBFC
had viewed it five times in the presence of medical
experts who, however, had been divided. Even though
the production showed the possibility of cure from
sympathetic treatment, it had been cut by over 1,000
feet (about eleven minutes running time) and a foreword had been added making it clear that the shown
mental hospital conditions did not apply in Britain.
The BBFC had considered the award of a 'H' certificate, but rather than carry out such action Watkins
had relied upon assurances from the distributors that
all cinemas showing The Snake Pit would prohibit the
admission of children below 16 under any circumstances. This condition had presented no difficulty
during the film's opening run at the Odeon, Marble
Arch. What Watkins omitted to state in his letter
was that the Minister of Health himself, Aneuran
Bevan, had viewed the film and given it the final
go ahead.[29] Three months elapsed before it was cut
sufficiently to satisfy the BBFC on 16 May 1949.
Possibly what proved to be over-caution in this
instance resulted from the public rumpus which had
already surrounded the BBFC's failure to ban Brighton
Rock (Associated British-Boulting Brothers, 1947, dir
John Boulting), No Orchids for Miss Blandish (Renown,
1948, dir St John L. Clowes) and Good Time Girl
(Gainsborough, 1947, dir David MacDonald).[30] However, the mental illness precedent Hanna had feared
three years previously was at last set. Whether The
Snake Pit would have survived a ban if the BBFC staff
in 1949 had been identical to 1946 must necessarily

remain a matter for speculation, but as it was, after
some initial criticism which included a Commons
question of 25 May 1949 and correspondence in the
quality press, controversy soon subsided.

However, to return to 1946, which was also noteworthy for the return of the 'H' certificate in
quantity. No fewer than nine such certificates were
awarded during the year, half as many again as
throughout the entire Second World War. All of the
1946 'H' films now strike one as routine offerings of
the horror genre and virtually indistinguishable from
the many horror films which had received an 'A' certificate during the war. The reason behind this
apparent reversal of 'H' certificate policy is not
altogether clear. It appears unlikely to have derived from a general BBFC inclination to tighten up
in the direction of the pre-1938 rules, for no features were banned in 1946 or 1947 when several controversial decisions to allow films were taken. The
most probable explanation is the real horror of the
Nazi concentration camps. Routine torture, inhuman
medical experiments and the full details of the
Jewish extermination policy in the Nazi gas chambers
and gas vans became public knowledge through the war
crimes trials and the subsequent lurid reporting in
the press and the uncensored newsreels. It was no
accident that in The Snake Pit scenario Hanna
compared the mental hospital methods with Nazi
tortures.[26] This background, together with rising
juvenile crime, probably accounts for what seems in
retrospect to have been an exaggerated BBFC concern
to protect youth from the image of horror when much
genuine horror existed for youngsters to see and read
about.

Such speculation is supported by the relative
absence of 'H' films over the next few years remaining before the abolition of the 'H' certificate -
only eight from 1947 to 1950 inclusive - and by BBFC
anxiety during 1946 over the insertion into feature
films of concentration camp newsreels. This was
first done in The Stranger (RKO, 1945, dir Orson
Welles) which the BBFC passed uncut on 29 May 1946.
This deals with an escaped Nazi war criminal (Orson
Welles) who is living in an American town as a
university professor before his discovery by a persistent American war crimes investigator (Edward G.
Robinson). The scene in which Robinson shows concentration camp newsreel constituted a precedent which
the BBFC apparently soon regretted. For example,
when a scenario called Hatton Garden Murder was submitted on 25 August 1946, it included a scene in

which the heroine was shown still photographs of
Belsen concentration camp during its liberation in
April 1945. Madge Kitchener recommended that the
actors should be shown looking at the stills, and
that the audience should be left to speculate as to
how horrific they were.[31] Hatton Garden Murder was
seemingly not filmed, but Madge Kitchener's approach
to its scenario was probably adopted in 1947 with
Frieda (Ealing, 1947, dir Basil Dearden). Since
Anglo-Soviet relations were now deteriorating, British attitudes to Germany had to be reappraised.
Frieda, undeservedly rarely screened and little
remembered, is nevertheless a sharp reminder of how
strong British feelings were against the German race
as such, without individual distinctions, during the
two years after the final defeat of Germany in May
1945. A British prisoner of war pilot (David Farrar)
is rescued by a German nurse (Mai Zetterling) whom he
marries in order to gain her entry into Britain. As
a German she is initially rejected by the local population of Farrar's village which, however, gradually
relents and responds to Frieda's personal charm and
humanity. In the film Farrar and Mai Zetterling
attend a cinema performance in which concentration
camp newsreels appear. In the original version and
the extant National Film Archive print the newsreels
are actually seen, but at the BBFC in 1947 Frieda
was cut by 30 feet on 22 May. This was approximately
the same running time as the newsreel shown on the
screen and almost certainly the BBFC cut, which left
only the anguished faces of husband and German wife
on which the cinema audience could judge the newsreel
content. Incidentally Frieda also marked the return
of the good, anti-Nazi German to the British screen
as most strikingly if implausibly depicted in a long
and powerful verbal confrontation scene between the
anti-Nazi, humanitarian Frieda and her dedicated Nazi
brother (Albert Lieven). He turns up in Britain mas-
querading as a Pole who had fought in the British
army after service in the German army and subsequent
capture.
     The sharp increase in juvenile offences and
violence as well as press coverage of some brutal
murders and the resulting trials had led in the
immediate post-war years to support in right-wing
political circles for the arming of the police, while
on the other political wing there were many Labour
MPs who were opposed in principle to capital punishment. Under such circumstances it was hardly surprising that the BBFC continued to be preoccupied with
crime and violence. In one scenario Madge Kitchener

was insistent that a police inspector who drew a gun
must be in plain clothes, while in another she objected to the use of milk bottles as weapons because
this was suggestive to young minds.[32] With hindsight
arguably the most interesting scenario for 1946 dealing with crime and the law is The Paradine Case
(Selznick, 1947-8, dir Sir Alfred Hitchcock). Set in
London in 1946, the plot concerns British barrister
Anthony Keane (Gregory Peck) who falls in love with a
woman client, Mrs Paradine (Alida Valli), accused of
poisoning and murdering her blind husband. Despite
the barrister's belief in her innocence she turns out
to be guilty. In the 1946 scenario the accused was
to be shown in open court receiving the death sentence as the judge dons the black cap, the ceremonial
procedure of the time. However, both Hanna and Madge
Kitchener objected, whereupon the scenario was
altered to make Mrs Paradine commit suicide so that
the black cap sequence could be omitted. Both
censors also took exception to the suggestion that
during the many court scenes the judge, Lord Horfield
(Charles Laughton), possessed a streak of cruelty,
but this issue remained unresolved for the time
being.[33] When the film encountered later production
problems, the plot underwent further changes. The
suicide idea was dropped, but the black cap scene was
not reinstated. Instead Horfield announces the
pronouncement of the death sentence on Mrs Paradine
in private to his wife (Ethel Barrymore) with great
relish. There is also a strong suggestion throughout
that the barrister's professional handling of the
case is influenced wholly by his love for his client
even though he is happily married. Moreover, the
portrayal of Lord Horfield is unflattering, to say
the least, in several respects. Early in the film
he makes sexual advances to Keane's wife (Ann Todd)
practically under the nose of his own wife. In the
pre-court case sequences the dialogue emphasises
hanging as the penalty for guilt, and Horfield's
court interventions against Keane hint at bias
against the accused, although eventually this turns
out to be justified. In The Paradine Case Hitchcock
paints the practitioners of contemporary British
justice in an utterly unprofessional light, even if
in the end justice is done. None the less the BBFC
allowed it in full in December 1948, possibly due to
the influence of Watkins as Secretary. He himself
was a minor playwright, probably in consequence
understood better than Brooke Wilkinson the yearnings
of film-makers and was more inclined to grant artistic licence a priority over wider social

considerations.

However sceptical the BBFC was in 1946 to anything that called into question the impartial exercise of the law, its more open attitude to sex was symbolised by the ultimate passing of The Outlaw (Howard Hughes, 1941, dir Howard Hughes). This now unremarkable western followed in the footsteps of Jesse James in 1939 in that the notorious Billy the Kid was portrayed sympathetically rather than as a criminal with no redeeming features. Howard Hughes had filmed it during the war, but after its San Francisco premiere in February 1943 he had lost interest in a wider release until 1946. Then it was banned in the United States by many local censorship bodies not because it tolerated law-breakers but because the half-breed girl Rio (Jane Russell) was shown totally bare breasted. Eventually Hughes had to eliminate these shots to gain the Legion of Decency's approval.[34] In this truncated version, which was the print submitted to the BBFC on 14 May 1946, only the top part of Miss Russell's breasts was seen. Even so this version ran into trouble, but ultimately the BBFC passed it on 14 October with only more minor cuts and, amazingly, a 'U' certificate. This was sufficient to lead to much lurid poster advertising which showed Rio in provocative pose above the caption of 'mean, moody and magnificent'. Such advertising was more titillating than anything shown in The Outlaw itself in Britain in 1946. Yet the film provoked a limited amount of public protest and the BBFC showed some courage in allowing it at all after the furore it had already caused on the other side of the Atlantic, where the controversy had come to centre on the MPPDA's powers.

As the crime rate continued to rise in Britain during 1947, British films progressively emphasised violence in both contemporary and historical settings. When Charter Films in July 1946 had put forward a scenario for Fame is the Spur (GFD-Two Cities-Charter Films, 1947, dir Roy Boulting), based upon Howard Spring's novel itself allegedly based upon the life of Ramsay MacDonald, both Hanna and Madge Kitchener expressed misgivings about clashes between working class demonstrators and mounted police in early 20th century Britain. The latter even compared these projected shots with the famous Odessa Steps massacre in Battleship Potemkin,[35] but she evidently overlooked the similar scene allowed in Love on the Dole.[36] In the event Fame is the Spur, filmed with the riot included, was passed uncut on 5 August 1947. However, this production, which

describes the rise to high office of a young working
class Socialist (Sir Michael Redgrave) and the
dilution of his political principles once he has
reached the summit of power, was basically an expres-
sion of disillusion with the lack of radicalism in
Attlee government policies. The riot scene was in
this context merely a peripheral reminder of how in
the past labour unrest had been quelled by force,
whereas the general tone of The Brothers (GFD-Sydney
Box, 1947, dir David MacDonald) was much starker in
its approach to violence.

      This film, which has fallen into a mystifying
obscurity, is set in 1900 on the Isle of Skye where
Mary Lawson (Patricia Roc), an 18-year-old orphan,
becomes a church ward and is settled in the home of
Hector Macrae (Finlay Currie). His two sons, John
(Duncan Macrae) and Fergus (Maxwell Reed), both come
to love her, while she returns Fergus's love but to
encourage his jealousy flirts with Willie McFarish
(Andrew Crawford), whose family is the Macraes' great
enemy. When Hector dies, Mary rejects John's offer
of marriage, whereupon he orders Fergus to kill her
on the pretext that she had brought unhappiness to
the entire Macrae family. Fergus murders Mary and
then commits suicide. However, John's order for the
murder has been overheard by a member of the Macrae
whisky smuggling gang who kill him by the same method
as, very early in the film, an informer on the gang
has been killed. He had been tied and made to float
on the water's surface by means of large corks bound
under both arms. A fish was attached to the top of
his head to attract a gull whose peck at the fish
cracks the informer's skull. This execution is
explicitly depicted, but not John's death in the same
manner, while in addition Mary is shown swimming nude
(but only from a distance) as Jean Kent had been
shown in Caravan and there is a fierce and prolonged
fist fight under a waterfall between Fergus and
Willie McFarish. All this and the emphasis on sexual
repression in isolated communities, supported by
splendid location filming, produced a meritorious
feature but one which might have been expected to
meet severe problems at the BBFC. Instead it was
passed uncut on 25 April 1947.

      In March 1947 Charter Films sent the BBFC a
scenario for Brighton Rock. Written by Graham Greene
and Terence Rattigan, it deals with the activities of
a ruthless teenage hoodlum leader (Sir Richard
Attenborough) of a racetrack gang in pre-Second
World War Brighton. Before 1939 BBFC policy had
been to discourage any film dealing with organised

crime in Britain, this particular 'exception' not
having been breached by 1945. However, neither
Fleetwood-Wilson nor Madge Kitchener challenged the
validity of the basic theme but rather the details of
gang warfare, especially the use of razors, razor
slashing and vitriol throwing into the face. Moreover, Madge Kitchener questioned whether Brighton
should be mentioned by name.[37] On this occasion the
BBFC comments apparently left little impression on
the Boulting brothers who went on to make Brighton
Rock along the main lines of the scenario. Brighton
was named of course, while a razor slash across a
man's cheek was specifically shown, yet the BBFC
passed the film in full on 23 September 1947. This
favourable decision represented a landmark in British
cinematic history, for it reversed all previous BBFC
policy in allowing the depiction of British organised
crime and in the process opened the way to more
supposedly 'realistic' British films of various
genres but more especially crime films like No
Orchids for Miss Blandish and Good Time Girl.
     This development was greatly assisted by the
simultaneous appearance of quality American crime
productions as, after the boom year of 1946, American
cinema attendances dropped when television was making
its first relentless advance. In 1946 there had been
only 7,000 television licences in the United States,
but the figure was due to rise to 200,000 by 1948,
five millions by 1950 and 50 millions by 1955.
Notable American crime features in 1946-7 included
the documentary-style Boomerang (TCF, 1946, dir Elia
Kazan) in which a conscientious district attorney
(Dana Andrews) proves that the accused (Arthur
Kennedy) was not guilty of a clergyman's murder without being able to unmask the real murderer. Contrary
to BBFC policy, justice was not seen to be done, but
presumably as the setting was American the BBFC
passed Boomerang on 21 January 1947. Crossfire (RKO,
1947, dir Edward Dmytryk) constitutes a blistering
attack on anti-Semitism in the guise of a thriller,
with Robert Ryan turning in a riveting performance as
the bigoted GI who had murdered a Jew for racial
motives. Despite an uncompromising approach to its
subject and the obvious fear that it might touch off
further anti-Semitism in the light of the Jewish
anti-British terrorist campaign in Palestine, the
BBFC passed Crossfire on 13 August 1947.
     Such films were tough in their approach, but
they did not linger on visual violence. This stood
in contrast to Brute Force (U-I, 1947, dir Jules
Dassin), on the surface a stark but routine jailbreak

drama but one with the prison serving as an allegory
for the modern nation-state from the clutches of
which no citizen ever escapes. A sadistic head
warder (Hume Cronyn, one of his finest performances)
at one point tortures a prisoner to the accompaniment
of gramophone record music to drown the prisoner's
screams, a thinly veiled analogy with the orchestras
established in some Nazi concentration camps. This
particular scene is essential to the plot, with the
result that the BBFC allowed the film with only minor
cuts on 30 June 1947. Yet more brutal still was Open
City (Italy, 1945, dir Roberto Rossellini) dealing
with Italian resistance to the German occupation of
Rome during the closing stages of the Second World
War. In the film a young girl betrays one of the
resistance group when her lesbian partner withholds
a drug from her at German instigation. The Germans
torture the resulting male prisoner with a blow torch
while he is tied to a chair stripped to the waist.
The torture is specifically shown, but only very
briefly, whereas the prisoner's screams are heard for
some time afterwards. Astonishingly in the light of
this scene the BBFC passed Open City uncut on 10 June
1947, although it took almost a year to reach this
decision which was probably influenced by the interim
general trend towards greater violence in both
American and British productions.

In other respects, too, BBFC policy in 1947 was
liberal. For example, sexual repression among nuns
was allowed in Black Narcissus (GFD-The Archers,
1946-7, dirs Michael Powell and Emeric Pressburger),
passed virtually in full on 3 February 1947. Yet an
entirely different and misleading impression of the
BBFC can be reached from the same year's scenarios.
One amusing instance can be found in June 1947 when
Gainsborough submitted a scenario for a mermaid
comedy entitled Miranda in which a doctor on holiday
in Cornwall (Griffith Jones) catches a mermaid
(Glynis Johns) and takes her to London disguised as
an invalid. Madge Kitchener wrote,[38] 'The mer-baby
is unexplained. We have seen no mer-man. Are we to
conclude it had a landsman father? or is this being
too fastidious?' In the event Miranda (GFD-Gainsborough, 1947, dir Ken Annakin) was passed in full on 1
January 1948.

BBFC memories of the 1936 abdication crisis must
have lingered long, for both Fleetwood-Wilson and
Madge Kitchener showed sensitivity to the subject of
British royalty. In February 1947 Columbia submitted
a scenario for The Private Life of the Virgin Queen,
based upon a book by two American authors which had

claimed that Queen Elizabeth I had given birth to
children. Fleetwood-Wilson regarded the topic as
prohibitive in principle, while Madge Kitchener, who
evidently considered herself something of an histor-
ian, dissected the historical content in some detail.
She concluded that the scenario 'misrepresents and
falsifies the character of one of England's greatest
sovereigns. It is a book to be shunned more especially as we are within sight of the reign of Queen
Elizabeth II'.39 The Private Life of the Virgin
Queen was never produced, unlike Saraband for Dead
Lovers (Ealing, 1948, dirs Basil Dearden and Michael
Relph) which likewise caused many qualms at scenario
stage within the BBFC. The plot takes place at the
Hanoverian court between 1682 and 1694 and centres
upon the odious character of George Louis (Peter
Bull), the son of the Elector of Hanover and the
future George I of England. He is married to Sophie
Dorothea (Francoise Rosay), by whom he has had two
children, but has a mistress (Joan Greenwood) while
his father is having an affair with the wife of his
chief minister, Countess Von Platen (Dame Flora
Robson). Königsmark (Stewart Granger), an advent-
urer, arrives at the Hanoverian court in 1689.
Countess Von Platen is attracted to him but is
spurned in favour of Sophie Dorothea who is suffering
from her husband's physical maltreatment. Desperate,
she agrees to leave Hanover with Königsmark who,
however, when leaving her apartment is killed by the
Elector's soldiers due to scheming by the jealous
Countess Von Platen. Sophie Dorothea is then compelled by her tyrannical husband to sign a deed of
separation and undergo incarceration for life before
dying in prison in 1726. Fleetwood-Wilson
observed,40 'Our reigning king is a distant decendant
(sic) of George Louis. Care should be taken that his
German attributes are not too blatant.' Madge
Kitchener recommended the omission of various
dialogue pieces which suggested that the accession of
George I to the English throne in 1714 was due to
politics at the Hanoverian court rather than to
British historical developments. She also equated
the court mistresses with prostitutes.41 However,
Ealing ignored many of the BBFC comments and Saraband
for Dead Lovers was allowed on 14 May 1948 with only
minor cuts. With Labour in office theoretically
committed to the destruction of social privilege, the
BBFC remained watchful about possible unfavourable
portrayals of past ruling class personalities other
than royalty. This can be seen in the reactions of
Fleetwood-Wilson and Madge Kitchener to the scenario

for The Bad Lord Byron (Rank-Sydney Box, 1948, dir
David MacDonald), eventually passed with minor cuts
on 7 March 1949. Both censors were concerned that
the 'more sordid' aspects of Byron's notorious sexual
life should not be depicted.[42]
     Towards the end of 1947 Harris, himself now over
70, appointed Watkins as BBFC Assistant Secretary to
take over from Brooke Wilkinson who was then 77.
According to John Trevelyan later,[43] Watkins was a
liberalising force within the BBFC, but if this is so
the process was gradual, for it is far from apparent
in his response to the scenario for No Room at the
Inn which British National submitted at the end of
1947. This was based upon a successful stage play of
1946 and focuses on a hardhearted woman (Freda
Jackson) who half-starves and mistreats child
evacuees during the Second World War as well as turns
her home into a brothel. Despite the implausible
plot Freda Jackson's rousing stage performance had
virtually guaranteed the play's success, and British
National was anxious to capitalise while the public
taste for screen 'realism' persisted. However, both
Fleetwood-Wilson and Madge Kitchener opposed anything
which showed that the central figure had let rooms
'for immoral purposes', the latter even proposing a
contemporary setting since child cruelty was much in
the news.[44] Watkins supported most of these comments
and went on to propose further restrictions of his
own which included the omission of, first, the word
'damn' when used by girls of 13 and 16 and, second,
the woman's unfavourable view of life in an approved
school or Borstal for juvenile offenders.[45] Very
much a product of its time and rescued from total
mediocrity purely by Freda Jackson's performance, No
Room at the Inn (British National, 1948, dir Dan
Birt) was only slightly cut when the BBFC passed it
on 19 August 1948. But by then it seemed tame by
comparison with No Orchids for Miss Blandish,[46] which
had already aroused much public criticism of the
BBFC.
     However, before considering the events surround-
ing No Orchids, it is noteworthy that by the end of
1947 international politics had scarcely intruded
into feature film censorship either in Britain or in
the United States. Up to that time almost all the
post-war productions with political connotations had
been derived from the legacy of the Second World War.
Only Frieda had trodden seriously on controversial
contemporary international ground. No features had
been made dealing with the tensions in India and
Palestine which had led to the British withdrawals,

although Crossfire might be considered by implication
as sympathetic to the Jewish cause in Palestine.
Furthermore, the mounting friction between the Soviet
Union and the western allies as they failed to resolve their differences over Germany's future had not
so far appeared on the screen. Unfortunately the
BBFC scenarios for 1948 have not survived to enable
one to judge how far the emerging 'cold war' influenced BBFC policy, but the registers of the films themselves reveal that international considerations on
film loomed larger in 1948 than in 1946-7. For
instance, a British Newsreels documentary dealing
with disputed territory between the newly founded
India and Pakistan, The Kashmir Story, was cut on 10
May 1948. The Murderers are Amongst Us, (East
Germany, 1948, dir Wolfgang Staudte), a gloomy pro-
Communist offering which suggests that a Nazi resur-
gence remained a constant threat in Germany and thus
inferred that a reunified German state would inevitably be a constant menace to European peace, and its
English sub-titles were cut on 5 April 1948. On the
other hand A Foreign Affair (Paramount, 1948, dir
Billy Wilder), a mild anti-American satire which
concentrates upon blundering, bureaucracy and
corruption in the American zone of West Berlin, was
passed uncut on 4 June 1948. Eventually this turned
out to be true for The Iron Curtain (TCF, 1948, dir
William Wellman), the first Hollywood 'cold war'
piece made against the background of the House of
Representatives Un-American Activities Committee
investigation into alleged Communist influence in the
American film industry. The film traces the real
life career of a recent Soviet defector, Igor
Gouzenko, who as a diplomatic official in Ottawa has
revealed secrets of a Soviet spy ring in the United
States. Viewed at the BBFC on 25 June 1948 by
Harris, Watkins and Home Office, Foreign Office and
Scotland Yard representatives, The Iron Curtain at
length emerged utterly unscathed, probably because
this wholesale official scrutiny took place when the
Soviet blockade of West Berlin had just begun. This
signified the abandonment of neutrality in international relations at the BBFC in the heat of the
moment, but a scenario for February 1949[7] produced
BBFC comments divulging that by then film satire on
the Soviet Union was considered as prohibitive. This
semblance of neutrality in American-Soviet relations
did not survive the Korean crisis of 1950 and the
host of Hollywood anti-Communist 'cold war' features
which ensued in the first half of the 1950s, not
entirely disappearing until the Cuban missile crisis

of October 1962.

In 1948 the most severe public film uproar came
to rest on No Orchids for Miss Blandish which Hanna
had previously rejected at scenario stage in 1944.
Since then this seedy crime novel by James Hadley
Chase had been converted into a successful stage play
which had a long run in London's West End. The story
is of a young and beautiful heiress, the Miss
Blandish of the title, who is kidnapped by the ruthless Grissom gang and then beaten and drugged into
submitting to the amorous attentions of psycopathic
gang leader Slim Grissom. The film is a heavily
diluted version of the book, to the point where Miss
Blandish (Linden Travers) actually falls in love with
Slim (Jack La Rue) and willingly accepts his
advances, but despite such major alterations the BBFC
imposed substantial cuts before No Orchids was let
through on 12 March 1948. It was released a month
later, but in the interval the Commons had voted to
suspend capital punishment for a five-year trial
period in the face of House of Lords and public
concern at rising crime and youthful violence. No
Orchids as passed at the BBFC contains many routine
beatings, several casual shootings and threats of
calculated torture. As a rare British attempt to
emulate a classic American gangster film, it now
seems grotesque and laughable, but at the time of its
release in mid-April 1948 Dr Edith Summerskill, the
Parliamentary Secretary to the Ministry of Food,
delivered a public protest. Furthermore, the LCC
uncharacteristically imposed additional cuts, while
Surrey County Council banned it altogether on the
ground that it was 'injurious to morality and offensive to public feeling'.[48] Bootle, Eastbourne and
Sheffield followed Surrey's lead, whereas Blackpool,
the Isle of Wight and Preston permitted No Orchids in
full. For the first time since the early 1930s a
number of local authorities diverged from the BBFC.
Harris on 21 April even apologised to the Home Office
for having 'failed to protect the public'[49] as
adequately as the BBFC would have wished. Harris's
humility before Whitehall, the product of his own
long Home Office career and relative inexperience at
the BBFC, would probably not be accepted as justified
by many today, for the publicity surrounding No
Orchids was short lived and on the evidence of the
film itself all but incomprehensible to later gener-
ations. Only the unfortunate political timing of its
release can explain its contemporary notoriety. The
attention lavished on No Orchids probably encouraged
the May 1948 release of Good Time Girl. This

narrates in flashback the life of a working class
sensual teenage girl (Jean Kent) who leaves home
after a quarrel with her father to go to London where
she becomes involved in night club life. Later she
is sent to an approved school and, after her escape,
eventually forms a liaison with an American deserter
(Bonar Colleano) which leads to murder and a fifteen-
year prison sentence for the girl. The story was
partly inspired by the real life association of a
Welsh teenager, Mrs Betty Jones, with an American
deserter, Karl Hulten, which produced the so-called
'cleft chin' murder case of January 1945. Both were
found guilty, but Hulten was executed whereas Mrs
Jones was reprieved. The film's background is full
of rich detail of sordid post-war Soho night club and
gang life, including razor slashing and vitriol
throwing. The production of Good Time Girl had pre-
ceded Brighton Rock by several months. It was submitted to the BBFC on 15 July 1947 but not passed
unless cuts were made until 26 September, three days
after Brighton Rock itself had been allowed uncut.
For some unclear reason Gainsborough held up the
release of Good Time Girl until the aftermath of No
Orchids. Thus it was not altogether surprising that
reviews of Good Time Girl were mixed, but in retrospect more than 30 years later it stands up to the
ravages of time much better than No Orchids and fully
justifies the BBFC decision to let it through without
further viewings in spite of the No Orchids furore.
According to Jean Kent herself at the National Film
Theatre when Good Time Girl was shown there in January 1983, the film was very heavily cut, which was
also rumoured in contemporary film journals. However, this is not borne out in the BBFC records, so
that Gainsborough itself must have imposed the cuts
without waiting for the BBFC to do so. Shortly after
the release of Good Time Girl Harris on 19 May 1948
wrote a cautionary letter to the British Film Producers Association. He warned in particular against
the50

> growing prevalence in films of brutal and
> sadistic incidents and the choice of themes
> which necessitate such undesirable features.
> This development no doubt to a certain extent
> reflects the aftermath of a war, when viol-
> ence became the familiar accompaniment of
> daily life, and, on the most charitable view,
> may represent an attempt to portray on the
> screen some of the more unpleasant features
> and characters of the post-war period. On

the general ground that an art should,
with certain limits, be allowed to
express the salient mood of a period,
stories and incidents have been permitted
which might not have been acceptable in
another period.

In future, Harris concluded, the BBFC would ban such
objectionable material. The implication of this
letter was that the BBFC had been too liberal since
1945, but still the trend towards more brutal violence on the screen continued as cinema attendances
dropped in both Britain and the United States, particularly the latter, where by 1950 the figures were
to be less than half of those for 1946. By 18
November 1949 Harris's warning of May 1948 had been
so little heeded that he felt obliged to repeat it in
a further letter.[51]
     Brooke Wilkinson died in July 1948. He had
contributed more to the development of the BBFC and
possibly of the cinema itself than any other individual. He outlived four BBFC Presidents and provided a
continuity of policy through their presidencies which
might otherwise have been lacking. While it is
certainly arguable that at times he was too ready to
accommodate government departments, particularly between the wars, it is equally plain that he was not
the dyed-in-the-wool reactionary who comes across in
the writings of John Trevelyan, Nicholas Pronay and
Jeffrey Richards.[52] Courageous decisions in favour
of the film companies suggest instead that he was an
adaptable conservative. Although his eyesight was
failing from at least the early 1930s,[53] he remained
active at the BBFC almost to the day of his death and
the BBFC records show that he could still view films
right up to a few months of that time. Although
O'Connor must take some share of the credit for the
BBFC's success during Brooke Wilkinson's long secretaryship, there can be no question of the latter's
enormous achievements. Liberal BBFC decisions within
the context of their time were present at every stage
of his 35 years of office. While such decisions were
often not those of Brooke Wilkinson in person, but
rather in outward form those of the censors, it is
impossible to believe that decisions with which he
disagreed would have been allowed to stand so consistently as to destroy the broad direction of BBFC
policy. Although in theory the President rather than
the Secretary took public responsibility for decisions before 1960, the fact remains that between 1913
and 1948 Brooke Wilkinson was a full-time official

whereas the BBFC Presidents, with the possible exception of Redford in the formative years to 1916, were either retired or active in another sphere of life. They held their presidencies to be called upon when required rather than to participate in day-to-day administrative routine, and only O'Connor gave the job more than the minimum effort beyond the viewing of films and defending the BBFC from outside criticism. In reality this situation gave Brooke Wilkinson a dominant position within the BBFC until Harris became President in 1947. Of the vast number of films which the BBFC viewed during Brooke Wilkinson's secretaryship only a handful provoked much external criticism, although controversy might have been much greater if the BBFC had published a list of banned films and the names of the individual censors. But even this possibility is questionable, for now and again, mostly in the early sound years, the press managed to obtain and publish accurate information both about named banned films and the identity of the censors without arousing much public clamour. Censorship must be judged by what it permits as well as by what it suppresses. By this yardstick the evidence from the BBFC registers, the scenarios and extant films indicates that the BBFC under Brooke Wilkinson's stewardship struck an admirable balance between the commercial propensities of the film industry, the ideal of artistic freedom, the demands of the government of the day and the overall public interest. The outcome was the striking development of the cinema in Britain as the prime medium of mass communication until the 1950s.

In any case, although Watkins at once succeeded Brooke Wilkinson, the new Harris-Watkins partnership did not immediately usher in a clean break with the past. This much is already evident even though the materials are not yet available for a full study of the BBFC after Brooke Wilkinson's death. For instance, the ten banned films from October 1948 to the end of 1950 exceeded the total for the previous nine years, while the surviving BBFC 1949 scenarios disclose that the BBFC still clung to remnants of its pre-1938 rules. An April 1949 scenario entitled The Jersey Lily, dealing with the life of Lily Langtry, produced a concern that monarchy should not be denigrated in any way through Lily Langtry's association with King Edward VII.[54] More revealing still, especially in the light of later events, are Fleetwood-Wilson's comments on the scenario for The Blue Lamp, submitted in April 1949. This now well-known documentary-style film (Ealing, 1949, dir Basil Dearden)

on the work of the British police relates how a young
recruit (Jimmy Hanley) is strongly influenced by the
veteran PC George Dixon (Jack Warner) who trains him
before the latter is gunned down at short range and
killed by a young thug (Dirk Bogarde). Fleetwood-
Wilson objected to the fundamental theme because it
showed crime methods which might be imitated and per-
fected. He further believed that the shooting of
Dixon in the stomach at close range should not be
explicitly shown, as it was a 'brutal murder'.[55]
Fortunately Ealing chose to ignore BBFC caution and
produced The Blue Lamp along the broad lines of the
scenario, with Dixon's murder as one of its more
memorable scenes. The BBFC allowed the film in full
on 3 November 1949, probably because Fleetwood-
Wilson's objections were overridden by the overall
favourable image of the police as a counter to the
supposed crime wave which worried so many contempor-
aries.

These 1949 scenarios alone divulge that Brooke
Wilkinson's death did not mark a specific dividing
line in BBFC policy. Indeed it is impossible to
measure his career by the work of his successors, for
they all were faced with a fundamentally different
situation. Whereas he functioned in an age when the
cinema in Britain and the United States became THE
medium of mass communication, the cinema in Britain
and the United States after 1948 was to suffer a
gradual but permanent and steady decline. With the
advent of television it would have been very surprising if the cinema had maintained its former supremacy
in visual communication. However, what is perhaps
even more surprising is that the cinema in Britain
has not died out altogether under the impact of the
technological changes which have made visual entertainment so readily available in the home. By the
early 1980s cinema attendances in Britain had shrunk
to approximately one million per week and the number
of cinemas had slumped to below one thousand compared
to about 4,700 in 1945. None the less, even though
many films were by then shown on television or could
be hired on video cassettes relatively soon after
release in the cinemas, enough people remained prepared to attend the cinema regularly and thus ensure
its survival, however precariously. This development surely owed something to the liberal BBFC
policies of the Brooke Wilkinson era.

The charge that the near disappearance of the
British film industry by the 1970s was due to repressive censorship from 1913 to 1948[56] is both inaccurate and preposterous. Even before the 1909

Cinematograph Act, when there was no British film
censorship, the British film producers had found it
increasingly difficult to hold off American and
European competition. As the Americans outstripped
all their film rivals in the ensuing years, the
British film industry was on the verge of collapse
until its rescue by the 1927 quota system. But even
with this legal protective umbrella British companies
could not fulfil the quota, and as a result the major
American studios penetrated the British film industry
on a grand scale, while most British films could make
little or no box office impact in the United
States.[57] Furthermore, from 1934 to 1956 the
American film industry operated under much the same
censorship constraints as its British counterpart,
yet the Americans retained their supremacy in the
British market.
    First the quota system (modified in 1937 and
again in 1947), then the relaxation of the pre-1938
BBFC rules and finally the Second World War afforded
the British film industry its one great chance to
compete on equal terms with the Americans. However,
sufficient capital was never forthcoming, and
although the quality of British films unquestionably
improved by leaps and bounds after the late 1930s,
quality was not produced in quantity and the fundam-
mental fact remained that American films usually made
more money in Britain than British films did in the
United States. It is hard to credit that even the
most enlightened BBFC outlook would have altered such
elementary business economics. The decline of the
American and British cinemas relative to television
simply exacerbated existing circumstances to hasten
the near extinction of the British film industry,
aided by mounting trade union power within the
industry and consequent soaring production costs.
The number of British productions generated solely
from British capital has dwindled by degrees since
the 1950s until the quota system had finally to be
abolished as superfluous in 1982. Those who see
censorship as a cause of the British film industry's
demise must first establish that the censorship was
in fact repressive and then explain why the American
film industry has survived the virtual collapse of
inter-war censorship since the 1950s whereas the
British industry has not.

APPENDIX I

The BBFC's codified grounds for banning or cutting
films as given in the 1926 annual report were as
follows:

RELIGIOUS

1.   The materialised figure of Christ.
2.   Irreverent quotations of religious texts.
3.   Travesties of familiar Biblical quotations and
     well-known hymns.
4.   Titles to which objection would be taken by
     religious organisations.
5.   Travesty and mockery of religious services.
6.   Holy vessels amidst incongruous surroundings,
     or shown used in a way which would be looked
     upon as desecration.
7.   Comic treatment of incidents connected with
     death.
8.   Painful insistence of realism in death bed
     scenes.

POLITICAL

1.   Lampoons of the institution of monarchy.
2.   Propaganda against monarchy and attacks on
     royal dynasties.
3.   Unauthorised use of royal and university arms.
4.   Themes which are likely to wound the just
     susceptibilities of our allies.
5.   White men in state of degredation amidst native
     surroundings.
6.   American law officers making arrests in this
     country.
7.   Inflammatory sub-titles and Bolshevist
     propaganda.
8.   Equivocal situations between white girls and

APPENDIX I

men of other races.

MILITARY

1. Officers in British regiments shown in a disgraceful light.
2. Horrors in warfare and realistic scenes of massacre.

SOCIAL

1. The improper use of the names of well-known British institutions.
2. Incidents which reflect a mistaken conception of the police forces in this country in the administration of justice.
3. Sub-titles in the nature of swearing, and expressions regarded as objectionable in this country.
4. Painful hospital scenes.
5. Scenes in lunatic asylums and particularly in padded cells.
6. Workhouse officials shown in an offensive light.
7. Girls and women in a state of intoxication.
8. Orgy scenes.
9. Subjects which are suitable only for scientific or professional audiences.
10. Suggestive, indecorous and semi-nude dancing.
11. Nude and semi-nude figures, both in actuality and shadowgraph.
12. Girls' clothes pulled off, leaving them in scanty undergarments.
13. Men leering at exposure of women's undergarments.
14. Abortion.
15. Criminal assault on girls.
16. Scenes in and connected with houses of ill repute.
17. Bargain cast for a human life which is to be terminated by murder.
18. Marital infidelity and collusive divorce.
19. Children following the example of a drunken and dissolute father.
20. Dangerous mischief easily imitated by children.
21. Subjects dealing with venereal disease.

QUESTIONS OF SEX

1. The use of the phrase 'sex appeal' in sub-titles.
2. Themes indicative of habitual immorality.

3. Women in alluring or provocative attitudes.
4. Procuration.
5. Degrading exhibitions of animal passion.
6. Passionate and unrestrained embraces.
7. Incidents intended to show clearly that an
   outrage has been perpetrated.
8. Lecherous old men.
9. White slave traffic.
10. Innuendoes with a direct indecent tendency.
11. Indecorous bathroom scenes.
12. Extenuation of a woman sacrificing her honour
    for money on the plea of some laudable object.
13. Female vamps.
14. Indecent wall decorations.
15. Men and women in bed together.

CRIME

1. Hanging, realistic or comic.
2. Executions and incidents connected therewith.
3. Objectionable prison scenes.
4. Methods of crime open to imitation.
5. Stories in which the criminal element is
   predominant.
6. Crime committed and condoned for an ostensibly
   good reason.
7. 'Crook' films in which sympathy is enlisted for
   the criminals.
8. 'Third degree' scenes.
9. Opium dens.
10. Scenes of, traffic in and distribution of
    illicit drugs.
11. The drugging and ruining of young girls.
12. Attempted suicide by asphyxiation.
13. Breaking bottles on men's heads.

CRUELTY

1. Cruel treatment of children.
2. Cruelty to animals.
3. Brutal fights carried to excess, including
   gouging of eyes, clawing of faces and
   throttling.
4. Knuckle fights.
5. Girls and women fighting.
6. Realistic scenes of torture.

APPENDIX 2

'H' Films, 1933-1950

1933: The Ghoul; The Invisible Man; King Klunk;
      Vampire (Vampyr); The Vampire Bat.
1934: The House of Doom; The Medium; The Ninth
      Guest; The Son of Kong; The Tell Tale Heart.
1935: The Bride of Frankenstein; The Hands of
      Orlac; The Mark of the Vampire; The Night on
      the Lonely Mountain; The Raven; The Werewolf
      of London.
1936: The Devil Doll; The Man Who Changed His Mind.
1937: The Thirteenth Chair.
1938: I Accuse (J'accuse).
1939: The Cat and the Canary ('A' certificate for
      cut version in April 1943); Boy Slaves; A
      Child is Born; The Dark Eyes of London; The
      Gorilla; Hell's Kitchen; The Man They Could
      Not Hang; The Monster Walks; On Borrowed
      Time ('A' certificate after July 1945); The
      Return of Doctor X; The Son of Frankenstein.
1940: NIL
1941: The Monster and the Girl.
1942: The Ghost of Frankenstein.
1943: NIL
1944: NIL
1945: The Invisible Man's Revenge; The Mad Ghoul;
      The Return of the Vampire; United Nations War
      Crimes Film.
1946: The Ape Man; The Body Disappears (alternative
      title The Corpse Vanishes); Frankenstein
      Meets The Wolf Man; The House of Franken-
      stein; The Jungle Captive; The Mummy's
      Curse; The Mysterious Doctor; The Vampire's
      Ghost; The Voodoo Man.
1947: The Mummy's Ghost; The Mummy's Tomb.
1948: Dead Men Walk; The Fall of the House of

APPENDIX 2

Usher; The House of Dracula; The Monster
Maker; Tall Dark and Gruesome.
1949: NIL
1950: The Captive Wild Woman.

APPENDIX 3

Films banned by the British Board of Film Censors,
1913-1950

1913:   The Crimson Cross; Frou Frou; Funnicus the
        Minister; The Good Preceptress; The Great
        Physician; His Only Son; La Culotte de
        Rigadier; The Lost Bag; The Love Adventures
        of the Faublas; Love is Blind; Mephisto;
        The Night Before; The Priest and Peter;
        Religion and Superstition in Beloochistan; A
        Salvage; A Shop Girl's Peril; A Snake's
        Meal; Spanish Bull Fight; The Story of
        Sister Ruth; Why Men Leave Home.
1914:   The Blue Room; Coralie and Co.; Dealers in
        Human Lives; The Diva in Straits; The Hand
        that Rules the World; The Last Supper;
        Little White Slaves; Miraculous Waters; My
        Wife and I; The Sins of Your Youth; Three
        Men and a Maid; The Word that Kills.
1915:   Cupid Arthur and Co.; Hearts in Exile; Human
        Wrecks; Hypocrites; The Inherited Burden;
        Innocent; The Lure; Nobody Would Believe;
        Vera; A Woman; The Yoke.
1916:   The Double Room Mystery; The Dragon; The
        Eel; The Fire; A Fool There Was; Greed, No.
        14; Glittering Broadway; A Hero of
        Gallipoli; Inspiration; The Kiss of Kate;
        Little Monte Carlo; A Man without a Soul; A
        Mother's Confession; Nabbed; A Night Out;
        A Parisian Romance; The Rack; Tanks; Those
        Who Toil; Toil and Tyranny; The Unpainted
        Portrait.
1917:   The Battle of Life; The Black Terror;
        Conscience; Fear; The Four Feathers; The
        Fourth Estate; The Girl from Chicago; It May
        Be Your Daughter; Just as He Thought; The

Land of Their Forefathers; The Libertine;
The Marionettes; The Scarlet Mark; Sealed
Lips; Skirts; A Splendid Waster; Strafing
the Kaiser; Trapped for Her Dough; Under The
Bed; The Wager; What Happened at 22; The
Whelp; The Whispered Name.

1918: Blindfolded; The Crimson Stain; God's Law;
Honor's Cross.

1919: At the Mercy of Men; The Case of a Doped
Actress; Damaged Goods; The Divided Law;
Free and Equal; Her White God; Mother, I
Need You; The One Woman; Riders of the
Night; The Spreading Evil; Woman, Woman.

1920: A Friend of the People; The Great Shadow.

1921: Beyond the Barricade; Greater than Love;
Leaves from the Book of Satan; Love; The
Price of Youth; The Women House of Brescia.

1922: A Batchelor Apartment; Bolshevism on Trial;
Cocaine (passed as While London Sleeps on 19
June 1922); A Daughter of the Don; Dracula
(now known as Nosferatu); Handcuffs and
Kisses; The Kitchener Film; The New Moon.

1923: Animals like Humans; The Batchelor Girl;
Boston Blackie; Children of Destiny; Fit to
Marry; I also Accuse; Nobody; A Royal Bull
Fight; A Scream in the Night; Shootin' for
Love.

1924: The Downfall; Getting Strong; Human
Wreckage; The Last Man on Earth; Love and
Sacrifice; Open All Night; Through the Dark;
A Truthful Liar; A Woman's Fate.

1925: Battling Bunyon; The End of the Road; Grit;
Lawful Cheaters; North of Fifty-Fifty; Our
Little Bell.

1926: The City of Sin; Flying Wheels; Irish
Destiny; Potemkin (now known as Battleship
Potemkin); The Red Kimona; Rose of the
Tenements.

1927: The Ace of Cads; Birds of Prey; Life's
Shadows; Outside the Law; Plusch and
Plumowski; Salvation Jane; Two-Time Mama;
The Weavers; The White Slave Traffic.

1928: Cabaret Nights; The Companionate Marriage;
Dawn; The Girl from Everywhere; The Haunted
Ship; Mother; Night Life; Two's Company;
You Can't Beat the Law.

1929: Below the Deadline; Casanova's Son; Love at
First Sight; Marriage; The Mysteries of
Birth; The Racketeers (passed in 1930 as
Love's Conquest); The Seashell and the
Clergyman.

APPENDIX 3

1930: Born Reckless; Gypsy Code; Her Unborn Child;
Hot Dog; Ingagi; Liliom; The Parlour Pests;
The Party Girl; Possession; The Stronger
Sex; Who Killed Rover?

1931: An American Tragedy; Are These Our Children?;
The Blue Express; Captain Lash;
Civilisation; Devil's Cabaret; Doorway to
Hell (passed with cuts in July 1932); Easy
to Get; Enemies of the Law; The Fainting
Lover; The Ghost that Never Returns; The
Gigolo Racket; Girls About Town; Hidden
Evidence; Just a Gigolo; Laugh it Off;
Leftover Ladies; The Miracle Woman; Morals
for Women (passed with cuts in 1935); The
Naggers; Night Shadows; The Public Enemy
(passed in 1932); The Road to Reno; Ships of
Hate; Siamese Twins; Song of the Market
Place; Take 'em and Shake 'em; Too Many
Husbands; Town Scandal; The Victim; The
Virtuous Husband; Women Go On For Ever.

1932: La Chienne; Divorce a la Mode; False Faces;
The Flirty Sleepwalker; Freaks; Good Sport;
Her Mad Night; Here Prince; Lady Please;
The Last Mile; Life Begins; The Line's Busy;
Minnie the Moocher; The Monster Walks; Night
Beat; Night Life in Reno; L'Opera de Quat'
Sous(French language version of Die Dreigros-
chenoper or The Threepenny Opera); The
Sultan's Cat; Tango.

1933: Alimony Madness; Bondage; Caliente Love;
The Deserter; The Face on the Bar-room Floor
(passed later in the same year); Fanny's
Wedding Day; Gold Diggers of Paris; Hello
Sister; Her Resale Value; India Speaks;
Island of Lost Souls (passed in 1958); Kiss
of Araby; Malay Nights; Picture Brides;
Poil de Carrotte; Private Wives; Red-Headed
Woman (passed in 1965); Terror Abroad;
Thirteen Steps; What Price Decency?; What
Price Tomorrow?

1934: Animal Life in the Chaparral; Black Moon;
Casanova; Elysia; The Expectant Father;
Flüchtlinge; Le Grand Jeu; La Guerre des
Valses; Hell's Fire; Hitler's Reign of
Terror; Honeymoon Hotel; Leningrad; March
of the Years No. 5; Medbury in India; Men in
Black; Nifty Nurses; Old Kentucky Hounds; A
Penny a Peep; Red Hot Mama; Struggle for Ex-
istence; Sultan Pepper; The Wandering Jew;
World in Revolt.

1935: Arlette et les Papas; The Crime of Dr Crespi;

Death Day; The Fighting Lady; Free Thälmann; Good Morning Eve; Harlem Harmony; Oh, What a Night; The Prodigal; Puppets; Show Them No Mercy; Storm; Suicide Club; Yiddish Father.

1936: Club de Femmes; Hunter's Paradise; Jenny; The Leavenworth Case (passed later in the same year); One Big Happy Family; Red Republic; Spring Night.

1937: Cloistered; Lucrezia Borgia; Skeleton Frolics; Sport's Greatest Thrill; Sunday Go to Meetin' Time; That Man Samson; Wrestling.

1938: Avec le Sourire; Wedding Yells.

1939: Entente Cordiale; I was a Captive of Nazi Germany (passed later in the same year); Professor Mamlock (passed later in the same year).

1940: Buried Alive.

1941: NIL.

1942: The Corpse Vanishes (passed in 1946 as The Body Disappears); The Mad Monster (passed in 1952); No Greater Sin (passed as Social Enemy No. 1 in 1943),

1943: NIL.

1944: The Mystic Circle Murder.

1945: NIL.

1946: NIL.

1947: NIL.

1948: Behind Locked Doors; The Horn Blows at Midnight (passed later in the same year).

1949: Body Hold; Dedee d'Anvers; Elysia (16mm); The Miracle; Sins of the Fathers; Street Corner.

1950: Devil's Weed; Occupe toi d'Amelie (passed later in the same year); Story of Birth.

REFERENCES

Chapter 1
THE FORMATIVE YEARS, 1896-1918

1. For the pre-1914 development of the
British film industry the present writer has drawn
heavily from P. Corrigan, 'Film Entertainment as
Ideology and Pleasure: a Preliminary Approach to a
History of Audiences' and M. Chanan, 'The Emergence
of an Industry' in J. Curran and V. Porter (eds.),
British Cinema History (Weidenfeld & Nicolson,
London, 1983), pp. 24-35, 39-58.
2. Public Record Office (PRO), Home Office (HO)
45/10551/163175/2, 4 & 7.
3. House of Commons debates, vol. 3, cols.
1595-9, 21 April 1909.
4. Ibid., vol. 9, cols. 2260-6.
5. PRO, HO45/10066/B4388/5, 19 August 1909.
6. Ibid., 45/10551/163175/26.
7. Ibid., 45/10551/163175/48.
8. Ibid., 45/10812/312397/45, 7 September 1916.
9. N.M. Hunnings, Film Censors and the Law
(Allen & Unwin, London, 1967), p. 55.
10. Not one is mentioned in the standard history
of the British cinema, R. Low, History of the British
Film, 1906-1914 (Allen & Unwin, London, 1958).
11. PRO, HO45/10551/163175/65.
12. Ibid., 45/10551/163175/69.
13. Ibid., 45/10812/312397.
14. Ibid., 45/10812/312397/35.
15. Ibid., 45/10812/312397/45.
16. Ibid., 45/10812/312397/57.
17. Ibid., 45/10812/312397/70.
18. Ibid., 45/11191/373422/47, 21 December 1921.
19. C.M. Hepworth, Came the Dawn (Phoenix House,
London, 1951), p. 109.
20. The full list can be found in Hunnings, op.

cit., pp. 408-9.
   21. PRO, HO45/10955/312971/55 & 69.

Chapter 2
THE CONSOLIDATION YEARS, 1919-1927

   1. BBFC annual report for 1919.
   2. The BBFC 1919 annual report states that 28
films were banned, but BBFC records show only eleven
and the annual report mentions only eleven grounds
for bans. The author cannot explain the discrepancy.
   3. PRO, HO45/10955/312971/45.
   4. Ibid., 45/10955/312971/92, 94, 95 and 98.
   5. Ibid., 45/10969/391637/7, 11, 12 and 13.
   6. Ibid., 45/11191/373422/11.
   7. Ibid., 45/11191/373422/29.
   8. PRO, Foreign Office (FO) 395/363, P2678/
2605/150; 395/370, P749/38/150; 395/418, P1181/7/150;
395/427, P344, 399/18/150.
   9. PRO, HO45/11191/373422/47.
   10. Ibid., 45/11599/433067/1.
   11. Ibid., 45/11599/433067/1-6.
   12. Ibid., 45/11191/373422/71.
   13. Ibid., 45/11382/446368/1 and 2.
   14. K. Brownlow, Hollywood: the Pioneers
(William Collins, London, 1979), p. 111.
   15. PRO, HO45/11599/433067/7.
   16. House of Commons debates, vol. 214, col.
1209, 8 March 1928.

Chapter 3
'DAWN' AND THE TALKIES, 1928-1939

   1. 'Dawn (1928): Edith Cavell and Anglo-German
Relations', Historical Journal of Film, Radio and
Television (1984), pp. 15-28.
   2. BBFC annual report for 1928.
   3. J. Curran and V. Porter (eds.), British
Cinema History (Weidenfeld and Nicolson, London,
1983), p. 372. N. Pronay, 'British Newsreels in the
1930s: 1. Audience and Producers', History (1971),
pp. 412-3.
   4. British Film Institute (BFI), BBFC verbatim
reports, miscellaneous 1931-8.
   5. Conference on animal films and the treatment
of animals in films, 31 May 1934, BFI, BBFC verbatim
reports 1932-5.
   6. The questionnaire and its answers in summary
form are in BFI, BBFC verbatim reports, miscellaneous

1931-8.
     7. See pp. 24-5 above.
     8. BFI, BBFC verbatim reports 1932-5.
     9. PRO, HO45/14275/551004/9A and 36.
     10. A. Field, Picture Palaces (Gentry Books,
London, 1974), p. 119.
     11. BBFC records do not tally with the number of
banned films given in the annual reports for 1930,
1931 and 1932. The author has relied on the information in Appendix 3.
     12. A. Field, op. cit., p. 120. For Tyrrell's
views on the importance of publicity in diplomacy
during the 1920s, see P.M. Taylor, The Projection of
Britain: British Overseas Publicity and Propaganda,
1919-1939 (Cambridge University Press, Cambridge,
1981), pp. 20-1, 27, 43, 53.

Chapter 4
THE TALKIES: SOME FILMS, GENRES AND THEMES, 1929-1939

     1. PRO, HO45/15208/593742/35 & 42.
     2. J. Richards, 'The British Board of Film
Censors and Content Control in the 1930s: Images of
Britain', Historical Journal of Film, Radio and
Television (1981), pp. 102-4.
     3. BFI, BBFC scenarios 1938, 11a, Red Wind, 31
January 1938.
     4. Ibid., 1937, 137 & 137a, 16 December 1937.
     5. Ibid., 1938, 81, 22 November 1938.
     6. Ibid., 26 & 26a, 23 & 18 March 1938.
     7. Ibid., 1934, 316, 11 July 1934.
     8. Ibid., 1933, 172, 12 June 1933.
     9. J. Richards, op. cit., p. 110.
     10. Ibid., p. 109.
     11. Ibid., pp. 109-11.
     12. BFI, BBFC scenarios 1937, 91 & 91a, 31 July
1937.
     13. K. Vidor, A Tree is a Tree (Longman, London,
1954), pp. 161-4.
     14. BFI, BBFC scenarios 1939, 7 & 7a, 25 & 26
January 1939.
     15. Ibid., 68 & 68a, 16 & 11 November 1939.
     16. J. Richards, op. cit., pp. 106-7.
     17. BFI, BBFC scenarios 1937, 79, 21 June 1937.
     18. J. Richards, op. cit., pp. 111-15.
     19. M. Seton, Paul Robeson (Dobson Books,
London, 1958), pp. 121-2.
     20. BFI, BBFC scenarios 1939, 45 & 45a, 29 June
& 1 July 1939.

REFERENCES

21. R. Findlater, <u>Michael Redgrave, Actor</u>
(Heinemann, London, 1956), p. 50.
22. J. Richards, op. cit., pp. 111-14.
23. BFI, BBFC scenarios 1933, 128, 8 February
1933.
24. Ibid., 1934, 349, 29 October 1934.
25. Ibid., 1935, 415, 7 May 1935.
26. Ibid., 1936, 46, 3 April 1936.
27. Ibid., 1938, 65, 29 July 1938.
28. Ibid., 1939, 28, 8 May 1939.
29. Ibid., 28b, 4 May 1939.
30. J. Richards, 'The British Board of Film
Censors and Content Control in the 1930s: Foreign
Affairs', <u>Historical Journal of Film, Radio and Tele-
vision</u> (1982), pp. 40-1.
31. Ibid., p. 41.
32. Ibid., pp. 41-2.
33. Ibid., p. 42. J.C. Robertson, 'British Film
Censorship Goes to War', <u>Historical Journal of Film,
Radio and Television</u> (1982), pp. 51-2.
34. BFI, BBFC scenarios 1939, 5a, 21 January
1939.
35. Ibid., 24, 20 April 1939.
36. Ibid., 26, 21 April 1939.
37. Ibid., 55, 4 August 1939.
38. Ibid., 1935, 518a, 31 December 1935.
39. Ibid., 1936, 30 & 30a, 2 March 1936, <u>Scarlet
Sultan</u>.
40. J. Richards & J. Hulbert, 'Censorship in
Action: the Case of <u>Lawrence of Arabia</u>', <u>Journal of
Contemporary History</u> (1984), pp. 153-70.
41. Ibid., p. 158.

Chapter 5
THE SECOND WORLD WAR

1. P.M. Taylor, '"If War should Come": Preparing the Fifth Arm for Total War, 1935-1939', <u>Journal
of Contemporary History</u>, (1981), p. 30.
2. PRO, Cabinet papers 16/128, folios 67 and
71.
3. Ibid., fos. 118-21, 4 February 1936.
4. Ibid., fo. 74, 6 February 1936. PRO,
Cabinet Papers 16/127 MIC5, fo. 121, 3 July 1936.
PRO, MoI INF 1/178, CN/4, part 1, chapter viii film
censorship, 24 July 1936.
5. Taylor, '"If War should Come"', p. 36.
6. F. Thorpe & N. Pronay with C. Coultass,
<u>British Official Films in the Second World War: a De-
scriptive Catalogue</u> (Clio Press, Oxford, 1980), p.17.

7. PRO, Cabinet Papers 16/127, fo.170, 23 February 1938.

8. Ibid.

9. Ibid., fo.43, 18 March 1938.

10. Ibid., MIC 12, fo.207, 12 May 1938.

11. PRO, MoI INF 1/178, CN/4, part 1, memorandum by D.B. Woodburn, 17 September 1938.

12. PRO, Cabinet Papers 16/127, MIC 16, fos. 281-2, 14 November 1938.

13. Ibid., fo.69.

14. PRO, MoI INF 1/178, CN/4, part 1, Home Office to Woodburn, 10 January 1939.

15. Ibid., part 2, memorandum by Ball, 6 September 1939.

16. Ibid., Tyrrell to Usborne, 16 September 1939.

17. Ibid., Tyrrell to Usborne, 4 October 1939

18. Ibid., Admiralty Press Division to Monckton, 8 March 1940.

19. Ibid., part 3, film censorship memorandum, 19 November 1941.

20. BFI, BBFC scenarios 1942, 43 and 43a.

21. PRO, MoI INF 1/178, CN/4, part 3, Commander Powell to F. Williams (Controller of Censorship), 30 September 1942.

22. Ibid.

23. Ibid., A. Nunn May (Assistant Director, Films Division) to W.G. Hall (Vice-President British Film Makers' Association), 20 January 1943.

24. BFI, BBFC scenarios 1939, 67 and 67a.

25. See J. Richards, op. cit.; (1982), pp. 42-3.

26. BFI, BBFC scenarios 1939, 69.

27. Ibid., 24. H.S. Wilcox, 25,000 Sunsets (Bodley Head, London, 1967), p. 124. A. Neagle, Anna Neagle says 'There's Always Towmorrow': an Autobiography (W.H. Allen, London, 1974), p. 116.

28. PRO, MoI INF 1/178, CN/4, part 3, Major T. Dugdale MP (Conservative Central Office) to Bracken, 24 May 1943 and Bracken to Dugdale, 28 May 1943.

29. In the last two paragraphs the author has drawn heavily upon R.A. Oehling, 'Hollywood and the Image of the Oriental, 1910-1950', Film and History, (1978), pp. 33-41, 59-67.

30. PRO, PREM 4 14/15.

31. The Times, 11 December 1942, p. 4d.

32. Ibid., 15 June 1942, p. 8a.

33. BFI, BBFC scenarios 1939, 36 and 36a.

34. Ibid., BBFC scenarios 1938, 80 and 80a.

35. Ibid., BBFC scenarios 1941, 8 and 8a.

36. Ibid., BBFC scenarios 1945, 111 and 111a.

REFERENCES

Chapter 6
THE AMERICAN CONNECTION AND A BRITISH PERSPECTIVE,
1907-1950

1. E. De Grazia & R.K. Newman, Banned Films:
Movies, Censors and the First Amendment (R.R. Bowker,
London, 1982), pp. 8-13.
2. Ibid., p. 15.
3. Ibid., p. 22.
4. R.S. Randall, Censorship of the Movies: the
Social and Political Control of a Mass Medium (University of Wisconsin Press, London, 1968), p. 17.
5. De Grazia & Newman, op. cit., pp. 27-8.
6. W.H. Hays, The Memoirs of Will H. Hays
(Doubleday, Garden City, New York, 1955), pp. 365-9.
7. Ibid., p. 438.
8. De Grazia & Newman, op. cit., p. 34. See
also Appendix 1.
9. Ibid., p. 35.
10. Ibid., p. 37.
11. Ibid., pp. 40-1.
12. Lord Tyrrell's address to the CEA, 23 June
1937, PRO, HO45/23091/802297/6.
13. BFI, BBFC verbatim reports 1930-1, record of
a LPMC deputation to Shortt, 3 April 1930.
14. Brooke Wilkinson to Home Office, 28 July
1931, PRO, HO45/14277/551004/127.
15. Ibid., HO45/14275/551004/36.
16. Ibid., HO45/14275/551004/9A.
17. Ibid., HO45/14275/551004/36.
18. Ibid., HO45/15208/593742/35.
19. Ibid., HO45/15247/802297/6.
20. BFI, BBFC scenarios 1945, 132 & 132a, 3
October 1945.
21. Ibid., 137.
22. BFI, BBFC scenarios 1943, 61, 16 March 1943.
23. Ibid., 61a, 20 March 1943.
24. BFI, BBFC scenarios 1946, 2 & 4, 17 & 18
January 1946.
25. Ibid., 9 & 9a, 12 April 1946.
26. Ibid., 11, 30 April 1946.
27. The Eminent Dr Deeves, Ibid., 13, 4 May
1946.
28. Watkins to Clerk of the Birmingham Justices,
1 June 1949, PRO, HO45/23091/802297/76.
29. Ibid., HO minute, 2 June 1949.
30. See below, pp. 168-9, 174-5.
31. BFI, BBFC scenarios 1946, 32a.
32. Ibid., 12a & 41a, 28 April & 23 December
1946.
33. Ibid., 22 & 22a, 8 & 12 July 1946.

194

34. De Grazia & Newman, op. cit., pp. 65-7.
35. BFI, BBFC scenarios 1946, 27 & 27a.
36. See above, p. 137.
37. BFI, BBFC scenarios 1947, 55 & 55a.
38. Ibid., 70a.
39. Ibid., 53a.
40. Ibid., 78.
41. Ibid., 78a.
42. Ibid., 105 & 105a.
43. J. Trevelyan, What the Censor Saw (Michael Joseph, London, 1973), p. 55.
44. BFI, BBFC scenarios 1947, 113a.
45. Ibid., 113b.
46. See below, p. 174.
47. Dress Optional, BFI, BBFC scenarios 1949, 11 & 11a.
48. The Times, 28 April 1948, p. 3c.
49. PRO, HO45/23091/802297/59.
50. Ibid., HO45/23091/802297/67.
51. Ibid.
52. J. Trevelyan, op. cit., p. 49. N. Pronay, 'The First Reality: Film Censorship in Liberal England' in K.R.M. Short (ed.), Feature Films as History (Croom Helm, London, 1981), pp. 113-37; 'The Political Censorship of Films in Britain between the Wars' in N. Pronay & D.W. Spring (eds.), Propaganda, Politics and Film, 1918-1945 (Macmillan, London, 1982), pp. 98-125; J. Richards, op. cit., (1981), pp. 95-116 & (1982), pp. 39-48.
53. PRO, HO45/15206/592519/27, 17 March 1932.
54. BFI, BBFC scenarios 1949, 22a.
55. Ibid., 24.
56. Charles Clover in Daily Telegraph, 8 July 1982.
57. See, for example, R. Murphy, 'Rank's Attempt on the American Market, 1944-1949' in J. Curran & V. Porter (eds.), British Cinema History (Weidenfeld & Nicolson, London, 1983), pp. 164-78.

SELECT BIBLIOGRAPHY

Unpublished Sources

British Board of Film Censors, scenarios 1930-47 and
    1949
British Board of Film Censors, Verbatim Reports
    1931-8
British Board of Film Censors, Registers of Films
    Passed and Rejected
British Board of Film Censors, Memorandum by Sir
    Sidney Harris (March 1960) on the Origin and
    Development of the BBFC, 1912-52
Verbal testimony to the author from Bert Mayell
Cabinet Conclusions (minutes)
Cabinet Papers
Foreign Office Papers
Home Office Papers
Ministry of Information Papers

Published Sources
Official Printed Material

British Board of Film Censors, annual reports, 1913-
    37
House of Commons Debates
House of Lords Debates

Secondary Works on Film Censorship

Hunnings, T.N.M., Film Censors and the Law (Allen &
    Unwin, London, 1967)
Knowles, D., The Censor, the Drama and the Film
    (Allen & Unwin, London, 1934)
McClelland, D., The Unkindest Cuts: the Scissors and
    the Cinema (Thomas Yoseloff, London, 1972)
Montagu, I.G.S., The Political Censorship of Films
    (Gollancz, London, 1929)
Newman, R.K. & De Grazia, E., Banned Films: Movies,

Censors and the First Amendment (R.R. Bowker,
    London, 1982)
Phelps, G., Film Censorship (Gollancz, London, 1975)
Randall, R.S., Censorship of the Movies: the Social
    and Political Control of a Mass Medium (Univer-
    sity of Wisconsin Press, London, 1968)
Schumach, M., The Face on the Cutting Room Floor
    (Morrow, New York, 1964)

Secondary Works on Film

Brownlow, K., Hollywood: The Pioneers (Collins,
    London, 1979)
Curran, J. & Porter, V. (eds.), British Cinema
    History (Weidenfeld & Nicolson, London, 1983)
Low, R., A History of the British Film, 1906-1914
    (Allen & Unwin, London, 1958)
Manvell, R., Films and the Second World War (Dent,
    London, 1974)
Richards, J., Visions of Yesterday (Routledge & Kegan
    Paul, London, 1973)
Richards, J., The Age of the Dream Palace (Routledge
    & Kegan Paul, London, 1984)
Shipman, D., The Story of Cinema, vol. i (Hodder &
    Stoughton, London, 1982)

Memoirs

Hays, W.H., The Memoirs of Will H. Hays (Doubleday,
    Garden City, New York, 1955)
Hepworth, C.M., Came the Dawn (Phoenix House, London,
    1951)
Neagle, A., Anna Neagle says 'There's Always
    Tomorrow': an Autobiography (W.H. Allen, London,
    1974)
Trevelyan, J., What the Censor Saw (Michael Joseph,
    London, 1973)
Vidor, K., A Tree is a Tree (Longman, London, 1954)
Wilcox, H.S., 25,000 Sunsets (Bodley Head, London,
    1967)

Miscellaneous

Field, A., Picture Palaces (Gentry Books, London,
    1974)
Findlater, R., Michael Redgrave, Actor (Heinemann,
    London, 1956)
Halliwell, L., Film Guide, 4th edition (Granada,
    London, 1983)
Halliwell, L., Filmgoers Companion, 7th edition
    (Granada, London, 1980)

SELECT BIBLIOGRAPHY

Pronay, N. & Thorpe, F. in association with Coultass,
    C., British Official Films in the Second World
    War: a Descriptive Catalogue (Clio Press,
    Oxford, 1980)
Pronay, N. & Spring, D.W. (eds.), Propaganda,
    Politics and Film, 1918-1945 (Macmillan, London,
    1982)
Seton, M., Paul Robeson (Dobson Books, London, 1958)
Short, K.R.M. (ed.), Feature Films as History (Croom
    Helm, London, 1981)
Taylor, P.M., The Projection of Britain: British
    Overseas Publicity and Propaganda, 1919-1939
    (Cambridge University Press, Cambridge, 1981)

Articles

Oehling, R.A., 'Hollywood and the Image of the
    Oriental, 1910-1950', Film and History (1978),
    pp. 33-41, 59-67
Pronay, N., 'British Newsreels in the 1930s', History
    (1971), pp. 411-18 and (1972), pp. 63-72
Richards, J., 'The British Board of Film Censors and
    Content Control in the 1930s: Images of Britain
    and Foreign Affairs', Historical Journal of
    Film, Radio and Television (1981), pp. 95-116
    and (1982), pp. 39-48
Richards, J., & Hulbert, J., 'Censorship in Action:
    the Case of Lawrence of Arabia', Journal of
    Contemporary History (1984), pp. 153-70
Robertson, J.C., 'British Film Censorship Goes to
    War', Historical Journal of Film, Radio and
    Television (1982), pp. 49-64
Robertson, J.C., 'Dawn (1928): Edith Cavell and
    Anglo-German Relations', Historical Journal of
    Film, Radio and Television (1984), pp. 15-28
Taylor, P.M., '"If War Should Come": Preparing the
    Fifth Arm for Total War, 1935-1939', Journal of
    Contemporary History (1981), pp. 27-51

INDEX OF FILM TITLES

GENERAL INDEX

abortion 21, 60
Admiralty 10, 28, 92,
  113, 117, 121
Air Ministry 28, 91,
  117, 119
Andrews, Dana 169
anti-Semitism 33, 92-5,
  97-9, 101, 124, 131-2,
  157, 164, 169, 172
Arbuckle, Roscoe (Fatty)
  29, 147
Arliss, George 94, 102,
  106
Arliss, Leslie 139, 143
Asquith, Anthony 70, 102,
  122, 124
Asther, Nils 66, 96
Attenborough, Sir Richard
  133, 168
Attlee, Clement 155, 160,
  168
Atwill, Lionel 134, 139
Aylmer, Felix 132, 143

Bacon, Lloyd 81
Ball, Sir Joseph 115-16
Bancroft, George 77
Banks, Leslie 58
Bara, Theda 61
Barrymore, Ethel 166
Barrymore, John 26
Baxter, John 132
Bendix, William 138
Bennett, Joan 142, 162
Bevan, Aneuran 163
birth control 32, 35, 60

Blaxland, Benham 6, 14
Bogarde, Dirk 178
Bogart, Humphrey 80-1,
  137
Boleslawski, Richard 69
Bond, Ward 100
Borzage, Frank 125
Bottome, Phyllis 125
Boulting, John 163, 169
Boulting, Roy 129, 163,
  167, 169
Bow, Clara 61
Boyer, Charles 126
Bracken, Brendan 127, 144
Bracken, Eddie 142
Brahm, John 142
Breen, Joseph 152
Brenon, Herbert 17
Bressart, Felix 127
British Board of Film
  Censors (BBFC) -
  establishment of 4-5,
  146; annual reports
  7-11, 16, 19-21, 31,
  37, 39, 43-4, 56, 58,
  60-2, 74, 76-9, 149,
  154, 158
Brook, Clive 77
Brooke Wilkinson, Joseph
  - see Wilkinson,
  Joseph Brooke
Brooke, Hillary 136
Brown, Clarence 40, 66,
  126, 151
Browning, Tod 57-8
Brunel, Adrian 43, 49, 96

205

GENERAL INDEX

80, 95, 137, 142, 162
Lang, Matheson 22, 33,
    59, 65
Laughton, Charles 136,
    166
Lawrence, Marc 138
Lawrence, T.E. 108
Lawson, Wilfrid 129
League of Nations Union
    24-5, 27
Lean, David 133, 160
Legion of Decency 151-2,
    154, 167
Leigh, Vivien 140
Leni, Paul 56
Leroy, Mervyn 69, 77, 79,
    129-30
Lieven, Albert 165
Litvak, Anatole 82, 100,
    126, 133, 162
Livesey, Roger 131
Lloyd George, David 2,
    16, 19, 49
Locarno treaties 36-7,
    42, 95, 154
Lockwood, Margaret 139,
    141, 143
Logan, Jacqueline 40
Lombard, Carole 65
London County Council
    (LCC) 27-30, 32, 35,
    40, 42, 48-52, 57, 96,
    99, 116, 152-3, 174
London Film Society - see
    Film Society, The
London Public Morality
    Council (LPMC, later
    Public Morality
    Council) 39, 45, 57,
    135, 152
Lord, Reverend Daniel A.
    150
Lorre, Peter 70, 95, 107
Loy, Myrna 66, 89
Lubitsch, Ernst 126
Lucan, Arthur 83
Lugosi, Bela 57, 134
Lukas, Paul 100
Lyon, Ben 91

McCarey, Leo 132, 159

McCrea, Joel 81
MacDonald, David 163,
    168, 172
MacDonald, Jeanette 62
MacDonald, Ramsay 48, 50,
    102, 167
MacGinnis, Niall 130
McLaglen, Victor 88
Macrae, Duncan 168
Mamoulian, Rouben 58, 62
Manchuria, crisis of
    1931-3: 102
Mander, Miles 93
Mannheim, Lucie 95
Marèze, Janie 62
marriage 7, 11, 21, 26,
    32, 35, 44, 60, 65-7,
    123-4, 140-2, 147,
    156, 159-60, 165, 168
Marshall, George 136
Mason, Herbert 105, 141
Mason, James 139, 143
Maugham, W. Somerset 140
Mayo, Archie 77, 79
medical ethics 7, 33-4,
    44, 60, 72-4, 134, 158
Mendes, Lothar 94
Menzies, William Cameron
    103
Merkel, Una 136
Metro-Goldwyn-Mayer (MGM)
    Studios 36, 40, 46,
    58, 61-2, 64, 69-71,
    73-5, 78, 81, 83, 91,
    118, 125-7, 129-31,
    140, 151, 159
Middlesex County Council
    13, 27, 32, 40, 48-9,
    57
Miles, Sir Bernard 135
Milestone, Lewis 91, 129,
    136
Milland, Ray 160
Ministry of Information
    (MoI) 109-22, 124,
    127-30, 132-3, 143-4,
    158
Minkin, Adolf 98
miscegenation 26, 65-7,
    105, 140
Monckton, Sir Walter 117

209

Montagu, Hon Ivor 43, 49,
    51, 54, 95-6
Morley, Karen 84
Morley, Robert 159
Morris, Chester 32, 64
Motion Picture Producers
    and Distributors
    Association of America
    (MPPDA) 147-52, 167
Muni, Paul 69, 79, 132
Murnau, Friedrich 29
Murray, Stephen 138, 141
Mussolini, Benito 97, 104

Nash, Percy 22, 28
National Council of
    Public Morals 15-17
Nazimova, Alla 130
Nazism 91-102, 119, 124-
    5, 128-32, 135, 137,
    139, 154, 157, 160,
    162, 164-5, 169, 173.
    See also Hitler, Adolf
Neagle, Dame Anna 72
Negri, Pola 61
Neill, Roy William 136,
    138
Newton, Robert 140
nudity 6, 10-11, 60-5,
    141, 161, 168.
    See also sex

O'Brien, Pat 76, 82
O'Casey, Sean 87-8
O'Connor, T.P., MP (BBFC
    President, 1916-29)
    16, 18, 24, 28-32, 37-
    42, 46, 49-50, 54, 75,
    147-9, 176-7
O'Hara, Maureen 136
Oland, Warner 68
Old Mother Riley - see
    Lucan, Arthur
Olivier, Sir Laurence 140

Pabst, Georg (G.W.) 92,
    102
pacifism 16-17, 25, 36-7,
    59, 91-2, 101-4, 132-3
Pakistan 157, 173
Palestine 108, 157, 169,
    172
Paramount Studios 26, 35,
    46, 54, 58-9, 62, 64,
    68-9, 77, 90-1, 129,
    134-5, 137-8, 140,
    142, 159, 173
Parker, Cecil 73, 98
Pascal, Gabriel 70, 133
Pathé Studios 40, 42
Peace Ballot 103
Peck, Gregory 129, 166
Pepper, Barbara 84
Pichel, Irving 58, 130
Pickford, Mary 147
Pidgeon, Walter 137
Pilbeam, Nova 138
Portman, Eric 119
Powell, Michael 99, 119-
    20, 122, 130, 170
Power, Tyrone 66, 82, 133
Preminger, Otto 130, 159
Pressburger, Emeric 120,
    130, 170
Price, Dennis 161
Priestley, J.B. 54, 141
prostitution 11, 23, 35,
    40, 58, 60, 62-3, 65,
    81, 142, 150, 162,
    171-2
Pudovkin, Vsevolod (V.I.)
    43, 51

Qualen, John 84
Quigley, Martin 150

racialism 11, 20-2, 33,
    60-1, 65-70, 75, 85,
    92-5, 97-9, 101, 105,
    124, 131-2, 157, 164,
    169, 172
Rainer, Luise 69
Rains, Claude 128
Rank, J. Arthur 144
rape 11-12, 26, 60, 128,
    140, 142
Rappaport, Herbert 98
Rathbone, Basil 93, 126,
    136, 138
Rattigan, Terence 168
Reagan, Ronald 134
Redford, G.A. (BBFC

President, 1913-16)
4-5, 9, 13, 15-16, 30-
1, 177
Redgrave, Sir Michael 168
Reed, Sir Carol 85, 124
Reid, Wallace 34
Reith, Sir John 117, 121,
144
Relph, Michael 171
Renoir, Jean 62, 104
Rhouma, Gypsy 66
Richards, Addison 84
Richardson, Sir Ralph 73
Rilla, Walter 97, 132
Rin Tin Tin 46
Ritz Brothers 59
RKO Studios 58-9, 65, 88,
90, 119, 128, 131,
134-6, 164, 169
Roach, Hal 136
Robertson, John 77
Robeson, Paul 85, 90
Robinson, Edward G. 69,
77, 80, 82, 100, 142,
162, 164
Robson, Dame Flora 132,
171
Roc, Patricia 168
Rosay, Francoise 171
Rossellini, Roberto 170
Ruggles, Wesley 64
Russell, Jane 167
Russell, Rosalind 73
Russia 19, 21-2, 25, 28,
36-7, 43, 49, 51, 83-
4, 96-9, 101, 106,
118-23, 125-8, 144,
156-8, 160, 165, 173
Ryan, Robert 169

St Valentine's Day
massacre 77
Samuel, Sir Herbert 3,
12-16, 28, 32, 146,
153
Sanders, George 137
Saville, Victor 71, 74,
91-2, 97-8
Schildkraut, Joseph 40
Scotland Yard 24-5, 49,
71, 173

Scott, Randolph 138-9
Seiler, Lewis 82
Seiter, William 69
sex 7, 10-12, 21, 23, 30,
34-5, 39-40, 44, 47-8,
57-8, 60-8, 78, 123-4,
136, 139-43, 147-8,
150-1, 154, 159-61,
166-8, 170, 172, 174-
5.
See also nudity
Shaw, George Bernard 54,
70, 133, 159
Sherman, Vincent 132
Shoedsack, Ernest 46, 58-
9, 135
Shortt, Edward (BBFC
President, 1929-35)
25, 28, 30, 49-50, 52-
4, 61-2, 68, 78-80,
88, 91, 97, 126, 150,
153-4
Shortt, Miss N. - see
Crouzet, Mrs N.
Sidney, Sylvia 80
Smith, Lady Eleanor 161
Soviet Union - see Russia
Spanish Civil War 54, 97-
8, 104-8, 112
Stahl, John M. 71, 129
Stalin, Joseph 126-8
Stanwyck, Barbara 63, 66,
88, 141
Steinbeck, John 130, 136
Sternberg - see Von
Sternberg, Josef
Stevens, George 90
Stewart, James 130, 136
Stopes, Dr Marie 32
Stroheim - see Von
Stroheim, Erich
Sturges, Preston 142
Sullavan, Margaret 130
Surrey County Council 48,
57, 153, 174

Tallents, Sir Stephen
112-14
Taurog, Norman 75
Taylor, Robert 71, 130
Taylor, William Dean 147

GENERAL INDEX